Seashells of Central New South Wales

A Survey of the Shelled Marine Molluscs of the Sydney Metropolitan Area and Adjacent Coasts

PATTY JANSEN

Published privately by the author

Townsville, Australia

1995

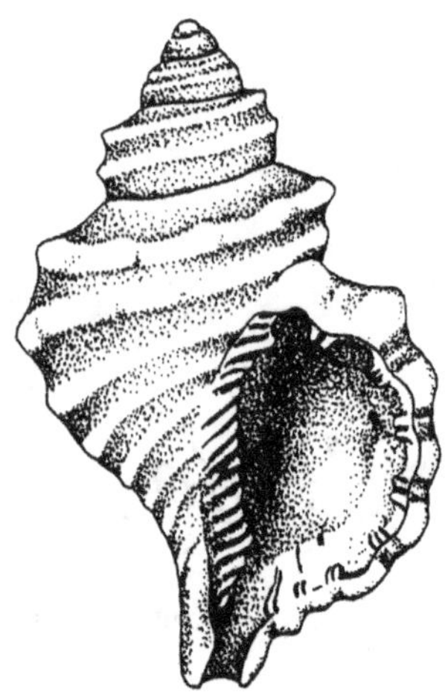

Front cover: View to the north over Botany Bay from the
Grand Parade, Brighton-le-Sands

Designed and published by
Patty Jansen
11 Eden St.
Belgian Gardens Qld. 4810, Australia

National Library of Australia Cataloguing-in-Publication entry

Jansen, Patty
  Seashells of central new South Wales: a survey of the
  shelled marine molluscs of the Sydney Metropolitan Area
  and adjacent coasts.

  Bibliography
  Includes index
  ISBN 0 646 23760 8

  1. Mollusks - New South Wales - Sydney Region-
  Identification. 2. Mollusks - New South Wales - Sydney
  Region - Collection and preservation. I. Title.

594.099441

Printed in Townsville, Australia by Townprint

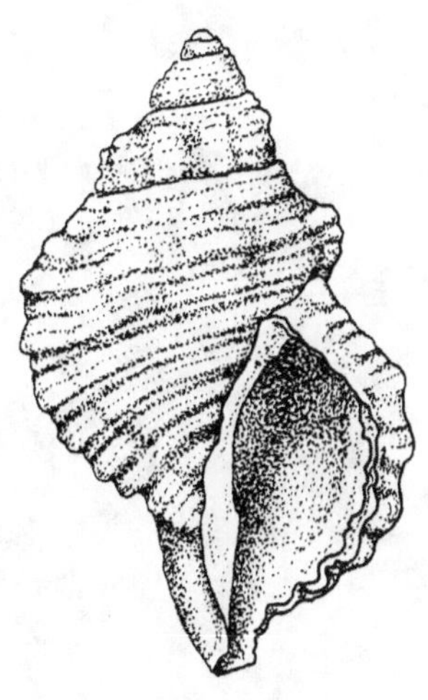

to Des, Michael and other friends at the Sydney Shell Club.
This may make it easier to identify your finds.

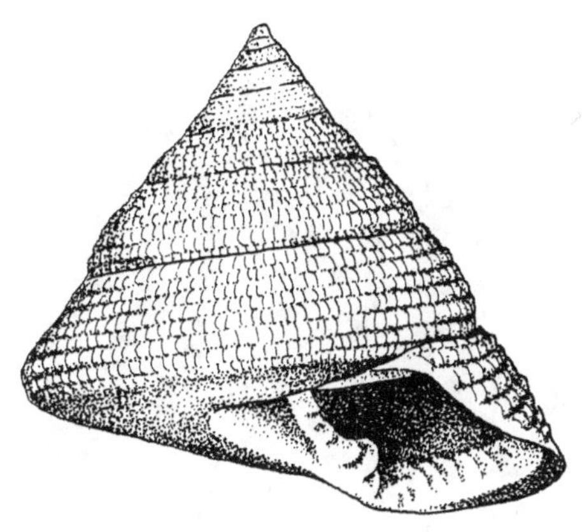

Contents

Foreword IX

Acknowlegdements XI

Introduction

   Collecting shells 1
   About the descriptions 2
   Map of collecting and observation sites in the Sydney metropolitan area 3
   Map of collecting and observation sites on the New South Wales coast. 4
   Features of the gastropod shell 6
   Features of the bivalve shell 7

Gastropoda

   Patellidae 8
   Lottiidae 9
   Neritidae 10
   Scissurellidae. 11
   Haliotidae. 12
   Fissurellidae 13
   Turbinidae 15
   Trochidae. 18
   Skeneidae 24
   Plesiotrochidae 25
   Dialidae. 26
   Litiopidae 26
   Cerithiidae 26
   Batillariidae 27
   Planaxidae 28
   Turritellidae. 28
   Siliquariidae 29
   Littorinidae 30
   Eatonellidae 31
   Cingulopsidae 32
   Anabathridae 32
   Emblandidae 34
   Rissoidae 34
   Assimineidae 37
   Iravadiidae 37
   Epigridae 37
   Vitrinellidae. 37
   Caecidae 38
   Struthiolariidae 38
   Strombidae 38
   Hipponicidae 40
   Vanikoridae. 40
   Calyptraeidae. 41
   Vermetidae 42

VI

Cypraeidae	43
Triviidae	44
Lamellariidae	45
Naticidae	46
Tonnidae	48
Cassidae	48
Ranellidae	48
Cerithiopsidae	50
Triphoridae	51
Epitoniidae	52
Janthinidae	54
Eulimidae	55
Aclididae	56
Muricidae	56
Buccinidae	59
Columbellidae	62
Volutidae	65
Olividae	66
Olivellidae	66
Pseudolividae	67
Marginellidae	67
Mitridae	70
Cancellariidae	71
Terebridae	72
Turridae	72
Conidae	74
Architectonicidae	77
Pyramidellidae	79
Amathinidae	82
Acteonidae	83
Ringiculidae	83
Hydatinidae	83
Bullinidae	83
Scaphandridae	85
Philinidae	85
Bullidae	85
Haminoeidae	85
Retusidae	86
Cylindrobullidae	86
Aplysiidae	87
Umbraculidae	88
Ellobiidae	88
Trimusculidae	89
Siphonariidae	89
Amphibolidae	90

Bivalvia

Nuculanidae	91
Arcidae	91
Glycymeridae	92
Philobryidae	92
Mytilidae	93
Pteriidae	94
Malleidae	94

Limidae 95
Ostreidae 96
Pectinidae 96
Anomiidae 97
Trigoniidae 98
Lucinidae 98
Diplodontidae 99
Thyasiridae 99
Kelliidae 99
Galeommatidae 99
Lasaeidae 100
Montacutidae 100
Leptonidae 100
Carditidae 100
Condylocardiidae 101
Crassatellidae 102
Cardiidae 102
Hemidonacidae 103
Mactridae 104
Mesodesmatidae 105
Solenidae 105
Cultellidae 105
Tellinidae 106
Semelidae 106
Psammobiidae 106
Donacidae 107
Veneridae 108
Corbulidae 111
Hiatellidae 112
Pholadidae 112
Laternulidae 112
Myochamidae 112
Cleidothaeridae 113

Cephalopoda

Dentaliidae 114
Spirulidae 114

References 115

Glossary 123

Index 125

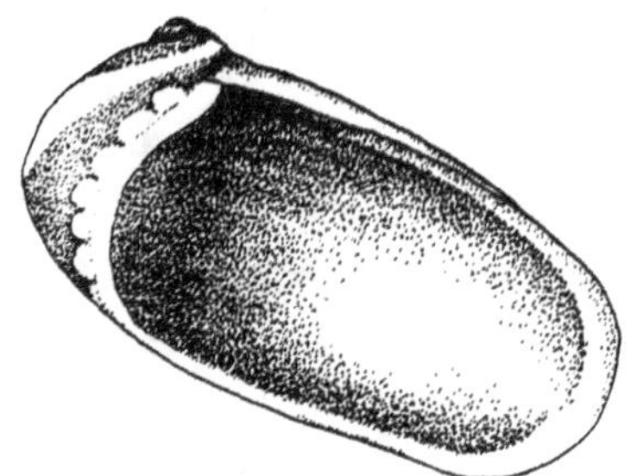

Foreword

With a molluscan fauna that exceeds that of the Atlantic coast of western Europe, it is surprising that the rich and varied fauna of the Sydney area has not inspired the production of an identification guide before now.

The area has had a long history of malacology, both from professional and amateur workers. Professional workers in the past, such as John Brazier, Charles Hedley, Tom Iredale, Joyce Allen and Don McMichael, were based at the Australian Museum and interacted with many notable amateurs. In more recent years these included Charles Laseron and Tom Garrard, well known through their numerous important publications. Others such as Gertie Thornley, Jacques Voorwinde, Joy Kerslake and Lee Woolacott not only provided published work but the large collections that they put together are now part of the Australian Museum research collection and provide a very valuable resource for future workers in the area. This collection was extensively used by Patty Jansen during the production of this work.

Patty has provided us with not only a delightful set of illustrations of our local shelled molluscs but a valuable resource in the form of an identification tool. Whereas some already available works cover many of the larger species treated in this book, the many small and minute species are better covered than in any other available work. These small shells can be readily obtained in considerable diversity from shores throughout the area with little or no environmental disturbance and require only a cheap microscope for study. There is a very great deal that we need to learn about the biology, distribution and
ecology of even our most common molluscs both large and small. This work should make it easier for some of that to be done.

Winston Ponder

Australian Museum, Sydney

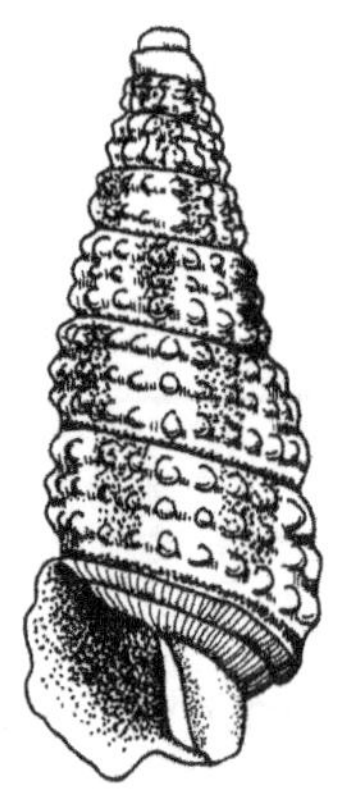

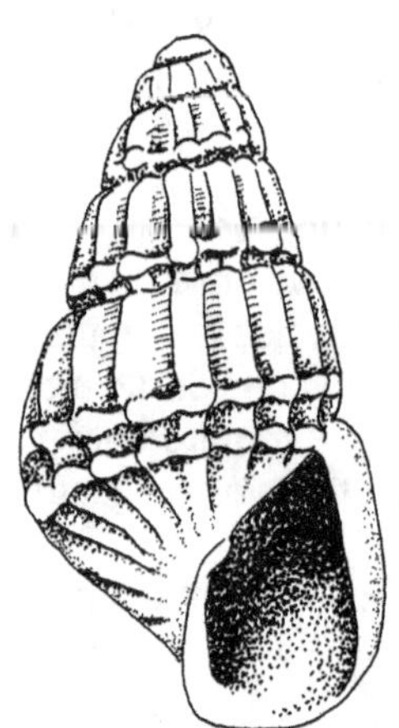

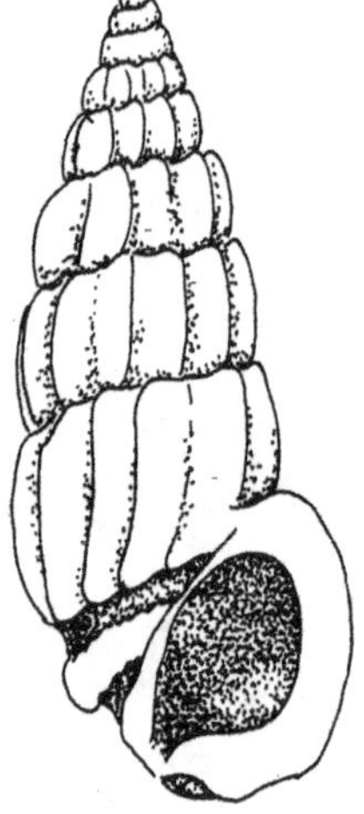

Acknowledgements

Publication of this book would not have been possible without the help of Dr. Winston Ponder, Dr. Bill Rudman, Ian Loch and Phil Colman from the Australian Museum, who have advised me on identification and taxonomy of many species and have allowed me to use the extensive research collection and the library of the Malacology Department.
A number of people have advised me on their areas of expertise. I especially wish to thank Dr. Carole Hickman and Dr. Bruce Marshall (Trochidae), Dr. Dean Hewish (Marginellidae), Thora Whitehead (Naticidae, bivalves), Dr. Winston Ponder (Rissoidae and related families, Muricidae, small bivalves), Dr. Bill Rudman (Ophistobranch molluscs), Kevin Lamprell (Scaphopods) and Ian Loch (a variety of species).
The members of the Sydney Shell Club (alias the Conchology Section of the Royal Zoological Society of New South Wales or the New South Wales branch of the Malacological Society of Australasia) have encouraged me to write this book. I especially wish to thank my friends Des and Bernice Beechey for reading parts of the manuscript and for their hospitality during my visit to Sydney in 1994.
This book was sponsored by the Keith Sutherland Award.
Finally, the publication of this book would not have been possible without the support of my husband, Jos Meulenbroeks. He has accompanied me on collecting trips and has encouraged me to write this book.

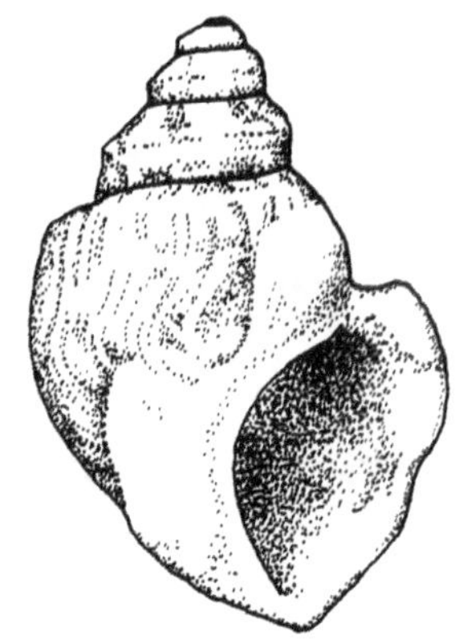

Introduction

Sydney is Australia's largest city with close to four million inhabitants. Sydney's varied and spectacular coastline has attracted attention from all over the world. Many Sydneysiders and tourists enjoy spending time on the beach and inevitably some of them will pick up some shells. Sydney has a rich molluscan fauna, probably as a result of the many different habitats within the metropolitan area. Iredale and McMichael's 1962 checklist of New South Wales molluscs contains 2063 species, many of which can be found on Sydney's beaches.

So, when I came to Sydney in 1988 and continued my hobby of shell collecting, I was astonished to find that a book on the shells of this area was not available; in fact, a book on shells of New South Wales had never been written. In my efforts to identify species that I had found, I had to consult many original descriptions, some of them dating from last century. I had to track down publications in scientific journals and I became a frequent visitor at the Australian Museum. Soon, I realised that the lack of interest in small shells, shown by local collectors, was probably caused by the lack of material to identify them with. This is why I started writing a series of articles in the 'Sydney Sheller', newsletter of the Conchology Section of the Royal Zoological Society of New South Wales. However, I felt that the type of material covered would probably interest a wider audience and I started thinking about joining them together in a book.

With this book, I hope to enable interested people, both amateur collectors and professionals, to easily identify shells found on beaches in central New South Wales. I have chosen to restrict the material covered to species that can be found on beaches, because they are readily accessible to everyone. A large number of micromolluscs are included; they are common in shell grit and previous books on Australian shells have largely ignored them. For the more advanced, I have included a long reference list of scientific publications relating to the taxonomy, and sometimes ecology, of families covered in this book. Many recent works are included. I hope that by publishing this book I will encourage collectors to look at smaller species, many of which are real gems. I have spent many hours sorting shell grit under a microscope and have always found it an enjoyable experience. One bag of shell grit can yield more exciting finds than a stroll on the beach at low tide.

Too often, shell collecting is seen as an environmentally undesirable activity and although many collectors prefer to collect live shells, I do not think that this is true. Most collectors are responsible and do not take more than they need, they will not collect immature, damaged or breeding specimens and will leave the habitat as they have found it, turning back stones and disposing of any rubbish in the appropriate places. It is in fact overcollecting for food that has prompted authorities to close part of the coast for shell collecting. But far more important threats to the molluscan population are habitat destruction and pollution.

I think shell collectors make an important contribution to the knowledge of the molluscan fauna. Many collectors choose to donate their collections to museums and in this way, a number of museums have built up large collections showing the variety and distribution of species, both in the past and present. In these times of financial cutbacks, a lot of work on museum collections is done by volunteers, many of whom are also shell collectors. And it is these very museums that government and environmental agencies rely on for information.

Collecting shells

The easiest way to find shells is to look for them on the beach. I find beach collecting the most enjoyable way of shell collecting. It is easy, quick and the shells generally do not need a lot of cleaning. A visit to the beach after strong winds or heavy rain may yield many good specimens. However, beach collecting has a number of drawbacks. Shells are often eroded and information about the habitat of species is lost. Thus, collecting live specimens may sometimes be desirable.

Finding live shells takes a lot of effort, knowledge and above all, patience. Those collectors who don masks and fins hoping to find the seabed moving with live shells will be disappointed. Most molluscs are nocturnal and hide during the daytime. In order to find them, you need to turn stones, look in crevices and dig in the sand. Knowledge about the habitat or food source of species is vital and even then, finding them is not easy.

Intertidal rock flats are a good place for live shells. Rock pools often harbour a variety of life so beautiful that I have often lost track of what I was looking for, preferring to take photographs instead.

Cleaning is important for the preservation of specimens in your collection. Beach shells should be washed in fresh water to rinse off any salt. If left on the shell, it will eat away at the shell surface, gradually destroying your specimens over time. Many species possess a periostracum a brownish, often hairy layer of material covering the shell. It is part of the shell and can be useful in identification. However, it can be removed by soaking the shell in pure bleach. Bleach, however, should not be used on shells with a polished surface and bivalves should not be left in bleach for too long, since it will also dissolve the ligament.

When you have collected and cleaned your shells, it is of vital importance that they are labelled correctly. The collecting locality, including the habitat, depth, collecting date and name of the collector should be recorded on the label. Label and specimen should be stored so that they cannot be separated, or be given an identical number if stored in open drawers or boxes. Storing shells in air-tight containers or plastic bags has a number of advantages. Firstly, it prevents separation of label and specimen. Secondly, it prevents deterioration of both label and specimen. Many private collections are stored in sheds or in dark and humid rooms under houses. Unless you live in a very arid climate, or your shell room is heated or airconditioned, these conditions will be detrimental to the quality of the shells if stored in open containers. Also, insects like silverfish and cockroaches will munch away at your labels, turning your collection into a mess that is of no use to anyone.

About the descriptions

The descriptions of species covered in this book are based on specimens from the central New South Wales coastline, but many species have a much wider distribution. Ranges are given clockwise, so a species with a range from New South Wales to Western Australia is a southern, temperate species and a species ranging from Western Australia to New South Wales is a tropical, northern species.

The sizes given in this book are based on the largest diameter of an average specimen found in central New South Wales and are meant only as an indication of the average size attained by the species. Because the terms 'large' and 'small' are relative and can be misleading, they are, in this book, used in the following way:

minute	< 5 mm
very small	5-10 mm
small	10-20 mm
medium-sized	20-50 mm
large	50-100 mm
very large	> 100 mm

Map of the Australian coastline

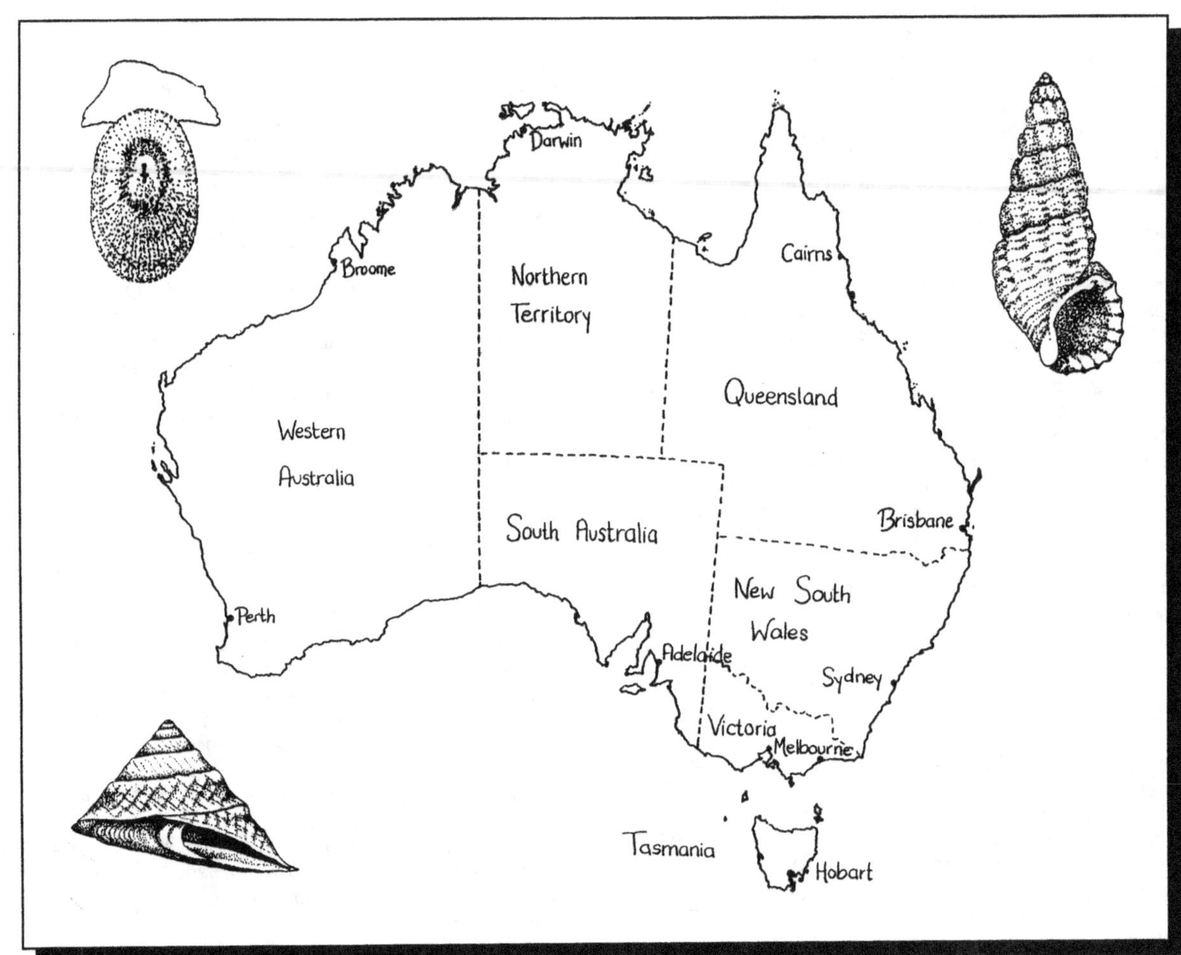

Map of collecting and observation sites in the Sydney metropolitan area

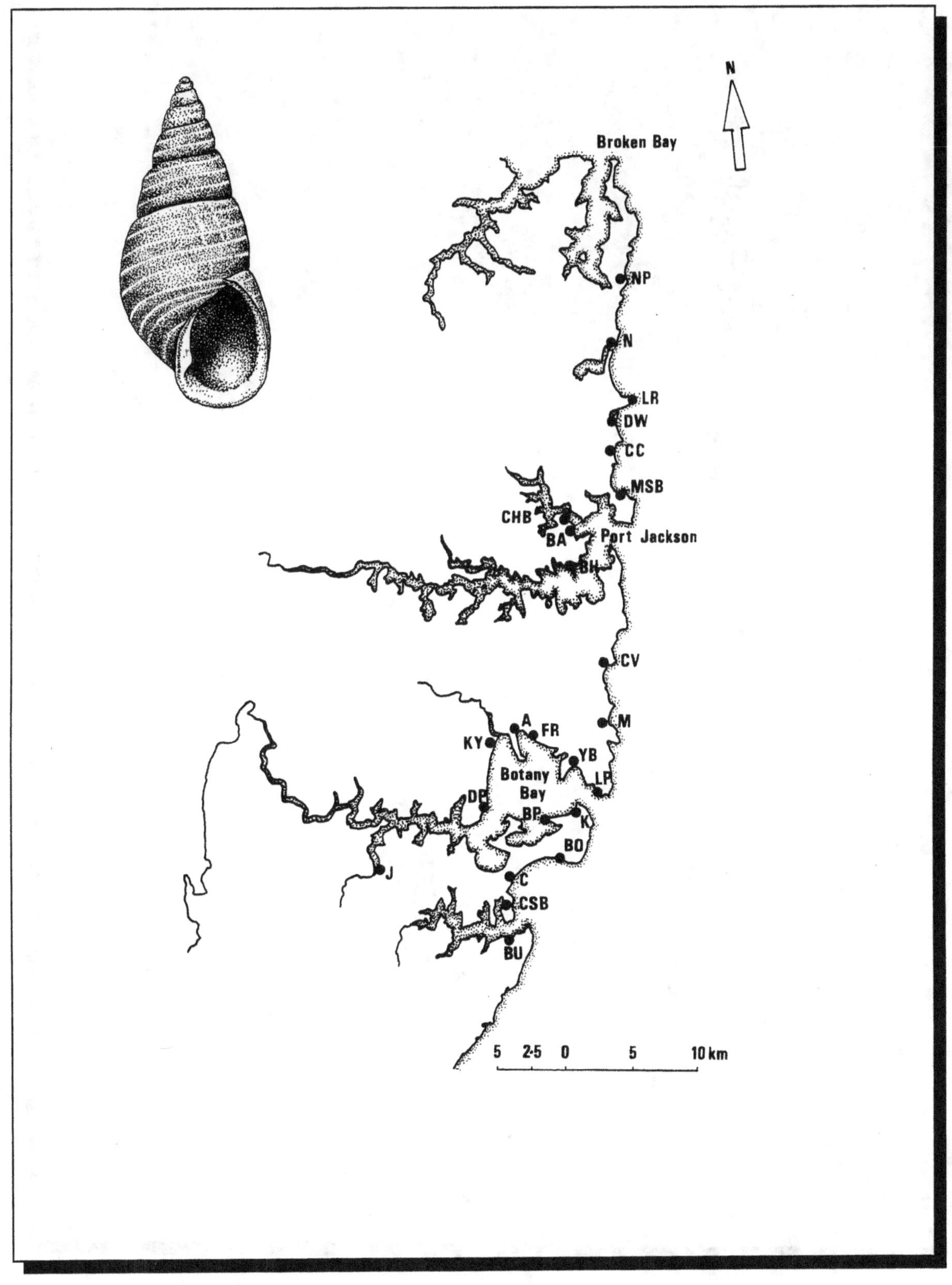

Map of collecting and observation sites on the New South Wales coast

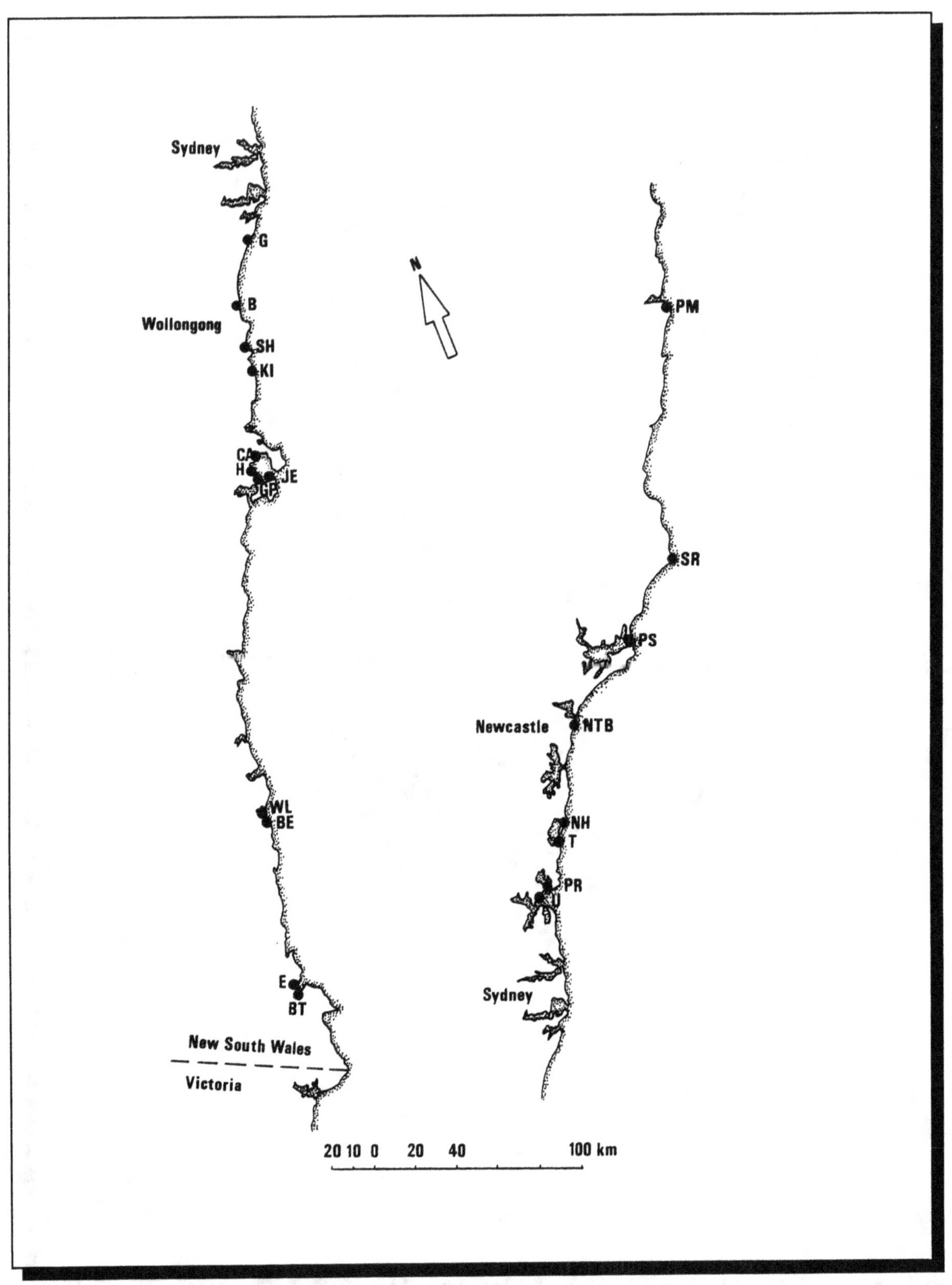

Legend to maps

A =   Airport (this beach no longer exists)
B =   Bulli
BA =   Balmoral
BE =   Bermagui
BH =   Bradleys Head
BO =   Boat Harbour
BP =   Bonna Point
BT =   Boydtown
BU =   Bundeena
C =   Cronulla
CA =   Callala Bay
CC =   Curl Curl
CHB =   Chinamens Beach
CSB =   Cronulla Shelly Beach
CV =   Clovelly
DP =   Dolls Point
DW =   Dee Why
E =   Eden
FR =   Foreshore Road
G =   Garie
GP =   Green Patch
H =   Huskisson
JE =   Bowen Island, Jervis Bay
K =   Kurnell
KI =   Kiama
KY =   Kyeemagh
LP =   La Perouse
LR =   Long Reef
M =   Maroubra
MSB =   Manly Shelly Beach
N =   Narrabeen
NH =   Norah Head
NP =   Newport
NTB =   Newcastle Town Beach
PM =   Port Macquarie
PR =   Pretty Beach
PS =   Tea Gardens, Port Stephens
SH =   Shellharbour
SR =   Seal Rocks
T =   Terrigal
U =   Umina
WL =   Wallagra Lake
YB =   Yarra Bay

Features of the gastropod shell

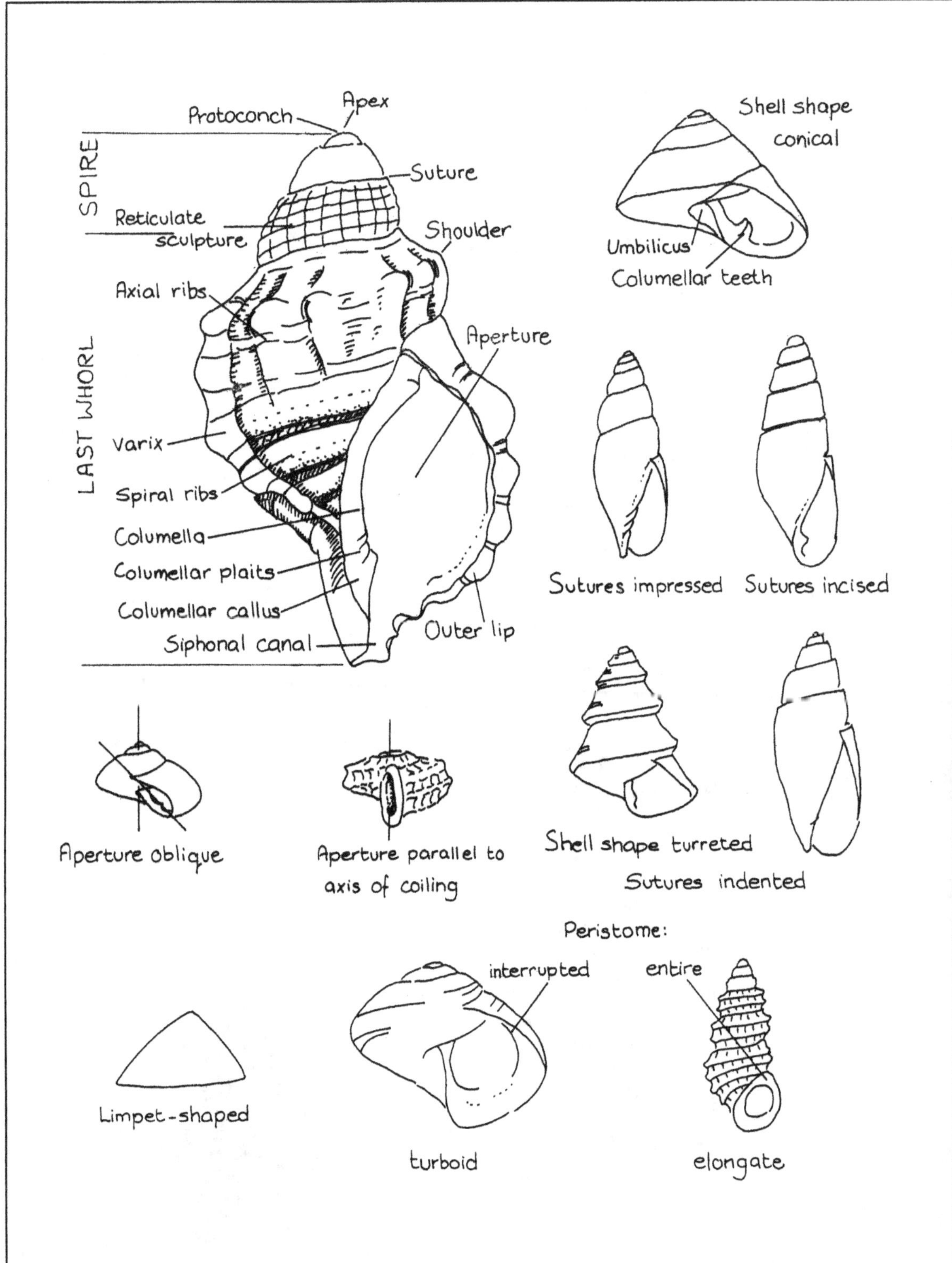

Features of the bivalve shell

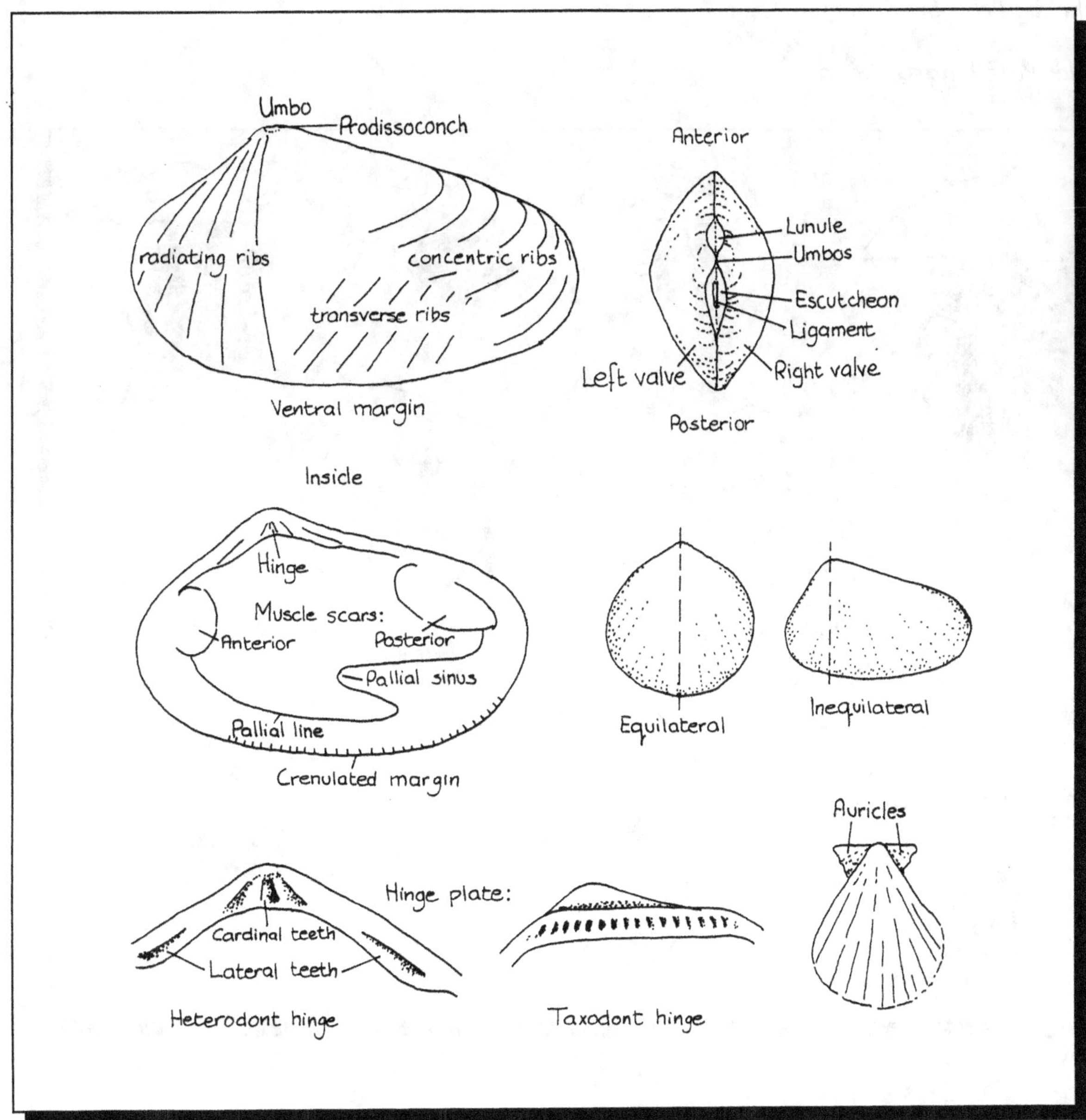

Class Gastropoda

Subclass Prosobranchia

Order Patellogastropoda

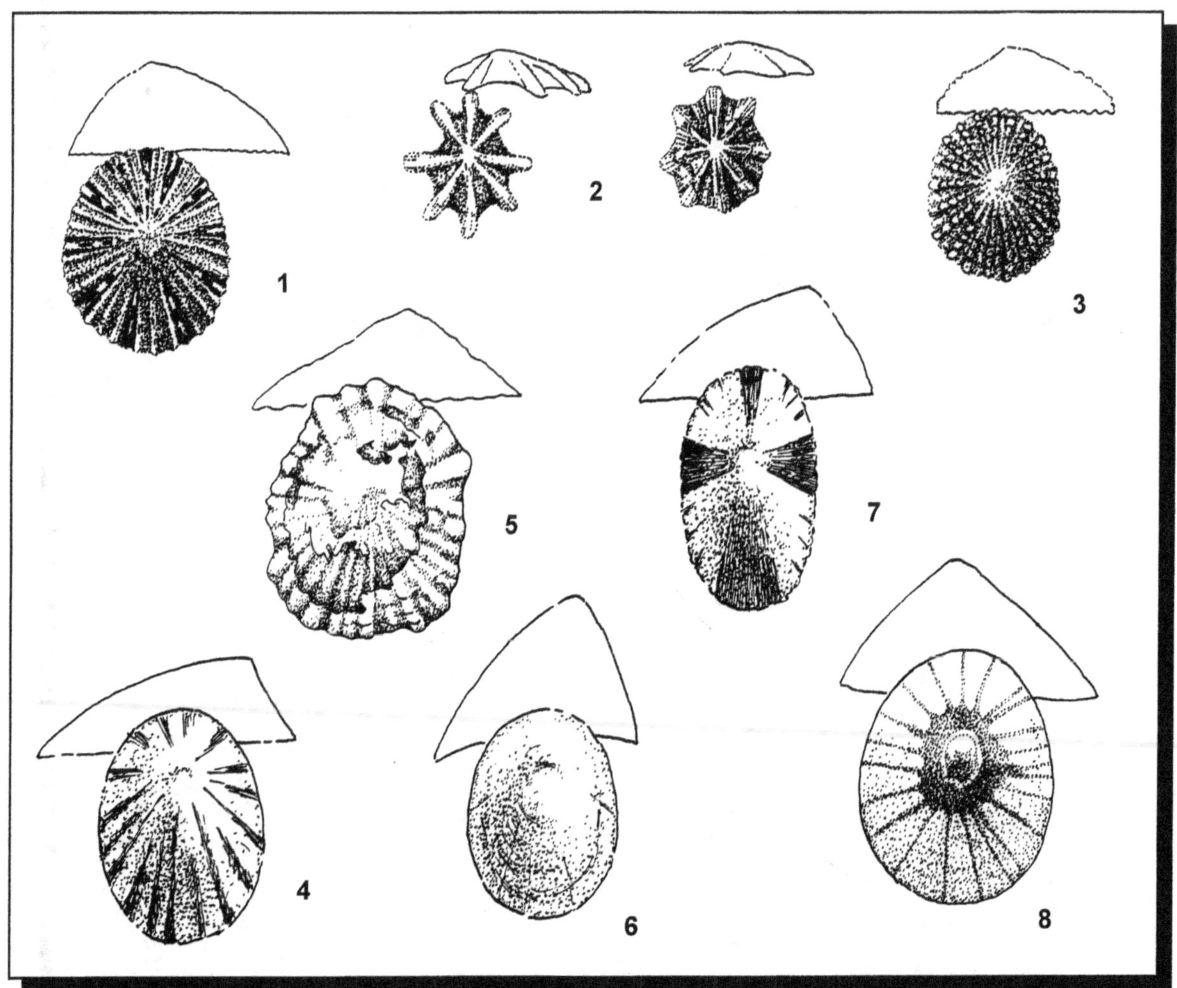

Superfamily Patelloidea

Family Patellidae

Members of the family Patellidae can be found worldwide
in both temperate and tropical seas. The shells are limpet-
shaped and often radially ribbed. The spatula (inside of
the apex) often has a different colour from the rest of the
shell, a feature used in identification.
The animals live intertidally on exposed shores. They
cling to a relatively smooth surface by means of their
powerful foot. Powell (1973) has reviewed the Patellidae
of the world and has included three species from New
South Wales. All three are described and figured here.

1. ***Cellana tramoserica*** (Holten, 1802)

The shell is almost circular, with its height about half its
largest diameter; the apex is slightly posteriorly placed;
the sides are slightly convex. The margin is scalloped by
about 20 radiating ribs. The colour is mostly yellow or
orange, with radiating bands of alternating white and
black. The inside reflects the colours of the outside, but is
often more bright. The spatula is bluish grey.
Size: 42mm.
Habitat: Common on exposed intertidal rocks.
Range: Southern Queensland to South Australia.
Remarks: The southern *C. solida* Blainville, 1825 is larger,

coarser and has a bright orange, much more strongly scalloped inner margin.

2. *Patella chapmani* Tenison-Woods, 1876

The shell is flat, star-shaped, with eight strong radiating ribs, the posterior five of which are larger than the others. The whole surface of the shell is covered in fine irregular radiating ribs. The colour is white, with thin brown lines on the large radiating ribs and irregular brown maculations in the interstices. The inside is porcellaneous and white.
Size: 30mm.

Habitat: Common below low tide level on bare rocks.
Range: Central New South Wales to southern Western Australia, including Tasmania.

3. *Patella peronii* Blainville, 1825

The shell is thick, elongate, with radiating ribs of irregular strength, ornamented with small nodules. The inner margin is finely crenulated. The colour is light brown, sometimes maculated with black. The inside is porcellaneous and white.
Size: 41mm.
Habitat: Common between rocks from low tide level down.
Range: Central New South Wales to southern Western Australia, including Tasmania.

Superfamily Acmaeoidea

Family Lottiidae

The Australian species of this family were formerly included in the Acmaeidae, but Lindberg (1986) has recently split this family into true Acmaeidae and Lottiidae based on characteristics of the animal. All Australian species were included in the Lottiidae.
The shells are smaller than those of the Patellidae, limpet-shaped and often almost smooth. The animals are inhabitants of the intertidal and shallow subtidal zone. The radula is only narrow and lacks a rachidian (central) tooth (Ponder and Creese, 1980). Macpherson (1955) has revised the Australian Lottiidae and Ponder and Creese (1980) revised the species of *Notoacmea*, *Collisella* and *Patelloida*. The status of the genus *Asteracmea* is unclear, but according to Ponder and Creese (1980) the radula of the species described here is like that of *Patelloida*.
Five species are described here. One or two additional species could be found on beaches in New South Wales (Ponder and Creese, 1980).

4. *Notoacmea petterdi* (Tenison-Woods, 1876)

This species has an almost circular shell with a low apex. It is sculptured with some distant radiating ribs. The colour is dark brown or black, characterised by a black inner margin. The spatula is black or dark brown.
Size: 12mm.
Habitat: On intertidal rocks, on vertical or sloping surfaces.
Range: Southern Queensland to eastern South Australia, including Tasmania.
Remarks: This species most resembles *N. flammea*, but can be separated by its smooth ribs and dark coloured spatula.

5. *Patelloida alticostata* (Angas, 1865)

The shell is large for the Australian members of the family, with an irregular margin. The outside is often eroded and sculptured with strong irregular radiating ribs. The colour is grey and white. The interstices between the ribs have fine concentric dark lines. The inside is white, the inner margin and the spatula are black or brown.
Size: 36mm.
Habitat: On bare rocks at or below low tide level.
Range: Southern Queensland to southern Western Australia, including Tasmania.

6. *Patelloida mimula* (Iredale, 1924)

The shell is elongate, with faint radiating ribs. The outside is often eroded; the inside is white with a dark brown inner margin.
Size: 13mm.
Habitat: Common in sheltered, estuarine habitats. The animal is yellow.
Range: Northern Australia from northern Western Australia to eastern Victoria.

7. *Patelloida mufria* (Hedley, 1915)

The shell is elongate, with faint radiating ribs. The colour is white with black or dark brown radiating bands, often displaying a 'Maltese cross' pattern. The interior is white; the spatula is brown.
Size: 18mm.
Habitat: Common on rocks at exposed ocean shores. The animal is grey.
Range: Northern New South Wales to southern Western Australia.
Remarks: This species is very similar to *P. mimula*, but the shell is more smooth, the inner margin has the same colour as the rest of the inside (as opposed to a black inner margin in *P. mimula*). Also, note differences in habitat and animal colours.

8. *Asteracmea illibrata* (Verco, 1906)

The shell is minute, conical and thin. The shell surface is almost smooth. The colour is pink with light brown radiating rays.
Size: 4mm.
Range: New South Wales.

Order Neritomorpha

Superfamily Neritoidea

Family Neritidae

The members of this family are mostly tropical, although a few species live in temperate waters. The shells are characterised by their blunt shape, with a short spire and large aperture. The operculum is half-moon shaped and bears a long, curved tooth on the inside, a feature that is characteristic for the family. The family is divided into two subfamilies (Baker, 1923), the Neritinae and Smaragdiinae, both of which are represented in the Sydney area. Komatsu (1986) revised the Neritidae of Japan and concluded that the subfamilies differ in both habitat and radular characteristics. The Smaragdiinae are associated with seagrass in sandy habitats and the Neritinae live on hard substrates.

Four species were found in the Sydney area, one of which is a tropical species.

Subfamily Neritinae

Shells medium-sized to small, thick-walled, with a thickened outer lip and often a rough or sculptured surface. For Australian species see Wilson (1993).

9. ***Nerita atramentosa*** Reeve, 1855

The shell is thick and heavy, with a smooth, often eroded surface. The spire is barely raised. The colour is black, the inside and the columella are white. The operculum is brown and bears small nodules.
Size: 28mm.
Habitat: Common on intertidal stones.
Range: New South Wales to southern Western Australia.

10. *Nerita albicilla* L., 1758

The shell is heavy, with a flat spire and a flaring outer lip. The sculpture consists of broad spiral ribs with narrow interstices. The colour is black with irregular white spots. The inside, the columella and columella callus are white.
Size: 29mm, but Sydney specimens are much smaller.
Habitat: Under intertidal stones.
Range: Western Australia to northern New South Wales, Indo-Pacific.

Subfamily Smaragdiinae

Shells small to very small, thin-walled, smooth, outer lip simple. Loch (1994) gives an overview of the genus *Smaragdia* in Australia.

11. *Smaragdia souverbiana* (Gassies, 1861)

This species has a much smaller and thinner shell than the above two species. The spire is somewhat raised, especially in large specimens. The shell surface is smooth and shiny.

The colour is light green or yellow with a fine pattern of darker lines.
Size: 8mm, but mostly smaller.
Range: Central Western Australia to southern New South Wales; widespread in the Indo-Pacific, from the east African coast to Fiji, Tonga and Samoa.
Synonyms: *Smaragdella pulcherrima* Angas, 1871

12. *Smaragdia tragena* (Iredale, 1936)

This species is similar in size and thickness to the previous species, but more bulbous in shape, with a short spire. The shell surface is smooth and polished. The colour is white, with a beautiful pattern of pink lines, often arranged in squares.
Size: 5mm.
Range: Queensland, central New South Wales, Papua New Guinea.
Synonyms: *Smaragdia abakionigraphis* Drivas & Jay, 1989 may be synonymous (Loch, 1994).

Order Vetigastropoda

Superfamily Scissurelloidea

Family Scissurellidae

The species belonging to this family have minute, turboid, thin, mostly translucent white shells. At or above the periphery of the last half to one-and-a-half whorl, there is a furrow (selenizone) which ends in a slit or a hole (foramen). Herbert (1986) has revised the Scissurellidae of South Africa, reviewing the existing genera. He has recognised the following three genera:
1. *Anatoma* - selenizone at the periphery.
2. *Scissurella* - selenizone ending in a slit at the outer lip.
3. *Sinezona* - selenizone ending in a hole behind the outer lip.
In addition, McLean (1989) divided the family into four subfamilies and described several new genera and species.

Two species that can be found in shell grit are discussed here. Additional species from New South Wales are:

Scissurellinae
Sinezona beddomei (Petterd, 1884) - see under *S. atkinsoni*
Scissurella rosea remota Iredale, 1924 - southern New South Wales. Sculptured with fine spiral ribs, becoming stronger on the base. Apex pink.

Anatominae
Anatoma australis (Hedley, 1903) - a deep water species, elevated-turboid, selenizone at periphery.

Subfamily Scissurellinae

13. *Sinezona atkinsoni* (Tenison-Woods, 1877)

This shell is depressed turboid and narrowly umbilicate. The shell surface is weakly and irregularly spirally ribbed, the ribs become progressively stronger on the base. The interstices between the ribs on the base are crossed by fine axial lamellae. The selenizone is on the shoulder of the last whorl, bordered by two sharp ribs and ends in an elongate hole. The protoconch is axially ribbed. The colour is translucent white.
Size: 2mm.
Range: Southern Queensland to southern Western Australia, including Tasmania; New Zealand.
Remarks: *Sinezona beddomei* (Petterd, 1884) has strong axial ribs and no spiral sculpture.

14. *Scissurella ornata* May, 1908

The shell is depressed turboid and umbilicate. The sculpture consists of strong axial ribs, the interstices between which are finely spirally ribbed, a feature becoming stronger on the base of the shell. The selenizone is at the shoulder of the last half of the last whorl and ends in a slit in the outer lip. The colour is translucent white.
Size: 1mm.
Range: Central New South Wales to Victoria, including Tasmania.

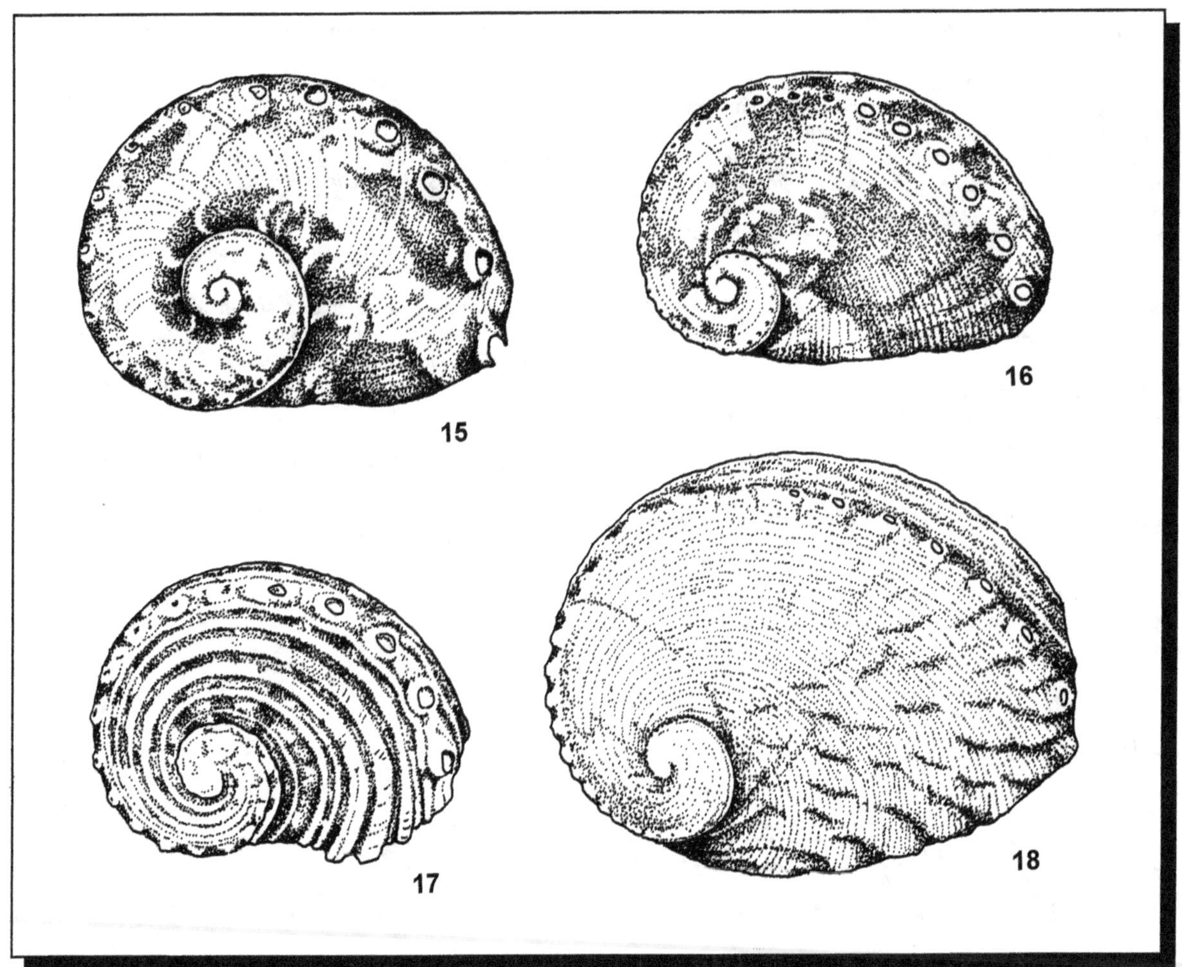

15

16

17

18

Family Haliotidae

The Haliotidae have medium-sized to very large, thick,
ear-shaped, low-spired shells, which possess a series of
holes on the shoulder of the last whorl. The recent
opinion is that the family has only one genus *Haliotis*
Linneaus, 1758. Generic or subgeneric names like
Notohaliotis Cotton and Godfrey, 1933, *Marinauris*
Iredale, 1927 and *Sanhaliotis* Iredale, 1929 have been
used in the past. Brown (1993) has investigated the
relationships between several Haliotidae, including some
Australian species. He concluded that division of the
genus may prove warranted after additional research, but
that the two common New South Wales species *H. rubra*
and *H. coccoradiata* are too genetically different to be
included in the same subgenus, *Notohaliotis*, as proposed
by Iredale and McMichael (1962).
Haliotidae live on or between stones intertidally or
subtidally. They cling to a relatively smooth substrate by
means of their powerful foot. Large specimens can be
almost impossible to remove.
Four species can be found in central New South Wales;
all are discussed and figured here.

15. *Haliotis brazieri* Angas, 1859

The shell is small and thin for the family. The apex is at
one third of the largest diameter from the shell margin.
There are three to five open holes on the shoulder, which
are situated on tubes. The shell surface above the
shoulder is almost smooth, there are some spiral ribs
below the shoulder. The colour is mostly red, maculated
with green or white.
Size: 23mm.
Habitat: Uncommon between stones subtidally.
Range: Southern Queensland to Central New South
Wales.

16. *Haliotis coccoradiata* Reeve, 1846

The shell is elongate and rather thin. The apex is at one
fourth of the largest diameter from the shell margin. There
are six or seven open holes on the shoulder. The shell
surface is sculptured with flat, irregular, fine spiral ribs,
which are wider than the interstices between them. The
colour is red with white and green maculations.
Size: 50mm.
Habitat: Common under intertidal stones.
Range: Southern Queensland to eastern Victoria.

17. *Haliotis hargravesi* Cox, 1869

This species is very similar to *H. brazieri*, from which it differs in possessing a sculpture of irregular high, flat-topped spiral ribs. There are three to four open holes on the shoulder. The colour is red with white and green maculations.
Size: 23mm.
Habitat: Uncommon under subtidal rocks.
Range: Southern Queensland to central New South Wales.
Remarks: The similarities with *H. brazieri* raise questions regarding the relationship between these species. *Marinauris melculus* and *M. ethologus* both Iredale, 1929 from southern Queensland also belong in this group.

Superfamily Fissurelloidea

Family Fissurellidae

Fissurellidae live worldwide from the intertidal zone down to deep water. They live on hard substrates, feeding mainly on algae or sponges, but the genus *Puncturella* was found to feed on Foraminifera (Herbert, 1991). The family has been divided into subfamilies based on morphological, radula and shell characteristics (e.g. McLean, 1984).
The shells are flat or limpet-shaped, often with either a hole in the apex or a slit in the anterior margin. The interior is usually porcellaneous and white, with a hoof-shaped muscle scar.
Ten species from central New South Wales are discussed here; some additional species can be found in southern New South Wales or in deep water (see Macpherson and Gabriel, 1962; Wilson, 1993).

Subfamily Fissurellinae

Shells with an apical hole, which is bordered by a rim of callus internally.

19. *Amblychilepas javanicensis* (Lamarck, 1822)

The shell is saddle-shaped, thin and roundly square, with a centrally placed elongate hole. The sculpture consists of concentric ribs. The colour is white with red radiating bands. The interior is white.
Size: 12mm.
Range: Southern Queensland to southern Western Australia.

20. *Amblychilepas nigrita* (Sowerby, 1834)

The shell is elongate, shield-shaped, with a centrally placed elongate hole. The shell surface is almost smooth except for some concentric growth lines. The colour is brownish pink with darker or lighter maculations or faint radiating bands. The interior is white.
Size: 19mm, but mostly smaller.
Habitat: Common under intertidal stones.
Range: Central New South Wales to southern Western

18. *Haliotis rubra* Leach, 1814

The shell is very large, heavy and rounded. The apex is at one fourth of the largest diameter from the shell margin. There are six or seven open holes on the shoulder. The sculpture consists of irregular rough spiral ribs crossed by fine axial lamellae forming small scales. The colour is uniform red.
Size: 131mm.
Habitat: Common between and under intertidal and subtidal rocks.
Range: Central New South Wales to eastern Victoria.
Remarks: Juveniles are separated from *H. coccoradiata* by their rounder shape, more pronounced ribs and more uniform colouration.

Australia.
Remarks: More common, narrower and more smooth than *A. javanicensis*.

21. *Cosmetalepas concatenatus* (Crosse & Fischer, 1864)

The shell is round and much flatter than most other species in this family. There is a hole in the middle of the shell, which is elongate, narrowed in the middle by two pieces of callus. The sculpture consists of small round pits in a smooth surface. The colour is entirely white.
Size: 16mm.
Range: Central New South Wales to central Western Australia.

Subfamily Diodorinae

Shells with a hole in the apex and a muscle scar with hook-shaped ends.

22. *Diodora ticaonica* (Reeve, 1850)

The shell is small, but thick. The sculpture consists of fine radiating ribs crossed by very fine concentric ribs. The hole is elongate and narrow and has two sets of knobs on the inside, dividing it into three compartments. The colour is off-white, often with grey radiating bands. The inside is white.
Size: 9mm, but grows larger.
Range: Central Western Australia to central New South Wales; Indo-Pacific.

23. *Diodora lineata* Sowerby, 1835

The shell is limpet-shaped and elongate. The hole in the apex is round or slightly elongate. The sculpture consists of radiating ribs crossed by finer concentric ribs. The inner margin is crenulate. The colour is light brown, often with red or dark brown radiating bands.

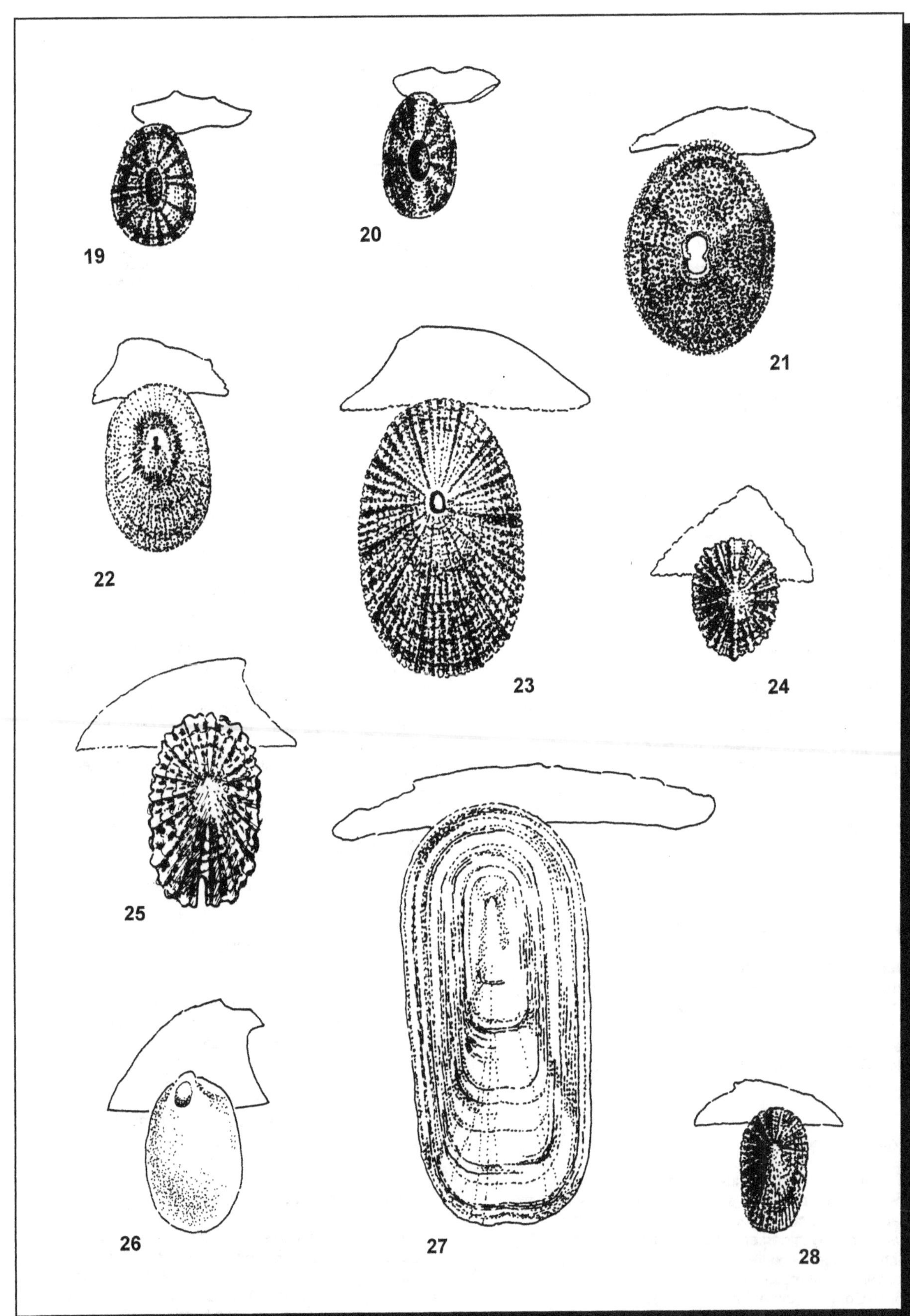

19
20
21
22
23
24
25
26
27
28

Size: 50mm, but mostly smaller.
Habitat: Under intertidal stones.
Range: Southern Queensland to Victoria.
Synonyms: *Elegidion audax* Iredale, 1924 (Ponder, 1975a).
Remarks: *D. jukesii* (Reeve, 1849) from Queensland and *D. lincolnensis* Cotton, 1930 from South Australia are rougher sculptured and the latter has a square hole.

Subfamily Emarginulinae

Shells with a slit or small excavation in the posterior margin. The shells are often white.

24. *Clypidina rugosa* (Quoy & Gaimard, 1834)

The shell is limpet-shaped and conical, with a very small notch in the anterior margin. The sculpture consists of strong irregular radiating ribs crossed by fine concentric ribs. The rib running from the apex to the notch in the anterior margin is enlarged. The inner margin is crenulated. The colour is greenish white, often with grey bands. The interior is white; the spatula is often darker.
Size: 25mm.
Habitat: Common on rocks intertidally, often eroded and overgrown with algae.
Range: Northern Queensland to southern Western Australia.

25. *Notomella candida* (A. Adams, 1851)

The shell is delicate and thin, with a slit in the anterior margin. The sculpture consists of delicate radiating and concentric ribs of about equal strength, with an elevated rib from the slit to the apex. The colour is uniform white.
Size: 14mm.
Range: Southern New South Wales to southern Western Australia.
Remarks: The Victorian *N. dilecta* (A. Adams, 1851) is more elongate, more finely sculptured and it has a furrow from the apex to the slit in the anterior margin.

26. *Puncturella kesteveni* Hedley, 1900

The shell is small for this family, fragile, with an elongate hole just below the apex; the hole is obscured from the inside by a plate-like process. The shell surface is rough, without obvious sculpture. The inside margin is smooth. The colour is white.
Size: 2.4mm.
Range: New South Wales.

27. *Scutus antipodes* Montfort, 1810

This species has the largest shell of all Australian shallow water Fissurellidae. It is flat and elongate in shape, with the apex placed at one fourth of the shell length from the posterior margin. The posterior margin is rounded; the anterior margin is concave. The sculpture consists of irregular concentric growth lines. The colour is white.
Size: 92mm.
Habitat: Common under large intertidal rocks. The animal is black and very slippery and much too big for its shell.
Range: New South Wales to southern Western Australia.

28. *Tugali parmophoidea* (Quoy & Gaimard, 1834)

The shell is elongate, limpet-shaped, with the apex at one third of the shell length from the posterior margin. There is a very faint notch in the anterior margin. The sculpture consists of a fine reticulate pattern of radiating and concentric ribs. The colour is white.
Size: 23mm.
Habitat: Under intertidal stones. The animal is orange.
Range: New South Wales and eastern Victoria.
Synonyms: *T. elegans* (Gray, 1843)
Remarks: *T. cicatricosa* A. Adams, 1852 from Victoria is more coarsely sculptured and some specimens have a scar-like impression around the apex.

Superfamily Trochoidea

Family Turbinidae

A large and diverse family of species with minute to very large turboid shells, with a high or low spire and a horny to heavy calcareous operculum.
Hickman and McLean (1990) have revised this family on the basis of animal and shell characteristics. The radula features, and especially the shape of the central tooth, are diagnostic for the family; some Turbinidae have a pronounced asymmetric radula. The animals are herbivorous and graze amongst seaweed and algae on hard substrates.
Nine subfamilies were recognised by Hickman and McLean (1990), seven of which live in Australia. Four are treated here. Additional Australian subfamilies are the Angariinae and Colloniinae, representatives of which live in tropical Australia, and the Gabrieloninae, one representative of which lives in Victoria and South Australia (Robertson, 1973).

Subfamily Liotiinae

Flat, umbilicate, small to medium-sized, low-spired shells mostly with reticulate sculpture and a thickened outer lip. The operculum is horny with a calcareous outer layer. The periostracum is calcified. The radula is symmetrical. Laseron (1954a) has included a number of species of this subfamily in his revision of the New South Wales 'Liotiidae', including some deep water species.

29. *Austroliotia botanica* (Hedley, 1915)

The shell is small, but thick, low-spired and widely umbilicate. The sculpture consists of a reticulate pattern of spiral and axial ribs, the spiral rib at the base is enlarged.

The aperture is circular; the outer lip is formed by a thickened axial rib, and is slightly oblique. The colour is dirty white.
Size: 8mm.
Range: Northern Queensland to South Australia, including northern Tasmania.

Subfamily Turbininae

Large to medium-sized, heavy shells. The aperture is oblique, but the angle to the axis of coiling can vary. The whorls are rounded or flat. The operculum is strongly calcified, often with ridges or pustules on the outside, or spectacularly coloured. The radula has a reduced central tooth, and is clearly asymmetrical.
Six members of this subfamily are described here, four of which are common. Species of the genus *Turbo* are especially widespread on the coast and coral reefs off Queensland, a few of these species range into northern New South Wales (Wilson, 1993).

30. *Astralium tentoriiforme* (Jonas, 1845)

The shell is heavy and conical, with a strong keel at its base, sculptured with fine irregular growth lines, but often eroded. The base is concave, with spiral ribs which bear fine lamellae. The aperture is very oblique, especially in large specimens. The columella is reflected and partly covers the base of the shell. The colour is light grey to pink. The operculum is white with a pink and blue rim.
Size: Up to 60mm.
Habitat: Intertidally to about 5m on large stones.
Range: Southern Queensland to Victoria.
Synonyms: *A. sirius* (Gould, 1849); this name has often been used for this species, but Ponder (1975*b*) found that the type specimen is a juvenile of the tropical *Astralium rhodostomus* (Lamarck, 1822).

31. *Astralium kesteveni* (Iredale, 1924)

The shell is depressed conical, with convex sides. The sculpture consists of a pattern of small nodules formed by oblique growth lines crossed by transverse axial grooves. The base is flat with slightly lamellose spiral ribs. The colour is dirty white; the columella is nacreous with a white, callous rim. The operculum is white with black.
Size: Up to 30mm.
Habitat: Subtidally on rocks.
Range: New South Wales and eastern Victoria.
Remarks: *Astraea tentoriiformis* has a much larger and higher spired shell. *A. squamifera* (Koch, 1844) from Victoria to Western Australia has a more convex base and is slightly indented in the umbilical area.

32. *Ninella torquata* (Gmelin, 1791)

The shell is turbiniform, umbilicate, large and heavy. The sculpture consists of faint broad ribs crossed by rough axial lamellae, often forming nodules immediately below the sutures. The colour is dirty grey to greenish grey. The operculum has a very distinct spiral rib and is white.
Size: Up to 100mm.

Habitat: Intertidally and subtidally on rocky shores. The animals are collected for food.
Range: New South Wales to southern Western Australia.
Synonyms: *N. whitleyi* Iredale, 1949

33. *Subninella undulata* (Lightfoot, 1786)

The shell is turbiniform, blunt, umbilicate and sculptured with broad spiral ribs. The colour is dark greenish, maculated with white. Fresh specimens have a thick, dark brown periostracum. The operculum is smooth and white.
Size: 39mm, but mostly smaller.
Habitat: Very common on intertidal rock flats.
Range: New South Wales to southern Western Australia.
Remarks: This species grows to a larger size, and is higher spired in Victoria, Tasmania and South Australia.

34. *Turbo exquisitus* Angas, 1877

The shell is thin and light-weight for the family, imperforate and rather high-spired. The whorls are shouldered; the sutures are indented. The sculpture consists of irregular spiral ribs with exquisite lamellae, which are often eroded in beach specimens. The columella is reflected over the umbilical area. The colour is dirty brownish pink with irregular darker and lighter maculations; the umbilical area is white.
Size: 31mm.
Range: Southern New South Wales to Victoria.

35. *Turbo imperialis* Gmelin, 1791

The shell is large and heavy and imperforate. The whorls are rounded and smooth, but not polished. The outside of the operculum bears small pustules. The colour is green with patterns of orange and brown. The columella and the inside of the shell are nacreous, the operculum is white.
Size: up to 80mm.
Range: Northern Queensland to southern New South Wales, Indo-Pacific.
Synonyms: *T. militaris* Reeve, 1848

Subfamily Tricoliinae

The shells are smaller than 10mm, high-spired for the family and colourful. The pigments fluoresce under ultraviolet light. The shell surface is mostly smooth. The operculum is calcareous. Sexual shell dimorphism is common in the genus *Tricolia* (Robertson, 1985).
The radula has a pronounced dip in the middle of each row of teeth.
Two species can be found in New South Wales, one is a very common Indo-Pacific species, the other is endemic to Australia.

36. *Tricolia variabilis* Pease, 1861

The shell is minute and thin, high-spired. The whorls are rounded; the last whorl is slightly inflated. The aperture is circular. The columella and the inside of the outer lip are

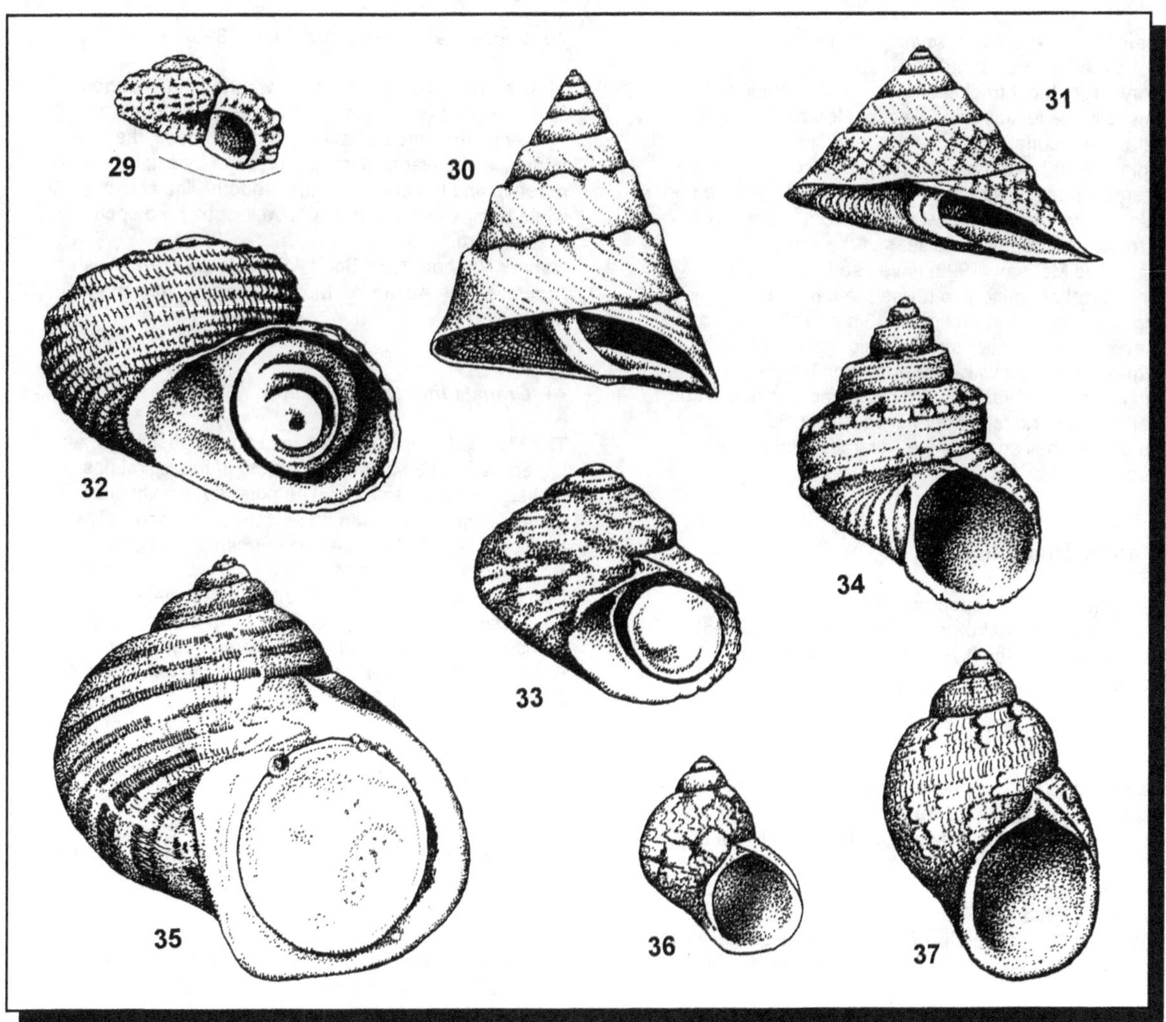

smooth. The shell surface is smooth and polished. The colour is pink marked with white and green.

Size: Up to 4mm.

Habitat: On algae intertidally. The female shells are much larger than the males and it is one of the few species in which radular sexual dimorphism is known.

Range: Central New South Wales to Victoria; widespread throughout the Indo-Pacific.

Remarks: *T. rosea* (Angas, 1867) is another species that can be found in New South Wales. It is more high spired than *T. variabilis*, is bright red or pink and has a sculptured protoconch.

Subfamily Phasianellidae

The shells are high-spired, thin, smooth, imperforate and often have beautiful colour patterns. The shell is brittle. The aperture is simple; the outer lip is thin. The operculum is calcareous and teardrop-shaped. The radula has no central tooth.

Phasianella australis Gmelin, 1791, which cannot be found in New South Wales, is a well-known Australian member of this subfamily. *P. variegata* Lamarck, 1822 is the Indo-Pacific representative of this genus.

37. *Phasianella ventricosa* Swainson, 1822

The shell is high-spired; the whorls are rounded and smooth, with a polished surface. The colour is pink or red with patterns of brown and white. The inside and the columella are white. The operculum is calcareous, white and teardrop-shaped.

Size: Up to 50mm, but Sydney specimens are much smaller.

Habitat: Between seaweed subtidally.

Range: Central New South Wales to southern Western Australia.

Remarks: *P. australis* Gmelin, 1791, from southern Australia, is higher-spired and grows to a larger size.

Family Trochidae

It is hard to give a quick description of a trochid shell. Most are medium sized, but some are minute and some are very large. Most trochids have a conical shell, but some shells are lenticular or elevate. Nearly all trochid shells are nacreous inside, but this also applies to most Turbinids. Most have a horny operculum, but some have no operculum at all. Needless to say, it is a very large and diverse family, members of which live from the intertidal zone to abyssal depths in all seas of the world. Hickman and McLean (1990) have used radular and morphological characters to revise the family at suprageneric level and recognise 13 subfamilies, divided into several tribes. Thirty species belonging to six subfamilies are dealt with here. Although the proper diagnosis of the subfamilies is through morphological and radular tooth characters, they will be briefly described based on the shell shape of the Australian members of the subfamily.

Subfamily Eucyclinae

There are two types of species in this subfamily: a group of species that live mainly in shallow water (described below) and a group that live in very deep water (tribe Calliotropini).

Tribe Chilodontini

Shells are thick, with reticulate or lamellose sculpture. The whorls are rounded; the sutures are impressed. The shape of the aperture is nearly circular. The outer lip is usually thickened, with denticles or lirae; the columella often possesses a tooth. Animals live mostly at shallow depths, although a deep water species, *Danilia telebathia* Hedley, 1911 lives at depths of 100m or more off the New South Wales coast (for description see Wilson, 1993).

38. *Euchelus aspersus* (Philippi, 1846)

The shell is thick, imperforate with rounded whorls and fine sculpture of spiral ribs crossed by very fine axial lamellae. The columella has a small nodule. The outer lip is crenulated. The colour is light brown or pink with small darker spots.
Size: 18mm.
Habitat: Common under stones intertidally.
Range: Northern New South Wales to southern Western Australia, including Tasmania.

39. *Herpetopoma scabriuscula* (A. Adams & Angas, 1867)

The shell is very small to minute, thick and narrowly umbilicate. The sculpture consists of about nine unequal spiral ribs on the last whorl, crossed by oblique axial lamellae. The columella has a tooth at its base, followed by a deep notch and another tooth. The aperture is circular. The inside of the outer lip is weakly lirate. The colour is brownish purple, often mottled with white. The columella and the umbilical area are white.
Size: 4mm.
Range: Central New South Wales to eastern Victoria.

40. *Vaceuchelus ampullus* (Tate, 1893)

The shell is thick, with rounded whorls, and imperforate. The sculpture on the last whorl consists of four strong spiral ribs and three weaker ribs on the base, the interstices between which are crossed by axial ribs. The outer lip and the columella are smooth. The colour is off-white to pink; the spiral ribs have irregular red spots.
Size: 13mm.
Range: Northern New South Wales to southern Western Australia. The Australian Museum has no specimens from Victoria.

41. *Granata imbricata* (Lamarck, 1822)

The shell is flat, ear-shaped, with a large last whorl, and imperforate. The sculpture consists of fine spiral ribs crossed by axial lamellae. The outer lip is crenulated. The colour is light brown with small dark brown spots. The interior is beautifully nacreous in fresh specimens.
Size: 39mm.
Habitat: Under stones intertidally. The animal is white and possesses numerous tentacles around the edges of the mantle. The animal has a small, horny operculum.
Range: Northern New South Wales to central Western Australia, including Tasmania.

Subfamily Trochinae

The shells of this subfamily are conical to elevate-conical and are common in the intertidal zone or shallow water.

Tribe Trochini

The shells are conical, with an incomplete peristome and often denticles on the columella. The Australian species of this tribe are members of the genera *Trochus*, *Tectus* (both tropical) and *Clanculus*.

42. *Clanculus brunneus* A. Adams, 1853

The shell is conical, sharply keeled and widely umbilicate. The spire whorls are flat. The sculpture consists of irregular spiral rows of nodules. The columella is straight and has one bifid tooth. The shell is mostly dirty brown, but may also be pink, and is mottled with blotches of dark brown, black or dark red. The base of the shell usually has a lighter colour. The apex is frequently green.
Size: 16mm.
Habitat: Intertidally under stones.
Range: Northern New South Wales to far eastern Victoria.
Remarks: The southern Australian *C. limbatus* Quoy & Gaimard, 1834, has a coarser sculpture and a nodulose rib around the umbilicus; it does not live in the Sydney area, but is common in Victoria, South Australia and Western Australia.

43. *Clanculus clangulus* (Wood, 1828)

The shell is conical, widely umbilicate and roundly keeled. The whorls are rounded, with impressed sutures. The last whorl has seven to eight narrow spiral nodulose cords, seven to eight; the cords become more crowded towards the periphery. The base has closely packed spiral cords. The inside of the outer lip has one tooth. The columella has a prominent bifid tooth near its base. The colour is dark green to olive brown, mottled with red. The base is much lighter in colour with many small red spots. The columella and the umbilical area are white.
Size: 14mm.
Habitat: Under stones intertidally and subtidally.
Range: Southern Queensland to far southern New South Wales.

44. *Clanculus floridus* (Philippi, 1848)

The shell is depressed conical, with rounded whorls and impressed sutures, and is widely umbilicate. The sculpture consists of spiral rows of nodules, which become smaller on the base. The inside of the outer lip is lirate, and has one tooth. The columella has one prominent bifid tooth. The colour is pink or light brown, with a pattern of darker blotches especially below the suture of the last whorl. The columella and the umbilical area are white.
Size: 12mm.
Habitat: Under stones intertidally.
Range: Northern New South Wales to eastern Victoria.

45. *Clanculus maugeri* (Wood, 1828)

The shell is conical and much larger than the other *Clanculus* species discussed here. It is roundly keeled, with a flat base. The sculpture consists of spiral rows of square nodules. The colour is reddish brown with small white spots. The apex is frequently green.
Size: 22mm.
Range: Northern New South Wales to eastern Victoria.

46. *Clanculus plebejus* (Philippi, 1851)

The shell is low-spired, with rounded whorls and impressed sutures. The sculpture consists of (from the suture down): two spiral cords close together, a wide space, a strong single cord, another wide space and two cords together at the periphery. There are some weak spiral grooves on the base. The outer lip is thickened. The columella has an insignificant tooth. The umbilicus is wide, but filled with callus and rather shallow. The colour is brown, mottled with black, white and pink. The columella and the area around the umbilicus are white.
Size: 10mm.
Habitat: Under intertidal stones.
Range: Southern New South Wales to southern Western Australia.

47. *Clanculus undatoides* Tenison-Woods, 1879

The shell is conical, with flat whorls and indented sutures. The sculpture consists of fine spiral cords with small nodules; the interstices are narrow. A broad spiral rib forms a sharp keel on the last whorl. The columella has a small tooth. The umbilicus is narrow and very shallow. The colour is purple, sometimes mottled with white. The keel on the last whorl has alternating white and purple spots.
Size: 11mm.
Range: Southern New South Wales.
Remarks: The Victorian *C. aloysii* Tenison-Woods, 1879 and South Australian *C. philippii* (Koch, 1843) are similar to this species. The first is lighter in colour, the second darker and is more coarsely sculptured. Cotton and Godfrey (1934) have synonymised these two species, but their status, and relationship with *C. undatoides*, remains unclear.

Tribe Gibbulini

The shells are depressed conical to conical, often with rounded whorls and impressed sutures. There is a wide range of genera and subgenera in the tribe, the status of some of which is unclear.

48. *Austrocochlea concamerata* (Wood, 1828)

The shell is roundly conical, heavy and thick-walled and imperforate. The sculpture consists of broad spiral ribs, the interstices between which are narrow. The columella is smooth except for a small tooth near the base of the shell. The colour is black; the spiral ribs bear small yellow, often triangular spots. The inside and the columella are white.
Size: 14mm.
Habitat: On intertidal rocks in sheltered bays.
Range: Southern New South Wales to southern Western Australia. Uncommon in Sydney.

49. *Austrocochlea constricta* (Lamarck, 1822)

This species is similar to *A. concamerata* but is more conical, higher-spired, more coarsely sculptured and has narrower ribs. The colour is purple with white bands.
Size: 25mm.
Habitat: Extremely common on exposed intertidal rocks.
Range: Southern Queensland to southern Western Australia.

50. *Nanula tasmanica* (Petterd, 1879)

The shell is very small, blunt and thin and narrowly umbilicate. The sides of the spire are convex; the whorls are slightly rounded. The shell surface is matt and almost smooth. The columella is slightly concave, reflected and smooth. The colour is off-white to yellowish, marked with darker coloured streaks or spots. The apical whorls are often darker than the rest of the shell.
Size: 5mm.
Range: Southern New South Wales to Victoria and Tasmania.
Remarks: *Cantharidella picturata* A. Adams & Angas, 1864 is similar but larger, has a straight columella and a more angular appearance.

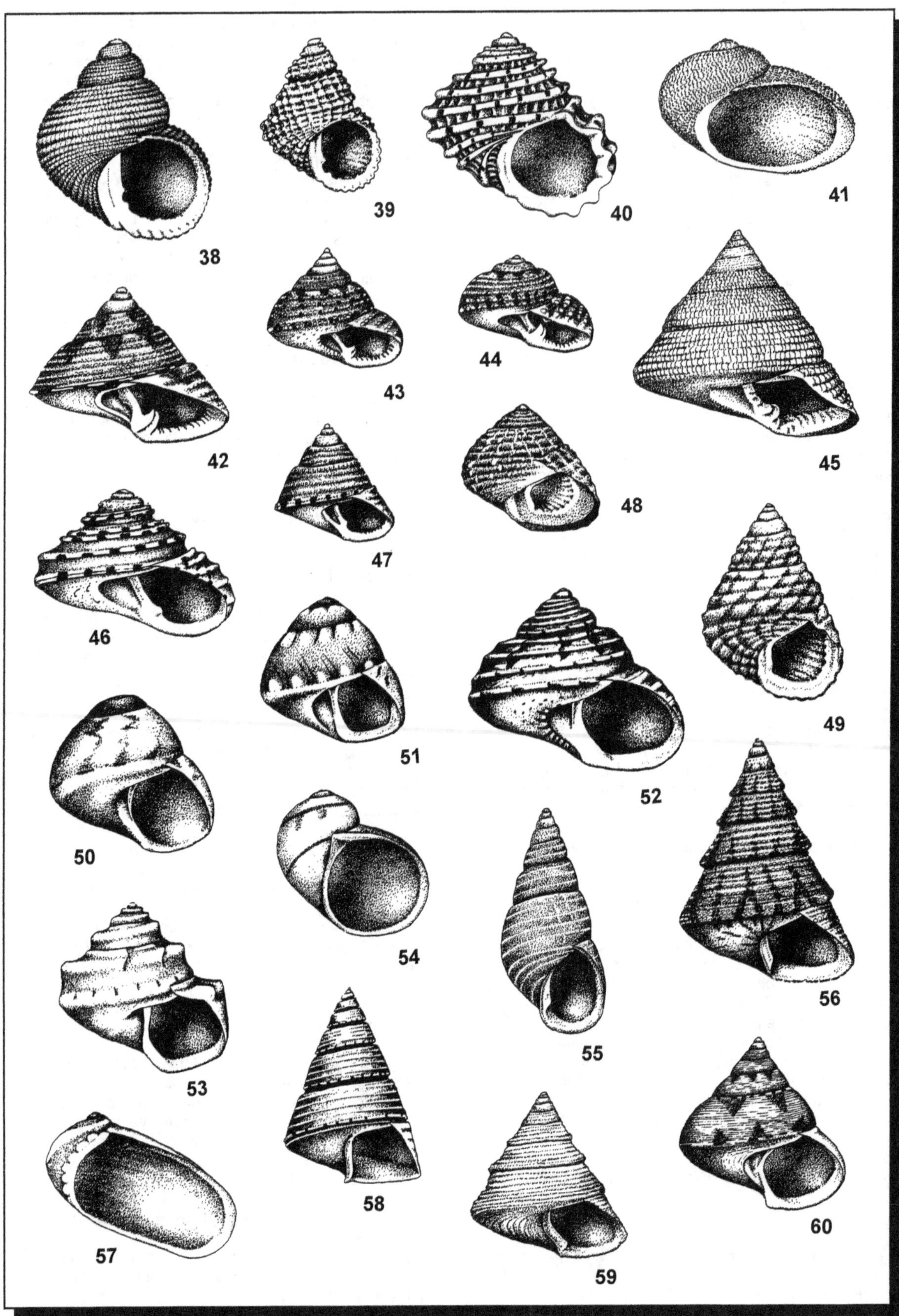

51. *Cantharidella picturata* (A. Adams and Angas, 1864)

The shell is very small, blunt and narrowly umbilicate. The spire whorls are flat; the sutures are barely impressed. The shell surface is smooth apart from two indistinct ribs at the periphery. The shell has red or brown patterns on a white background. The columella is white.
Size: 7mm.
Habitat: Common under intertidal stones.
Range: Northern New South Wales to eastern Victoria.

52. *Eurytrochus strangei* (A. Adams, 1853)

The shell is small, conical, thick and narrowly umbilicate. The whorls are rounded, with impressed sutures. The sculpture consists of four to five prominent narrow ribs above the periphery. The base has weak ribs. The outer lip is dentate within; the columella is slightly reflected. The colour is dark olive brown mottled with black and white. The base is covered in pink lines, which are most prominent near the umbilicus, where the background is white. The apex and columella are often tinted green.
Size: 8mm.
Habitat: Common under intertidal stones.
Range: Northern Queensland to eastern Victoria.

53. *Notogibbula bicarinata* (A. Adams, 1854)

The shell is thick and turbiniform; the whorls are angular, with both a shoulder and a keel. The shell surface is smooth, but not polished. The outer lip and columella are smooth; the umbilicus is narrow but deep. The colour is a delicate pink with dark purple or brown markings. Sometimes there is a pattern of darker pink zigzag lines.
Size: 10mm.
Range: Southern New South Wales to southern Western Australia.

54. *Fossarina patula* A. Adams and Angas, 1863

The shell is small and narrowly umbilicate. The last whorl is inflated and rapidly expanding; the spire is short. The shell surface is smooth, but not polished. The outer lip is sharp and smooth inside; the columella is smooth. The colour is off-white to yellow, irregularly mottled with bands or spots of chocolate brown, which also appear on the inside of the shell. This species is unusual in the Trochidae in that the inside is not nacreous. The columella is white.
Size: 5mm.
Range: New South Wales.
Remarks: *F. petterdi* Crosse, 1870 is a southern Australian species, which does not live in Sydney.

Tribe Cantharidini

The shells are elevate-conical, often with straight sides. A wide range of genera exists in this tribe and shell sizes range from medium-sized to minute.

55. *Phasianotrochus eximius* (Perry, 1811)

A well-known and common southern Australian species, characterised by its elongate shell with flat whorls and only slightly impressed sutures. The shell surface is polished and smooth. The colour is olive brown, sometimes maculated with a few white spots, especially in small specimens. The inside is bright iridescent blue.
Size: 33mm, but mostly much smaller.
Habitat: On seaweed at or below the low-tide mark on rocky ocean shores.
Range: Southern Queensland to southern Western Australia.
Remarks: This is the only species of *Phasianotrochus* that can be found in New South Wales; there are four additional species that are commonly found along the south coast of Australia.

56. *Odontotrochus indistinctus* (Wood, 1828)

The shell is thick and conical, and imperforate. The sutures are indented, each whorl starting below the widest point of the previous whorl. The sculpture consists of irregular spiral threads of rounded nodules, which become more closely packed towards the periphery, which is roundly keeled. The base is convex, bearing fine spiral cords of nodules. The columella is smooth except for one insignificant tooth at its base. The colour is grey, mottled with dark purple or red and white spots.
Size: 21mm.
Habitat: On seaweed in sheltered habitats.
Range: Southern Queensland to eastern Victoria.
Synonyms: *Thalotia marginata* Tenison-Woods, 1879 and *T. comtessei* Iredale, 1931 (Jansen, 1993).

Subfamily Stomatellinae

The shells are flat with a large aperture. The operculum is lost. The foot is very large and cannot be fully retracted in the shell. Instead, the animal is capable of autotomy (= shedding of body parts), a feature often observed in *Gena impertusa*, the only New South Wales representative of the subfamily (Loch, 1989). The species belonging to this subfamily live mostly in shallow water.

57. *Gena impertusa* (Burrows, 1815)

A common species, characterised by its thin almost smooth, ear-shaped shell, which is similar in shape to a *Haliotis*, but lacks the row of holes in the last whorl. The sculpture consists of fine spiral grooves. The colour is variable, usually dark with patterns of lighter dots, streaks or waves.
Size: 18mm.
Habitat: On the underside of rocks. The animal is very active.
Range: Southern Queensland to Victoria, probably to southern Western Australia (see below).
Remarks: The status of the species of *Gena* in Australia is unclear (Jansen, 1994). *S. auricula* Lamarck, 1816 from Victoria to Western Australia is possibly a synonym.

Subfamily Calliostomatinae

The shells in this subfamily are conical, with straight sides. An important diagnostic feature of the subfamily is the honeycombed pattern on the protoconch, which can be distinguished under a binocular microscope. Iredale (e.g. 1924, 1929a) and Cotton and Godfrey have caused a proliferation of genera, the status of which is currently under revision (B. Marshall, personal communication). Most Australian species live in offshore waters, although a few can be found intertidally.

58. *Calliostoma (Fautor) comptum* (A. Adams, 1854)

The shell is small, conical, and imperforate. The spire whorls are flat; the sutures are incised. The last whorl has a strong keel. The sculpture above the periphery consists of four spiral cords bearing small nodules. The base of the shell has very fine spiral ribs. The outer lip is sharp; the columella is straight and smooth. The colour is light brown. The spiral cord closest to the periphery bears alternating white and pink spots. The apex is often purple.
Size: 5mm.
Range: Northern Queensland to southern New South Wales, New Caledonia.
Synonyms: *Calliostoma purpureocinctum* Hedley, 1894.

59. *Calliostoma speciosum* (A. Adams, 1854)

The shell is medium-sized, conical, thick, stout and imperforate; the sutures are slightly indented. The sculpture consists of many irregular fine spiral ribs, which may bear small granules. The base is flat; the periphery is roundly angulate and marked by an enlarged rib. The columella is simple and reflected. The colour is dirty white, marked with irregular large red or purplish maculations. The columella and the inside are nacreous.
Size: 25mm.
Range: Southern Queensland to central New South Wales.
Remarks: Iredale and McMichael (1962) place *C. speciosum* in the genus *Pulchrastele* Iredale, 1929. However, the type species of that genus, *Calliostoma septenarium* Melvill and Standen, 1899, is a *Clanculus* and belongs in an entirely different subfamily.

60. *Astelena scitula* (A. Adams, 1855)

The shell is conical, narrowly umbilicate, with the sutures impressed. The sides of the spire are concave. The sculpture consists of many fine irregular spiral cords. A more prominent cord encircles the periphery. The colour is light brown, mottled with red; the apex is often dark purple. The base of the shell is usually much more uniformly coloured, bearing only thin bands of red spots.
Size: 12mm.
Habitat: Under stones intertidally and subtidally.
Range: Northern New South Wales to eastern Victoria.

Subfamily Solariellinae

The shells belonging to this subfamily are mostly low-spired, with a simple, almost circular aperture and rounded whorls. The peristome is nearly complete. Most species are widely umbilicate. The animal has long tentacles and the anterior end of the foot is split into two well-developed lobes. Most Australian species live in deeper water, but a few can be found on the beach.

61. *Minolops pulcherrima pulcherrima* (Angas, 1869)

The shell is thin, depressed conical and widely umbilicate. The spire whorls are rounded, each with two strong spiral ribs; the last whorl has three such spiral ribs. The entire shell surface is covered in fine spiral ribs crossed by very fine axial lamellae, giving the shell surface a felt-like appearance (best observed under a microscope). The aperture is circular and simple. The colour is off-white; the large spiral ribs have irregular bright pink spots.
Size: 14mm.
Range: Southern Queensland to southern New South Wales.
Synonyms: *M. rosulenta* (Watson, 1886)
Remarks: *M. pulcherrima emendata* Iredale, 1924 is similar but flatter and has more than three large spiral ribs on the last whorl. *M. arata* Hedley, 1903 is similar, but larger, coarser and lacks the felt-like sculpture.

62. *Spectamen bellulum* (Angas, 1869)

The shell is conical, thin and widely umbilicate. The whorls are slightly shouldered; the sutures are indented. The surface is smooth and shiny except for a nodulose rib around the umbilicus. In some specimens the shell surface has fine spiral grooves; this form has been named *S. epitheca* Iredale, 1929. The colour is milky white, translucent, marked with distinct axial bands of pink, which stop abruptly at the periphery. The base is white.
Size: 14mm.
Range: Southern Queensland to southern New South Wales.
Remarks: *S. philippense* (Watson, 1881) from Victoria and Tasmania is flatter, more widely umbilicate, larger and more red in colour. It lacks the row of nodules around the umbilicus. Also, the red axial bands continue on the base of the shell.

Subfamily Umboniinae

The shell shape in this subfamily ranges from lenticular to elevate. The apertural characteristics are simple. Most live in sand or on seagrass in sandy habitats.

Tribe Monileini

Shells lenticular, with a wide range of apertural characters. Common in tropical and subtropical shallow waters of Australia.

63. *Ethminolia probabilis* Iredale, 1924

The shell is depressed conical and widely umbilicate. The whorls are strongly shouldered, with indented sutures. The shell surface is smooth but not polished. The aperture is circular and simple. The colour is a dirty white mottled

with pink.
Size: 8mm.
Range: Central New South Wales to eastern Victoria.

64. *Monilea callifera* (Lamarck, 1822)

The shell is heavy and depressed conical. The whorls are
flatly rounded, with impressed sutures. The sculpture
consists of double spiral ribs, which are crossed by fine
growth lines. The aperture is almost circular; the outer lip
is crenulated; the columella bears a single tooth formed
by a spiral groove around the umbilicus. The umbilicus is
wide and deep, sometimes partially obscured by callus.
The colour is a dirty white, mottled with pink or purple.
Size: 24mm.
Range: Southern Western Australia to central New South
Wales, Indo-Pacific.
Synonyms: *Monilea lentiginosa* A. Adams, 1853, *Talopia
dividua* Iredale, 1927, *Talopia morti* Iredale, 1927.
Remarks: It appears that *M. callifera* no longer lives in the
Sydney area (C. Hickman, personal communication). It is
a common species throughout the Indo-Pacific.

65. *Talopena gloriola* Iredale, 1929

The shell is conical and umbilicate. The whorls are
rounded and slightly shouldered; the sutures are
impressed. The sculpture consists of many weak spiral
ribs. The colour is a dirty brown, with irregular markings of
darker brown; the area around the umbilicus is white.
Size: 11mm.
Range: New South Wales.

Tribe Bankiviini

Hickman and McLean (1990) created this tribe for the
southern Australian genus *Bankivia*, because of its
unusual, mostly smooth high-spired shells and unusual
mode of life. Animals live burrowed in sand and use their
modified neck lobes to inhale and exhale water. The eye
stalks are reduced and some species have no eyes at all.
The shells have lost the interior nacreous layer.

66. *Bankivia fasciata* (Menke, 1830)

A common species on sandy beaches, characterised by
its high-spired, thin, smooth and polished shell with
straight sides. The whorls are only slightly rounded. The
aperture is typically teardrop-shaped. The colour is
variable, and may be white with bands or patterns of
purple, pink or brown.
Size: 18mm.
Habitat: in large aggregations in fine sand down to 15m.
Range: Northern New South Wales to South Australia.

67. *Leiopyrga lineolaris* (Gould, 1861)

The shell is high-spired, thin, and imperforate or narrowly
umbilicate. The whorls are rounded with impressed
sutures. The shell surface is smooth, but some shells
have a single spiral rib just above the suture. The outer lip
is thin; the columella is reflected. The colour is mostly
white with patterns of pink and brown lines, which often
have a smudged appearance.
Size: 10mm.
Range: Northern New South Wales to Victoria.
Remarks: This species is similar to *Bankivia fasciata*, but
is smaller, broader and has impressed sutures.

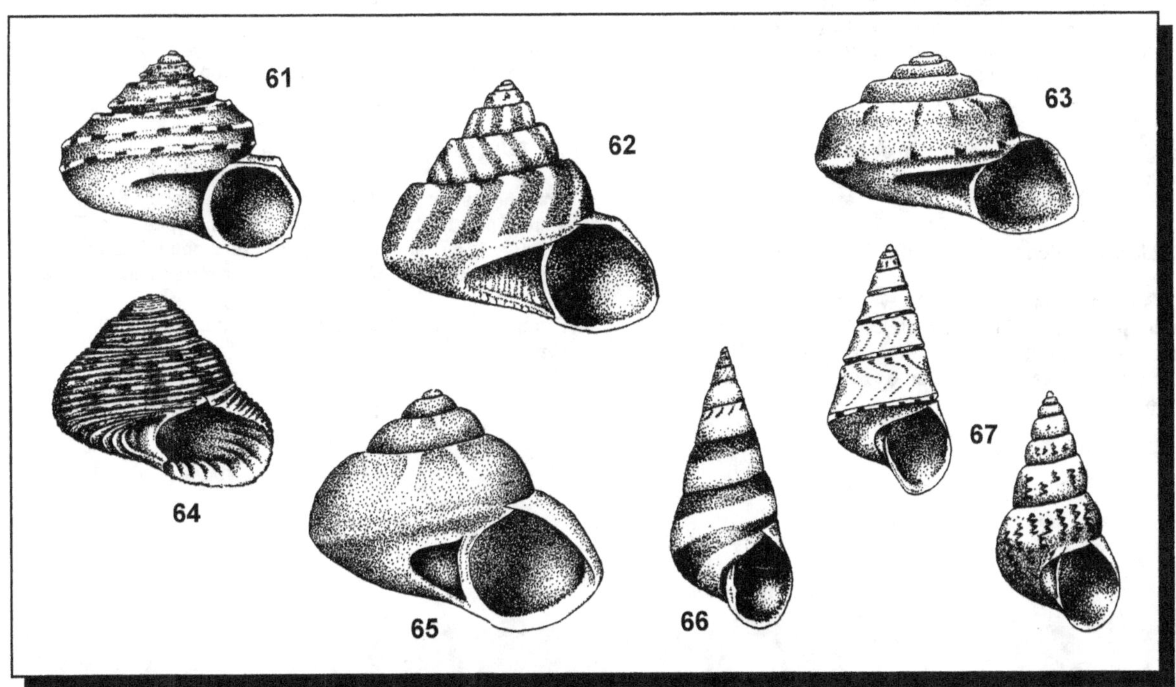

Family Skeneidae

Very small to minute shells, which are conical to lenticular in shape. They may be perforate or imperforate. Skeneidae can be separated from the Trochidae by their small size and the loss of the interior nacreous layer. However, species in this family have a variety of shell, anatomical and radular characters (Hickman and McLean, 1990). The family has been used as a dumping ground for small flat species removed from other families. A review of the genera, currently underway (W. Ponder, personal communication) is likely to prove that there are more than one family within the group. Skeneidae are generally associated with hard substrates and live from shallow to deep water (Marshall, 1988). There has been no review of the Australian species, but Laseron (1954a) has described and figured some New South Wales Skeneidae under the family name Liotiidae.

68. *Cirsonella weldii* Tenison-Woods, 1877

The shell is small and turboid. The whorls are rounded, with impressed sutures. The shell surface is smooth but matt, crossed by irregular growth lines. The peristome is entire; the aperture is circular. The umbilicus is deep but narrow. The colour is white.
Size: 3mm.
Range: Central New South Wales to Victoria, including Tasmania.
Synonyms: *Cirsonella australis* Angas, 1877

69. *Crossea concinna* (Angas, 1868)

The shell is turboid and narrowly umbilicate. The whorls are rounded with impressed sutures. The shell surface is polished and crossed by many very fine grooves. The aperture is circular. The columella is reflected. The umbilicus is a narrow slit, surrounded by a thickened rib. The colour is translucent white.
Size: 6mm.
Range: Southern Queensland to eastern Victoria, including Tasmania.

70. *Liotella pulcherrima* (Henn & Brazier, 1894)

The shell is minute and flat. The whorls are rounded with impressed sutures. The sculpture consists of fine axial lamellae, the interstices crossed by spiral striae. The aperture is circular; the peristome is entire. The colour is white.
Size: 2mm.
Range: Central New South Wales.

71. *Lodderena minima* (Tenison-Woods, 1878)

A thick, flat shell, characterised by its fine spiral sculpture and two keels, one on the base and one at the periphery. The umbilicus is narrow, bordered by a rib of small spines. The aperture is circular, bordered by an enlarged rib. The colour is translucent white.
Size: 1.8mm.
Range: Southern Queensland to southern New South Wales.

72. *Microcarina surgerea* Laseron, 1954

The shell is minute, flat and widely umbilicate; the aperture is circular. The sculpture consists of two strong spiral keels on the last whorl. The colour is translucent white.
Size: 1.1mm.
Range: New South Wales.

73. *Notosetia porcellana* (Tate & May, 1900)

The shell is broad and much higher-spired than the previous species. The whorls are slightly convex; the sutures are hardly impressed. The shell surface is smooth and polished, with an opaque band below the sutures and a well-defined area of callus on the base. The columella is partly reflected over a narrow but deep umbilical fissure. The colour is translucent white.
Size: 3mm.
Range: New South Wales.
Synonyms: *Wanganella fissura* Laseron, 1954.

74. *Teinostoma solida* (Laseron, 1954)

The shell is flat. The last whorl nearly envelops the entire spire. The sculpture consists of very fine spiral ribs. The aperture is circular; the outer lip is thickened. The umbilicus is closed by callus. The colour is translucent white.
Size: 2mm.
Range: Southern Queensland to central New South Wales.

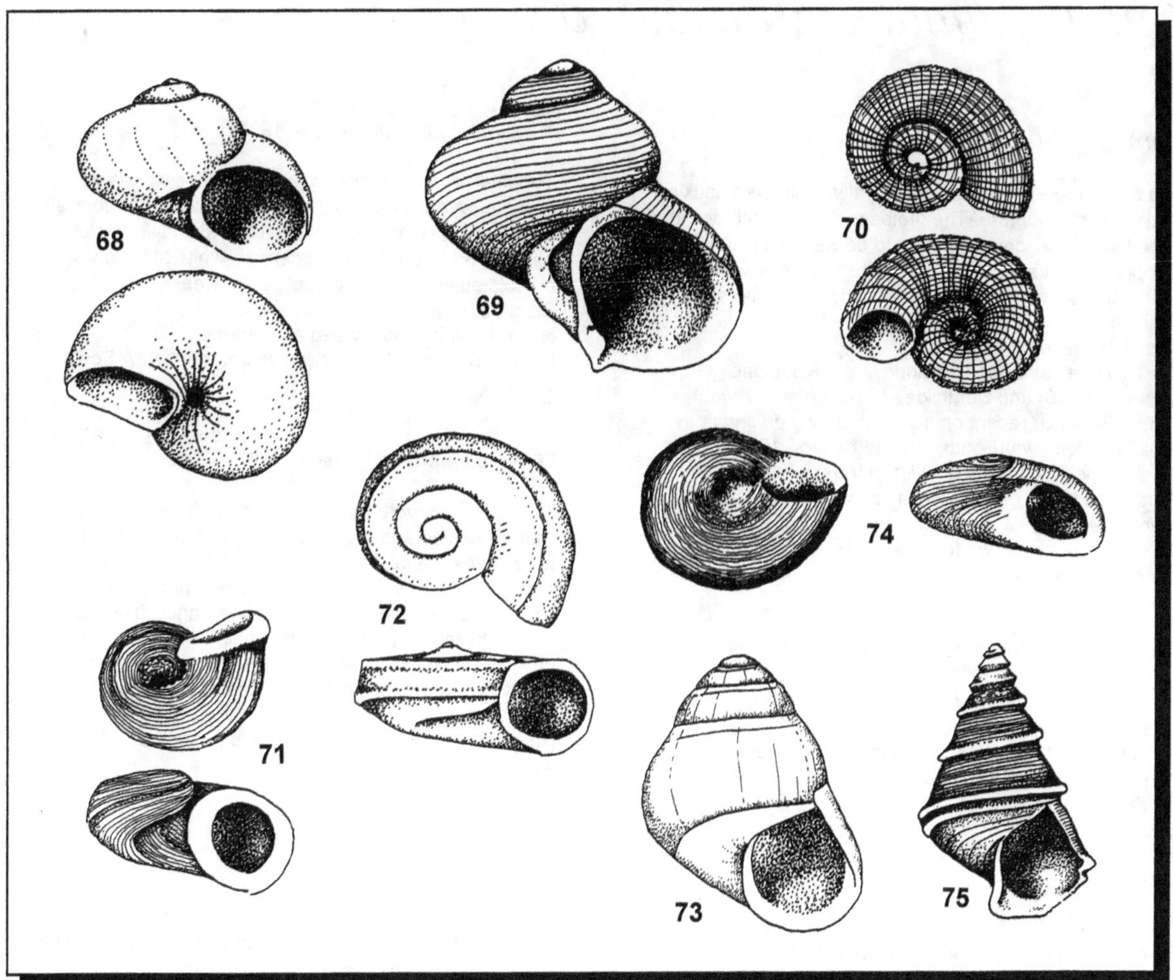

Superorder Caenogastropoda

Order Neotaenioglossa

Suborder Discopoda

Superfamily Campaniloidea

Family Plesiotrochidae

The shells are very small to minute, elevate-conical, with a periostracum consisting of very small hairs. The whorls are keeled and axial and/or spiral sculpture is often present. The animals have a mantle edge with many long papillae. Houbrick (1990a) has created this family based on anatomical characters of the animal and Healy (1993) has recently transferred it to the Campaniloidea based on sperm ultrastructure.

75. *Plesiotrochus pagodiformis* Hedley, 1907

The shell is elevate-conical and thin. The whorls are keeled, giving the shell a turreted appearance. The sculpture consists of fine spiral lines, with two larger spiral ribs at the periphery, the top one of which is visible in previous whorls. The base is convex, also with fine spiral lines. The colour is translucent yellowish.
Size: 3mm.
Range: Queensland to central New South Wales.

Superfamily Cerithioidea

Family Dialidae

The shells are elevate-conical, spirally sculptured, lacking distinct axial sculpture. The protoconch is smooth or with a median spiral ridge. Ponder and de Keyzer (1992) recognise eight species, most of which have a wide distribution throughout the Indo-Pacific, but some are restricted to a smaller range. They live in shallow water, mostly in sheltered habitats.
The Dialidae have been included in the Rissoidae (Laseron, 1950) and Cerithiidae (Cunningham-Vaught, 1989). The most recent opinion is that they belong in a family on their own (Ponder and de Keyzer, 1992). Several species, placed in *Diala* in the past, have been transferred to the genera *Alaba* and *Styliferina* (Litiopidae).
Two species are known from the Sydney region; both are common in seagrass intertidally.

76. *Diala megapicalis* Ponder & de Keyzer, 1992

The shell is thin and elevate-conical. The whorls are flat; the sutures are slightly impressed. The shell surface is smooth but not polished. Two spiral grooves run around the periphery. The columella has a thin callus. The colour is light brown.
Size: 5mm.
Range: Central New South Wales to central Western Australia.

77. *Diala sulcifera scobina* Laseron, 1950

The shell is rather thick and high-spired. The sculpture consists of about six strong spiral ribs on the last whorl; this sculpture continues on the base. The apertural characteristics are simple. The colour is white or light brown, irregularly mottled with darker brown.
Size: 5.2mm.
Range: Central to southern New South Wales.

Family Litiopidae

This is a family of very small shells that used to be placed in the Cerithiidae. Houbrick (1987*a*) has studied the animals of two species and placed the genera *Litiopa* and *Alaba* in a separate family.
Diagnostic features for the family are: a mucus gland on the foot that produces a mucus thread attaching the snail to its habitat, long retractile tentacles around the foot and an unusual protoconch sculptured with many axial riblets and subsutural plaits (Luque *et al.*, 1988).
The mature shells are relatively featureless, high-spired and thin. Three species are commonly found in estuarine habitats in the Sydney area; all three are described here.

78. *Alaba opiniosa* (Iredale, 1936)

The shell is elevate-conical and thin. The whorls are rounded with impressed sutures. The sculpture consists of fine spiral striae. The columella is slightly reflected below. The colour is translucent off-white to yellowish, maculated with very fine spots and streaks.
Size: 7mm.
Habitat: On intertidal weed and stones.
Range: Southern Queensland to southern New South Wales.

79. *Alaba monile* A. Adams, 1862

The shell is elevate-conical and thin. The whorls are roundly keeled and the keel is visible in previous whorls; the sutures are impressed. The sculpture is variable: some shells are smooth, others have small axial folds, which give the shell a knobbed appearance. The columella is reflected, covered by a thin callus. The colour is milky white, slightly translucent. A single dark brown interrupted band runs along the keel of the periphery.
Size: 7mm.
Range: Northern New South Wales to southern Western Australia including Tasmania.

80. *Alaba translucida* (Hedley, 1906)

The shell is elevate-conical and thin. The whorls are rounded; the sutures are impressed. The shell surface is smooth but not polished. The columella is reflected. The colour is translucent white.
Size: 7mm.
Range: Southern Queensland to southern Western Australia, including Tasmania.

Family Cerithiidae

The Australian species of this family are mostly tropical. Shells are typically high-spired, many-whorled, sculptured with spiral rows of nodules. Some species possess only axial folds. The sculpture and colouration are very variable within species. The animals are gregarious detritus feeders and commonly live in shallow water. They are often very common on intertidal reefs.
Several genera, such as *Argyropeza* (Houbrick, 1980), *Clypeomorus* (Houbrick, 1985), *Colina* (Houbrick, 1990*b*) and *Cerithium* (Houbrick, 1992) and the subfamily Bittiinae (Houbrick, 1993) have been revised. Only two species were found in the Sydney area.

81. *Cerithidium* sp.

The shell is minute and high-spired; the spire whorls are rounded; the sutures are impressed. The sculpture consists of three nodulose spiral cords on the last whorl

and the previous whorls and another three smooth spiral cords on the base. The aperture is simple. The peristome is almost entire; the columella is slightly reflected. The colour is light brown with a dark brown base.
Size: 2.8mm.
Range: New South Wales.

Subfamily Bittiinae

Houbrick (1993) has recently recognised seven genera in this subfamily based on anatomical evidence. The species are typically small-shelled, have cancellate sculpture and a short anterior canal.

82. *Cacozeliana granarium* (Kiener, 1842)

The shell is high-spired. The sides of the spire are slightly convex; the sutures are hardly visible. The sculpture consists of about five granulose spiral ribs, crossed by axial waves, which fade at the periphery. The base has about five more granulose spiral ribs. The columella is smooth, covered with a thin callus. The outer lip is slightly flaring and thin. The colour is greyish light brown, marked with white longitudinal streaks. The columella is lighter coloured.
Size: 19mm.
Habitat: In shallow bays under intertidal stones.
Range: New South Wales to South Australia, including Tasmania.

Family Batillariidae

Formerly placed in the Potamididae, these genera were placed in the family Batillariidae by Houbrick (1991) based on the anatomy of the animal. The shells are heavy and high-spired, somewhat similar in shape to those of the Cerithiidae, with spiral and axial sculpture, but usually with a flaring outer lip. The animals inhabit estuarine habitats, and are often found in mud between mangroves.

83. *Pyrazus ebeninus* (Bruguière, 1792)

The shell is high-spired and heavy, often very much eroded. The sculpture consists of large axial knobs, which are most obvious on the last whorl, crossed by many crowded spiral ribs. A recognition mark for this species is the large, thickened, flaring outer lip. The operculum is thick and circular. The colour is dark brown.
Size: 70mm.
Habitat: In mud between mangroves. The animals leave tracks in the mud at low tide.
Range: Queensland to eastern Victoria.

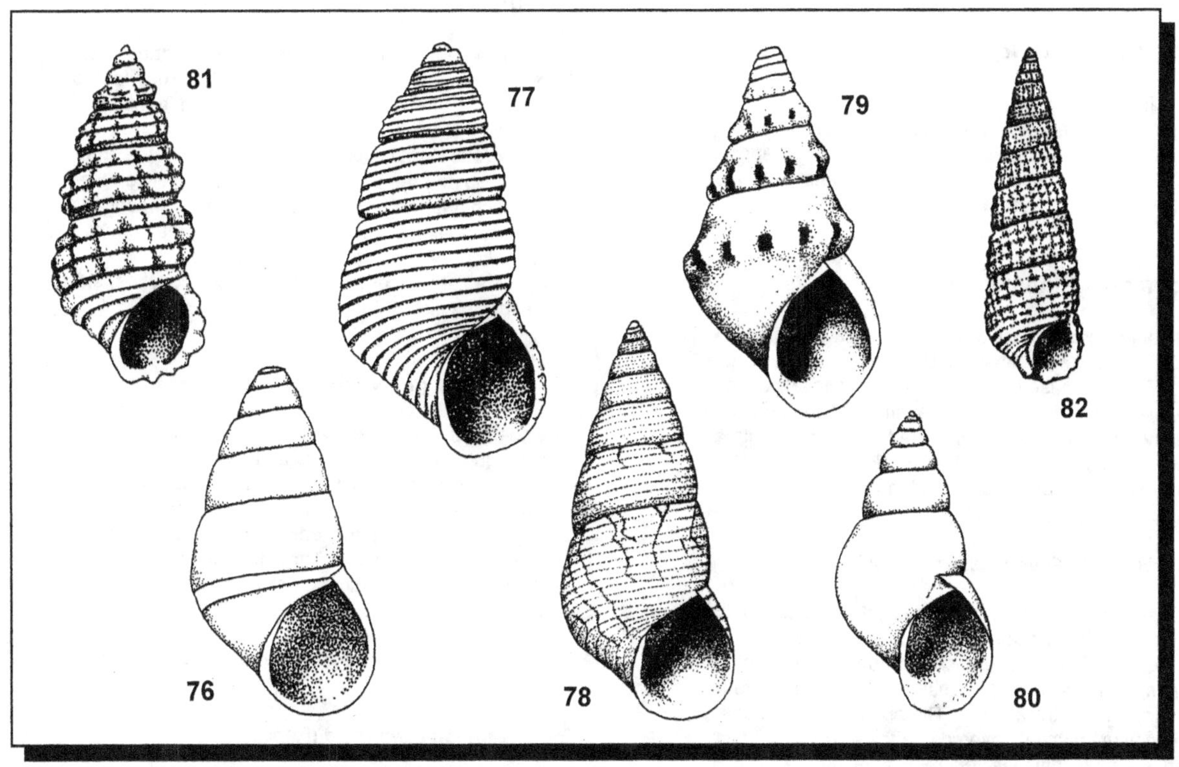

84. *Velacumantus australis* Quoy & Gaimard, 1834

The shell is thick. The sculpture consists of broad axial folds crossed by numerous beaded spiral ribs. The columella has thickened callus. The outer lip is slightly flaring. The colour is dark brown, with the spiral ribs lighter in colour. White banded specimens do exist, but according to Ewers and Rose (1966) these have a higher mortality rate than uniformly coloured specimens and are therefore underrepresented in the adult population.
Size: 37mm.
Habitat: On stones and intertidal sand flats.
Range: Queensland to South Australia, including Tasmania.

85. *Zeacumantus subcarinatus* Sowerby, 1855

The shell is small for the family, high spired and thick. The whorls are rounded; the sutures are impressed. The sculpture consists of broad axial folds, about 14 on the last whorl. These are crossed by one or more spiral grooves in some shells. The axial sculpture fades at the periphery, where a sculpture of strong, irregular spiral ribs takes over and continues on the base. The columella is simple; the outer lip is thin. The colour is black or dark brown; the columella and outer lip are lighter in colour.
Size: 15mm.
Habitat: in colonies on intertidal stones in sheltered bays, where it feeds on seaweed (McClatchie, 1979).
Range: New South Wales. This species was introduced from New Zealand.

Family Planaxidae

This family comprises two, previously considered separate, subfamilies. The animals are unique in that the females possess a cephalic brood pouch. The eggs are deposited in this pouch and develop at least until late veliger stage (Ponder, 1980).

Subfamily Planaxinae

The species of this subfamily have thick shells and live in the intertidal zone, mostly in tropical regions. Houbrick (1987*b*) has revised this group and recognises seven genera, three of which live in Australia. The animals are herbivores. They have high-spired, thick shells with a short anterior canal and a thick periostracum. Only one species lives in the Sydney region.

86. *Hinea brasiliana* (Lamarck, 1822)

The shell is thick and elevate-conical. The sides of the whorls are flat; the sutures are visible but hardly impressed. The shell surface is smooth but not polished. The aperture is relatively small. The columella is reflected, covered with a thick callus. The outer lip is blunt and thick. The colour is white, covered in a thick yellow periostracum, which is very persistent.
Size: 19mm.
Habitat: Under intertidal stones in colonies.
Range: Northern New South Wales to Victoria, Indo-

Pacific (see below).
Remarks: Beechey (1991) has discussed the unusual distribution of this species, which includes the New South Wales coastline and a narrow band across the Pacific Ocean to Easter Island.

Subfamily Fossariinae

Relatively little is known about this group of small to minute, white shells, which have a narrow umbilicus and angular whorls. Previously, they were considered to be related to the Calyptraeidae. As in that family, tiny males are often found on the shells of much larger females, suggesting that individuals probably change sex during their life. However, this happens in many mollusc species. One species was found in shell grit on Sydney's beaches; it is uncommon.

87. *Fossarus sydneyensis* Hedley, 1925

The shell is elevate-conical and thin. The spire whorls are rounded; the sutures are impressed. The sculpture consists of thin spiral ribs, the interstices crossed by very fine axial striae. The outer lip is slightly thickened. The umbilicus is narrow, with the three last spiral ribs disappearing into it. The colour is yellowish off-white.
Size: 4mm.
Range: New South Wales.

Family Turritellidae

Turritellidae have high-spired and many-whorled shells. They live in mud, usually in deeper water. They feed on fine particles of detritus, which are trapped in mucus sheets on the gills.
Marwick (1957) revised the genera based on the shape of the outer lip and the primary spirals, especially on the protoconch. Garrard (1972) has revised the recent and tertiary Australian Turritellidae based on protoconchs and the basal and lateral sinus in the outer lip.
Turritellidae are uncommon on Sydney's beaches, since most species live in deep water.

88. *Gazameda gunnii* (Reeve, 1849)

The shell is thin and needle-like. The aperture is quadrangular; the periphery is angulate and the base is flat. The sculpture consists of several spiral ribs, which are variable in size. The top and the bottom rib are often enlarged in Sydney specimens, rendering the sides of individual whorls concave. The colour is light brown, maculated with white flames, especially just below the sutures.
Size: 25mm, but grows larger.
Range: New South Wales to Victoria, including Tasmania.

89. *Gazameda tasmanica* (Reeve, 1849)

The shell is high-spired and thick. The sides of the spire are completely straight; the sutures are only slightly incised. The aperture is circular; the base is flat. The

sculpture consists of fine spiral cords crossed by curved growth lines. The colour is white, maculated with light brown.
Size: 35mm, but grows larger.
Range: New South Wales to Victoria, including Tasmania.

Family Siliquariidae

Siliquariidae have irregularly coiled, tube-like shells. They are mostly, but not always, distinguished by longitudinal shell slits or a series of holes in the top of the whorls. The status of many genera is unclear and awaiting anatomical study, but a revision of the family is currently underway (Bieler, 1992).

90. *Pyxipoma weldii* Tenison-Woods, 1875

The shell is elongate, irregularly coiled and the axis of coiling is often bent. The whorls do not touch each other. The aperture is irregularly shaped. The shell surface is almost smooth. In the top of the whorls there is a series of small holes. The colour is white to purple or brown, translucent.
Size: 19mm.
Range: New South Wales to southern Western Australia, including Tasmania.

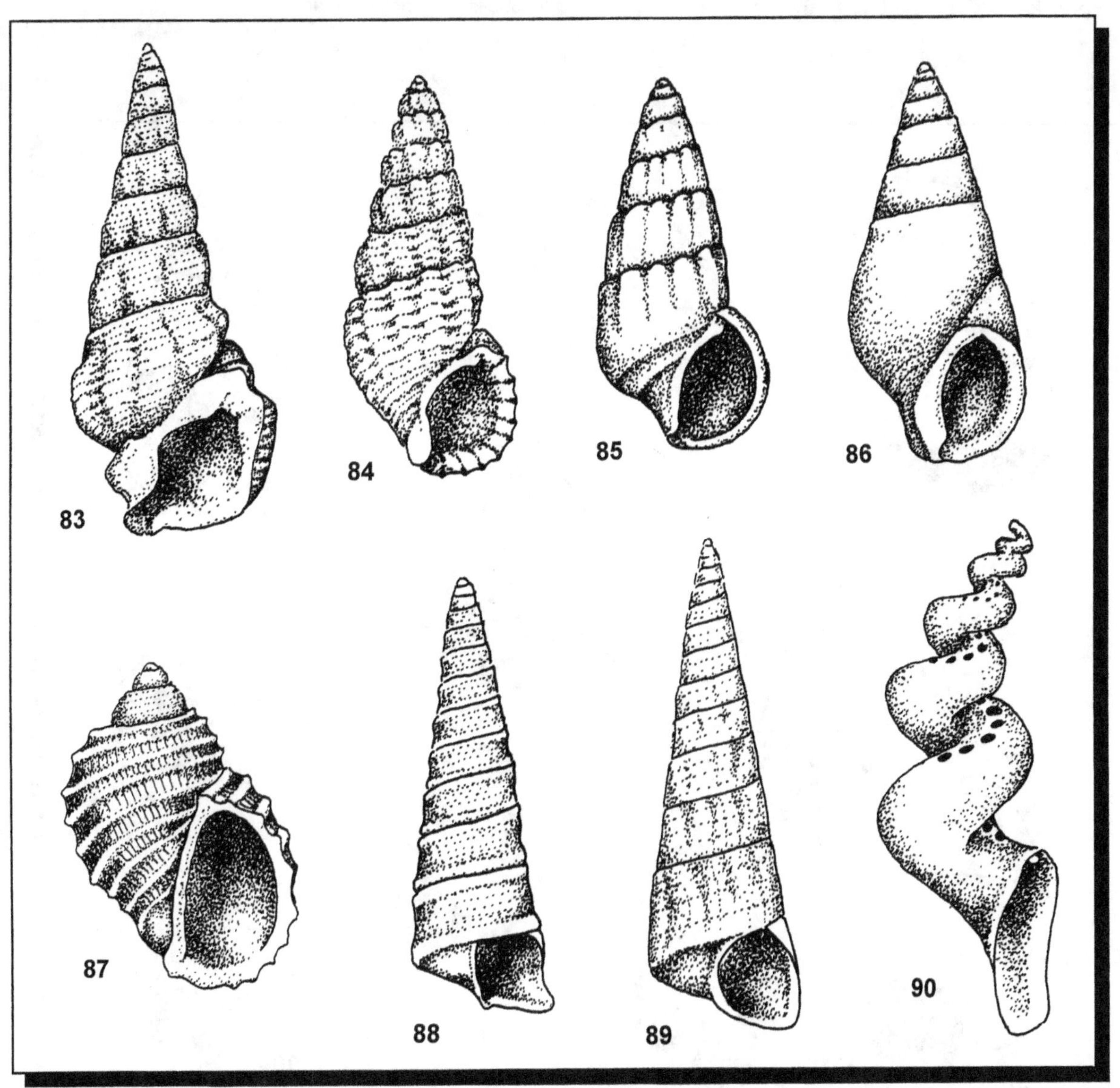

Superfamily Littorinoidea

Family Littorinidae

Littorinidae are found worldwide intertidally. They live on hard substrates such as exposed rocks and mangrove trunks. The Littorinidae have dull, imperforate shells, without any characteristic features. Rosewater (1970, 1972) and Reid (1986) have reviewed the Indo-Pacific Littorinidae. All species have distinct males and females. Fertilisation is internal, with some species having developed ovoviviparity.

Eight species of Littorinidae have been reported from Sydney; six are described here. Besides these, *Littoraria filosa* (Sowerby, 1832) and *L. philippiana* (Reeve, 1857) have been found (see under *L. luteola*)

91. ***Bembicium auratum*** (Quoy & Gaimard, 1834)

The shell is conical and sharply keeled. The sculpture consists of broad irregular nodules, which are most obvious at the keel. Most shells are heavily eroded. The base is flat, with irregular spiral ribs. The colour is dirty white, with irregular dark brown maculations. The columella and inside of the shell are creamy yellow.
Size: 25mm.
Habitat: On intertidal stones in sheltered bays.
Range: Southern Queensland to southern Western Australia, including Tasmania.

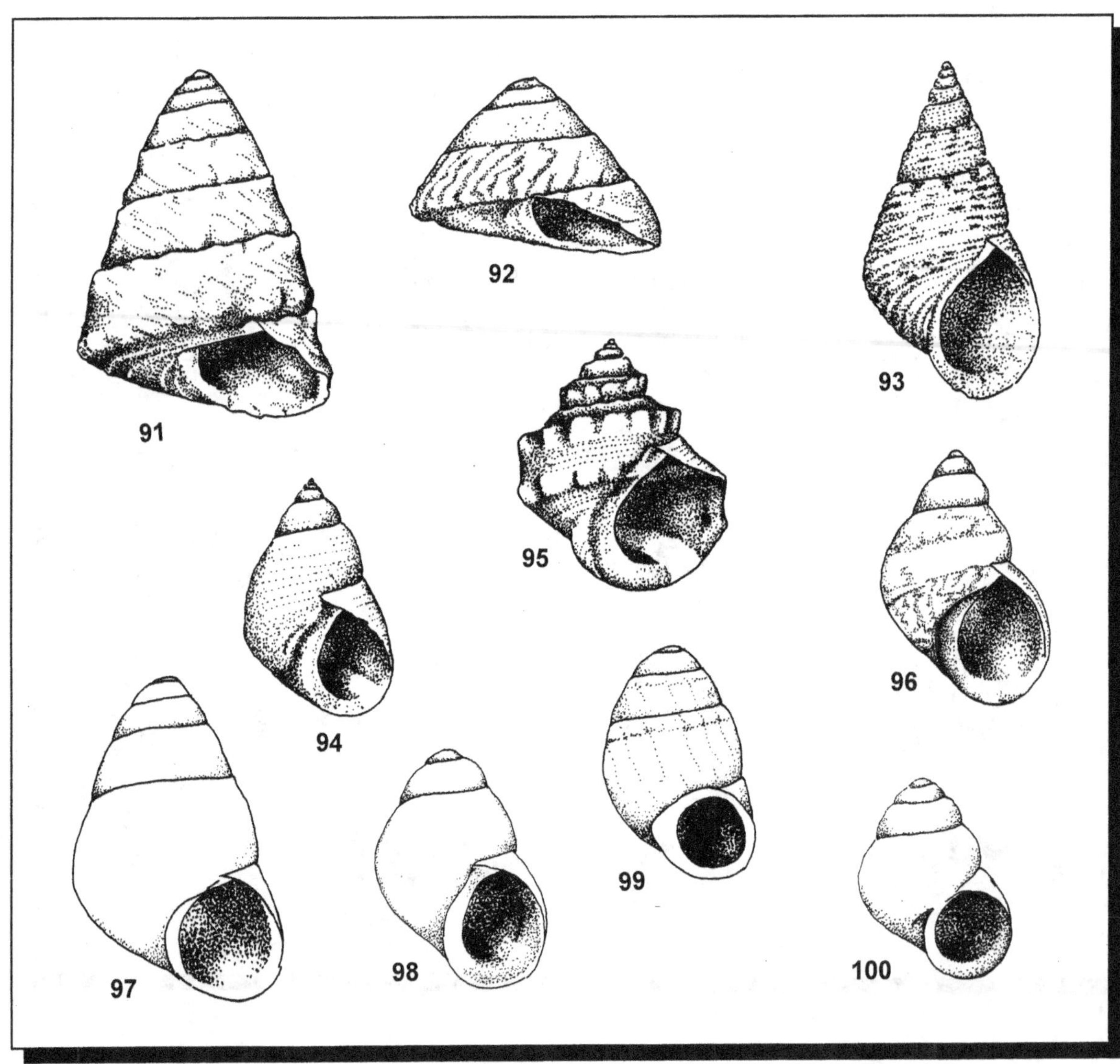

92. ***Bembicium nanum*** (Lamarck, 1822)

The shell is conical and keeled. The shell surface is rough
without any obvious sculpture. The colour is whitish with
oblique axial dark brown bands. The base is white with
black spots. The inside is yellowish, with some dark
brown axial lines shining through from the outside.
Size: 23mm.
Habitat: On intertidal rocks on exposed shores.
Range: Southern Queensland to South Australia,
including Tasmania.
Remarks: This species is more smooth and lower spired
than *B. auratum*. Reid (1988) describes the differences
between these, and other species of *Bembicium*, in more
detail.

93. ***Littoraria luteola*** Quoy & Gaimard, 1834

The shell is thin and elevate. The whorls are rounded; the
sutures are impressed. The sculpture consists of about
nine spiral ribs on the last whorl, with another seven ribs
on the base. The rib encircling the periphery may be
slightly enlarged. The columella has a thin layer of callus.
The colour is light brown to yellowish, maculated with dark
brown spots. The columella callus is chocolate brown.
Some specimens are completely yellow or orange.
Size: 18mm.
Habitat: On mangrove trunks, around the high tide line.
Range: Northern Queensland to southern New South
Wales.
Remarks: this species is part of the *L. scabra* (L. 1758)
complex, that has been divided into several species over
the years, joined back together (Rosewater, 1980) and
again subdivided based on animal characteristics (Reid,
1986). *L. filosa* (Sowerby, 1832) and *L. philippiana*
(Reeve, 1857) are two other species belonging to this
complex that could possibly be found in Sydney, but are
much rarer.

94. ***Nodilittorina unifasciata*** Gray, 1826

The shell is conical, with a rounded periphery, and an
almost smooth surface. The colour is whitish with a band
of bluish grey in the middle of the last whorl and often
another band of grey at the base of the shell. The inside
of the aperture and the columella are dark chocolate
brown, except for a white spiral band inside the aperture.
Size: up to 17mm, but mostly smaller.
Habitat: Common on rocks above high-tide level.
Range: Southern Queensland to southern Western
Australia, including Tasmania, New Zealand.

95. ***Nodilittorina pyramidalis*** Quoy & Gaimard, 1833

The shell is conical, with a rounded periphery. The
sculpture on the last whorl consists of two spiral rows of
sharp nodules, only one of which is visible in previous
whorls. The colour is a dirty bluish grey. The inside of the
aperture is chocolate brown except for two narrow white
spiral bands, one at the base and one just above the
widest point of the aperture.
Size: 20mm.
Habitat: Common above high-tide level, in colonies.
Range: Northern Queensland to Victoria.

96. ***Nodilittorina acutispira*** Smith, 1892

The shell is small for the family and high-spired. The
whorls are rounded; the sutures are deeply impressed.
The shell surface is matt, without obvious sculpture. The
columella has a thin callus. The colour is dark brown,
becoming greyish when eroded. The columella is
chocolate brown; the outer lip is yellowish.
Size: 4mm.
Habitat: on intertidal stones near rock pools, in colonies.
Range: New South Wales.

Superfamily Cingulopsoidea

Family Eatonellidae

The family name Eatonellidae was introduced by Ponder
(1965) for a group of minute molluscs common in
Australian and New Zealand. Members of this family had
previously been placed in the Rissoidae (Laseron, 1950).
The shells are simple, conical to elongate, with smooth
rounded whorls and simple apertural characteristics.
The animals live in the littoral and sublittoral zone and
graze on algae. They possess a pair of tentacles that
move about vigorously when the animal is in motion.
Ponder and Yoo (1977) have revised the Australian
species and found 20 recent species, most of which live in
temperate Australia. Two common species from New
South Wales are described here; some additional species
can be found in shell grit (Ponder and Yoo, 1977).

97. ***Crassitoniella flammea*** (Frauenfeld, 1867)

The shell is thick and conical. The sutures are hardly
impressed. The sculpture consists of axial growth lines.

The aperture is circular; the columella is reflected. The
colour is completely red.
Size: 3mm.
Range: Southern Queensland to Victoria, including
Tasmania.

98. ***Eatoniella (Eatoniella) atropurpurea*** (Frauenfeld,
1867)

The shell is very small and blunt. The whorls are rounded;
the sutures are impressed. The shell surface is smooth
and shiny. The apertural characteristics are simple. The
colour is purple; the protoconch is white.
Size: 1.5mm.
Range: Southern Queensland to central Western
Australia, including Tasmania.

Family Cingulopsidae

The Cingulopsidae is a family of minute shells commonly found in littoral and sublittoral algae. Until recently, when Ponder and Yoo (1980) revised the family, the existence of the family in Australia was not recognised and species were treated as members of the Rissoidae (Laseron, 1950).

The shells are simple, conical to depressed conical, often smooth or with very little sculpture. The apertural characteristics are simple. Shells resemble those of some Rissoidae, but the anatomical characters of the animals are quite distinctive. Ponder and Yoo (1980) describe 30 recent Australian species; two common species from shell grit from Sydney's beaches are described here. Additional species may be found (Ponder and Yoo, 1980).

99. *Pseudopisinna gregaria* Laseron, 1950

The shell is minute, relatively low-spired and blunt. The sculpture consists of irregular oblique axial ribs and a spiral groove beneath the suture. The peristome is complete; the columella is a little expanded over the last whorl; the aperture is circular. The colour is light brown.
Size: 1.0mm.
Range: Southern Queensland to southern Western Australia, including Tasmania.

100. *Eatoniopsis (Rufodardanula) castanea* Laseron, 1950

The shell is very small and conical. The spire whorls are rounded; the sutures are indented. The shell surface is completely smooth. The colour is entirely translucent dark brown.
Size: 1.3mm.
Range: Southern Queensland to eastern Victoria; Tasmania.

Superfamily Rissooidea

Family Anabathridae

This family was formerly a subfamily of the family Barleeidae (Ponder, 1983), but was given family status by Ponder (1988). The shells are conical to high-spired and typically possess a pitted protoconch and a chitinous inner shell layer. They live in shallow water on hard substrates. Ponder (1983) has revised the genera of the then Barleeidae and Ponder and Yoo (1976) have reviewed the genus *Pisinna*. Several species are extremely common on Sydney's beaches. Besides the species described here, some additional species could be found. Laseron (1950), and the two references mentioned above, deal with species from New South Wales.

101. *Anabathron (Anabathron) contabulatum* Frauenfeld, 1867

The shell is minute, elongate, with a characteristic turreted shape, formed by a very strong keel on the shoulders of the whorls. A second, weaker, keel is visible on the base of the last whorl. The rest of the shell is smooth. The aperture is almost circular; the outer lip is thickened. The colour is a deep translucent brown in fresh specimens, fading to white in beach shells.
Size: 1.7mm.
Range: Southern Queensland to South Australia.

102. *Anabathron (Anabathron) lene* (Hedley, 1915)

The shell is minute and elongate. The shell surface is smooth except for two spiral keels on the last whorl and one on previous whorls. The aperture is simple and nearly circular. The colour is translucent pink in fresh specimens, fading to white in beach shells.
Size: 1.6mm.
Range: Southern Queensland to southern Western Australia, including Tasmania.
Remarks: This species can be separated from *A. contabulatum* by its much weaker spiral keels and by its pink colour.

103. *Anabathron (Scrobs) delta* Laseron, 1950

The shell is minute, elongate and blunt. The last whorl is drawn out and elongate. The shell surface is weakly spirally ribbed. The peristome does not touch the last whorl. Between the inner lip and the last whorl there is a furrow, which widens with increasing distance from the axis of coiling. The colour is translucent white.
Size: 1.4mm.
Range: New South Wales.

104. *Anabathron (Scrobs) sp.*

The shell is short-spired, thick and smooth. The last whorl is drawn out; the peristome is entire, connected to the last whorl by extensions of the outer lip. Between the columella and the last whorl there is a wide and deep furrow. The colour is brown.
Size: 2.0mm.
Range: Central New South Wales to eastern Victoria.
Remarks: This species somewhat resembles *A. (Scrobs) pluteus* Laseron, 1950, but that species is larger and white.

105. *Badepigrus pupoideus* (A. Adams, 1865)

The shell is high-spired and blunt. The shell surface is smooth. The peristome is entire; the outer lip is thickened. The furrow between the peristome and the last whorl is reduced to a narrow line. The colour is red-brown.

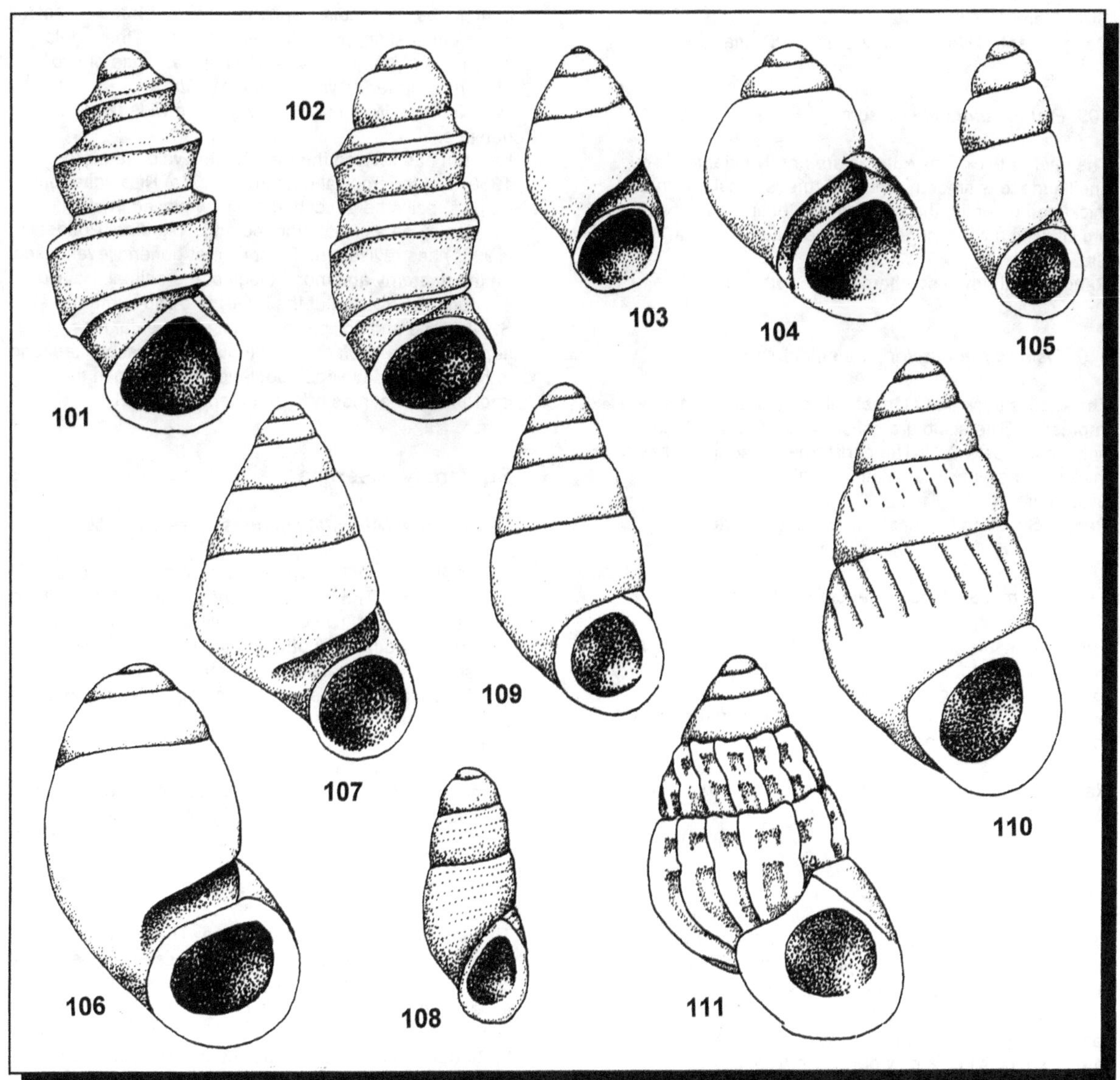

Size: 1.6mm.
Range: Northern New South Wales to northern Western Australia, including Tasmania.
Synonyms: *Scrobs petterdi* Brazier, 1894

106. *Amphithalamus (Microfossa) jacksoni* (Brazier, 1894)

The shell is minute, blunt and thick. The last whorl is drawn out, occupying about two-thirds of the entire shell height. The peristome is entire, and does not touch the last whorl, but is connected to it by two ribs, which extend from the outer lip. Between these ribs, there is a furrow. The colour is light brown.
Size: 2.7mm.
Range: Southern Queensland to central New South Wales.

107. *Amphithalamus (Microfossa) pyramis* (Laseron, 1950)

The shell is high-spired, conical and thick. The whorls are flat; the sutures are hardly impressed. The last whorl is roundly angulate. The shell surface is smooth. The peristome is complete, there is a furrow between the peristome and the last whorl. The colour is light brown.
Size: 2.5mm.
Range: Southern Queensland to eastern Victoria, including Tasmania.

108. *Microdryas iravadioides* (Gatliff & Gabriel, 1913)

The shell is minute and pupiform. The sides of the spire are convex; the individual whorls are slightly impressed. The sculpture consists of fine spiral grooves. The aperture is relatively large and roundly triangular. The outer lip is flaring and only slightly thickened. The colour is white.

Size: 2mm.
Range: Central New South Wales to Victoria.

109. *Pisinna albizona* (Laseron, 1950)

The shell is thick. The sutures are hardly indented. The shell surface is smooth. The aperture is circular with a thickened outer lip; the peristome is entire. The colour is brown, with a white band below the sutures.
Size: 4mm.
Range: Northern to southern New South Wales.

110. *Pisinna frauenfeldi* (Frauenfeld, 1867)

The shell is thick and elongate. The sutures are hardly impressed. The sculpture consists of axial folds, often only on the last whorl. The peristome is entire and has a thick rim of callus. The colour is light brown.
Size: 5mm.
Range: Southern Queensland to eastern Victoria.

111. *Pisinna salebrosa* (Frauenfeld, 1867)

The shell is short-spired, broad and thick. The sutures are hardly impressed. The sculpture consists of broad axial folds, which are slightly indented in the middle. The peristome is entire; the aperture is circular, bordered by a thick rim of callus. The colour is light brown.
Size: 3mm.
Range: Southern Queensland to southern New South Wales.

Family Emblandidae

This family was created by Ponder (1985*a*) for the species described here. It used to be placed in the Rissoidae (Laseron, 1950) and its shell bears resemblance to those of that family. However, its unusual radula and anatomical features separate it from this family. There are no other known species in the only genus *Emblanda*.

112. *Emblanda emblematicum* (Hedley, 1906)

The shell is thick, high-spired and turreted. The sculpture consists of a strong spiral keel forming a shoulder, crossed by strong axial ribs. There is a second, much weaker keel around the base of the shell. The peristome is entire; the aperture is nearly circular. The colour is light brown.
Size: 1.9mm.
Range: New South Wales.

Family Rissoidae

The family Rissoidae has many species worldwide. All are small to minute, which accounts for the lack of attention this family has received in the popular literature. The shells are elongate, their height larger than their width. The sculpture is variable, lacking, spiral or axial or both, weak or strong. There is no umbilicus. The aperture is oval to D-shaped. The outer lip is often thickened and continuous. The main diagnostic feature for the Rissoidae is the unusual shape of the central tooth of the radula, which has a prominent serrated cusp and one or two pairs of spines further down (Ponder, 1985*b*).
Most animals live in shallow water in a wide range of habitats.
Laseron has revised the New South Wales (Laseron, 1950) and the tropical (Laseron, 1956*a*) Rissoidae, but many species he described are now placed in other families, such as Anabathridae and Epigridae. Ponder (1985*b*) has revised the Rissoidae at generic level based on the anatomy and morphology of the animal. His work supports the division of the family into two subfamilies. Shell shape and sculpture are not very useful for separating the subfamilies, although the Rissoininae tend to have a well-developed posterior angulation in the aperture, sometimes with an anterior channel.

Subfamily Rissoinae

113. *Alvania (Alvania) eminens* (Laseron, 1950)

The shell is blunt. The whorls are rounded; the sutures are impressed. The sculpture consists of five spiral ribs on the last whorl and two on the previous whorls, crossed by axial ribs of equal strength, forming nodules at the intersections. The peristome is entire; the outer lip is slightly thickened. The colour is completely translucent white.
Size: 3mm.
Range: New South Wales.
Remarks: The shorter spire separates this species from the species of *Merelina*, especially *M. elegans*.

114. *Alvania (Alvania) novarensis* (Frauenfeld, 1867)

The shell is blunt with convex sides. The whorls are slightly rounded; the sutures are impressed. The sculpture consists of microscopic spiral striae crossing broad axial folds, which fade towards the base of the shell. The columella is reflected at its base. The outer lip is slightly thickened. The colour is translucent yellowish brown, mottled with darker brown at the top and base of the whorls. A white spiral band runs around the periphery and is partly visible on previous whorls. The outer lip is white.
Size: 3mm.
Habitat: In sheltered bays.
Range: Southern Western Australia to eastern Victoria.

115. *Onoba (Subestea) australiae* (Frauenfeld, 1867)

The shell is high-spired and blunt. The whorls are rounded; the sutures are impressed. The sculpture on the last whorl and two previous whorls consists of four weak spiral ribs, crossed by axial ribs of equal strength, forming nodules at the intersections. The base has nine smooth spiral ribs. The apical whorls are sculptured with smooth spiral ribs. The colour is uniform light brown.
Size: 2.9mm.
Synonyms: *Rissoina apicilirata* Tate & May, 1901 and *Rissoina ochroleuca* Brazier, 1894.
Range: Central New South Wales to eastern Victoria, Tasmania.

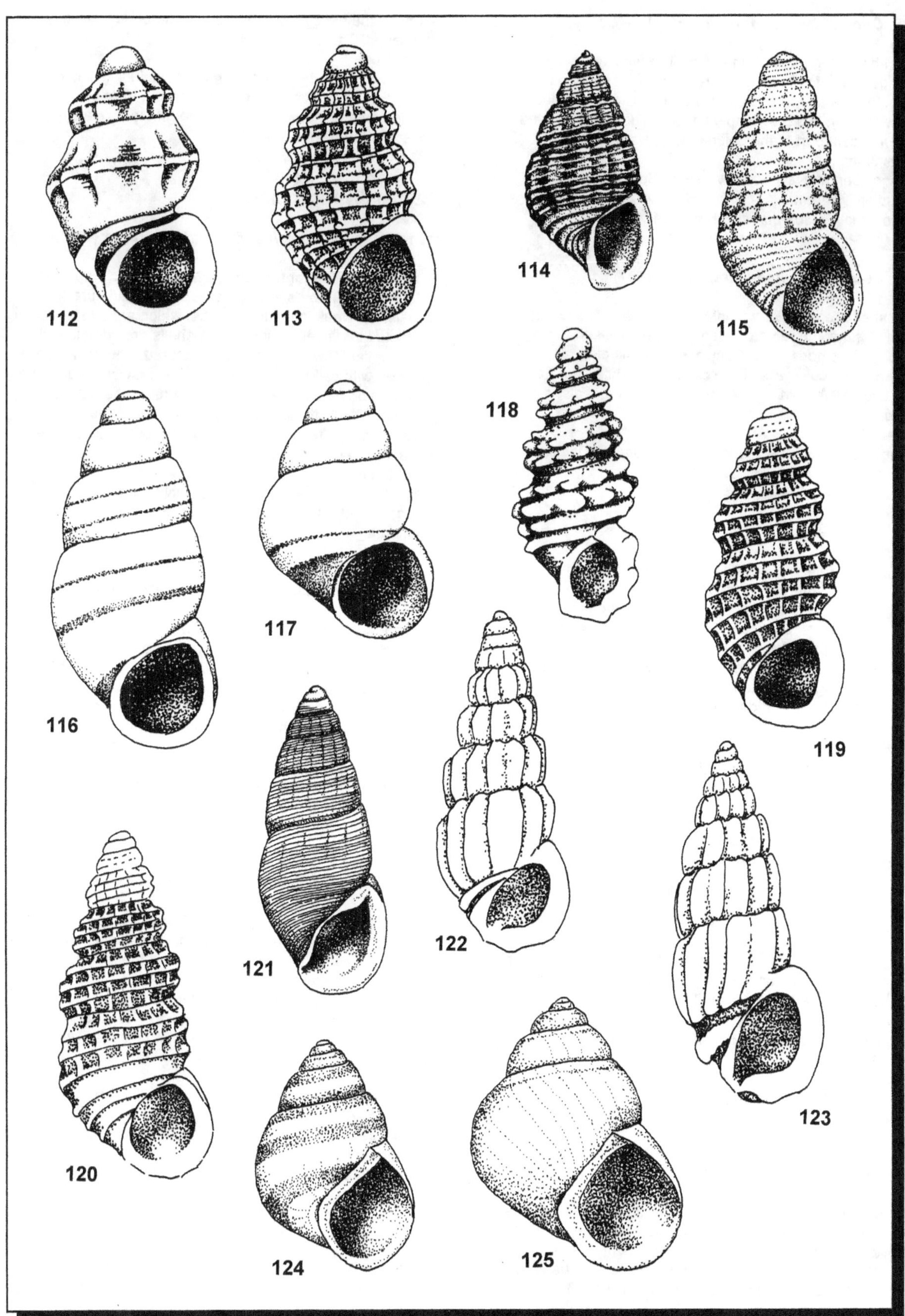

112
113
114
115
116
117
118
119
120
121
122
123
124
125

116. *Onoba (Ovirissoa) rubicunda* (Tate & May, 1900)

The shell is high-spired and blunt. The whorls are rounded, with impressed sutures. The shell surface is smooth. The aperture is circular and simple. The colour is off-white with two brown spiral bands. The umbilical area and adjacent part of the columella are dark brown.
Size: 3mm.
Range: Central New South Wales to South Australia, including Tasmania.
Synonyms: *Rissoa purvillus* Hedley, 1906.

117. *Lucidestea nitens* (Frauenfeld, 1867)

The shell is conical and blunt. The spire whorls are rounded; the sutures are indented. The shell surface is smooth. The peristome is entire, with a thin glaze covering the columella. The colour is off-white. The base has two dark brown bands and the columella is also brown.
Size: 2.3mm.
Range: Central Queensland to South Australia, including Tasmania.

118. *Merelina sp.*

The shell is thin and elongate. The whorls are squarely rounded; the sutures are deeply impressed. The sculpture consists of three strong spiral ribs on the last whorl and two on previous whorls. These ribs bear large, sometimes spine-like nodules. The peristome is entire; the columella is slightly reflected below, the outer lip is flaring and slightly thickened. The colour is yellowish translucent, often with darker bands at the top and base of each whorl.
Size: 3mm.
Habitat: Under stones on rocky shores.
Range: Southern Queensland to Victoria, including Tasmania.
Remarks: This species has been confused with *Merelina cheilostoma* (Tenison-Woods, 1877), but that species is much larger and does not live in New South Wales.

119. *Merelina elegans* (Angas, 1877)

The shell is elongate. The whorls are rounded; the sutures are impressed. The sculpture consists of spiral ribs, five on the last whorl and three on the previous whorl, crossed by axial ribs of equal size. The aperture is circular; the peristome is entire; the outer lip is thickened. The colour is white.
Size: 3.5mm.
Range: Southern Queensland to southern New South Wales.

120. *Merelina gracilis* (Angas, 1877)

The shell is elongate. The whorls are rounded; the sutures are impressed. The sculpture consists of three spiral ribs above the periphery, crossed by axial ribs of equal strength, forming peaks at the intersections. The base has a further three spiral ribs, but no axial sculpture. The aperture is

circular; the peristome is entire. The outer lip is slightly thickened. The colour is yellow.
Size: 5mm.
Range: New South Wales to Victoria, including Tasmania.
Remarks: This species can be separated from *M. cheilostoma* by its weaker sculpture and less deeply incised sutures.

Subfamily Rissoininae

121. *Rissoina (Rissoina) fasciata* (A. Adams, 1853)

The shell is large for the family and thick. The whorls are rounded; the sutures are impressed. The sculpture consists of weak longitudinal folds, which are often restricted to earlier whorls. Some shells are completely smooth; very few are strongly sculptured. The columella is covered with callus, which tends to be heavier towards the anterior and posterior end of the aperture. The outer lip is smooth, slightly thickened and flaring. The colour is mostly white, often marked with continuous or interrupted spiral bands of brown or purple.
Size: 8mm.
Habitat: Under stones at intertidal rock platforms.
Range: Southern Queensland to Victoria, including Tasmania.

122. *Rissoina (Rissolina) angasi* Pease, 1872

The shell is slender and thin. The whorls are rounded and shouldered, giving the shell a turreted appearance; the sutures are deeply impressed. The sculpture consists of about 14 oblique axial ribs on the last whorl, fusing into a spiral rib at the base on the shell. The columella is covered with a thin callus. The outer lip is flaring, thickened. The colour is translucent white.
Size: 5mm.
Habitat: Under intertidal stones at rock platforms.
Range: Northern New South Wales to northern Western Australia, including Tasmania.

123. *Rissoina (Rissolina) crassa* Angas, 1871

The shell is high-spired and thick. The whorls are squarely rounded; the sutures are impressed. The sculpture consists of about 14 strong axial ribs on the last whorl, fusing into a spiral rib at the base of the shell. The ribs are slightly oblique and continuous over the whorls. The columella is covered with a thick callus. The outer lip is flaring, thickened, with a small notch at its base. The colour is completely white.
Size: 7mm.
Habitat: Under stones at intertidal rock platforms.
Range: Northern New South Wales to South Australia.
Remarks: This species is larger, broader, shorter spired and more heavily build than *R. angasi*. A similar, but different species lives in southern Western Australia.

Family Assimineidae

The members of this family have very small to minute, smooth, conical, relatively featureless shells. The last whorl is rounded and there is a small umbilical chink. This family is unusual in that it contains species that live in estuarine habitats, in freshwater as well as terrestrial species. The absence of gills in this family is an adaptation to life outside the water. Two species can be found in the Sydney region; both are described here.

124. ***Assiminea buccinoides*** Quoy & Gaimard, 1835

The shell is blunt, with convex sides, and umbilicate. The whorls are rounded; the sutures are impressed. The shell surface is smooth except for some fine axial growth lines. The columella is reflected, leaving a narrow slit of the umbilicus uncovered. The outer lip is simple. The colour is yellowish brown with three brown spiral bands on the last whorl.
Size: 4mm.
Range: Northern New South Wales to southern Western Australia, including Tasmania.

125. ***Assiminea siennae*** (Tenison-Woods, 1877)

The shell is minute, blunt and umbilicate. The shell surface is smooth and shiny. The colour is uniform brown.
Size: 3 mm
Range: New South Wales.

Family Iravadiidae

Shells elongate, always higher than broad and mostly smaller than 5mm. Shells smooth or with spiral sculpture. A diagnostic feature for the family is the planorbid or depressed dome-shaped protoconch, which has two whorls, the first one of which is minute.
The animals live in shallow water, mostly in mangrove habitats, some live in brackish water, but some live in deep water.
Ponder (1984) has revised the genera of the Iravadiidae. One species was found in the Sydney area. *Iravadia (Pseudonoba) subquadrata* (Laseron, 1950) is another species that could be found in the area; numerous species can be found in northern Australia (see Ponder, 1984 for figures).

126. ***Nozeba topaziaca*** (Hedley, 1908)

The shell is blunt. The spire whorls are flat; the sutures are slightly indented. The shell surface is entirely smooth and polished. The apertural characteristics are simple; the columella is slightly reflected. The colour is white.
Size: 4mm.
Range: Southern Queensland to southern New South Wales, Tasmania.
Remarks: This species has in the past been placed in the Eulimidae (Laseron, 1955a) because of its general appearance and shiny surface.

Family Epigridae

Shells small, with hardly any sculpture, high-spired and elongate. The last whorl is often drawn-out as if it has been 'uncoiled'. Laseron (1950) has described the New South Wales species of *Epigrus*, for which a separate family was erected by Ponder (1985b) based on animal and radular characteristics. The radula is unusual; the radular ribbon is broad and short and very small in relation to the size of the animal. The central tooth is minute and very narrow. The lateral teeth are rectangular with several cusps. *Epigrus* feeds on Foraminifera and the unusual radula is probably an adaptation to this food source. One species was found in the Sydney region.

127. ***Epigrus dissimilis*** (Watson, 1886)

The shell is elongate; the sides of the spire are slightly convex. The whorls are rounded; the sutures are only very slightly impressed. The sculpture consists of fine axial growth lines and a narrow spiral groove just below the sutures. The colour is translucent white.
Size: 4mm.
Range: Central Queensland to Victoria, including Tasmania.

Family Vitrinellidae

Very small to minute, flat, mostly umbilicate shells. Laseron (1954a) has described most of the Sydney species under the Liotiidae. The species described here are now placed in the Vitrinellidae (Cunningham-Vaught, 1989).
Most species live in shallow water, but Marshall (1988) describes a new genus of Vitrinellidae from submerged wood in deep water off the New South Wales coast. There has been no revision of the Australian species and the taxonomic status of many species remains unclear. Four species commonly found in shell grit in the Sydney area are described here. For additional species see Laseron (1954a).

128. ***Callomphala lucida*** Angas, 1864

The shell is large for the family, flat and imperforate. The shell surface is completely smooth and polished. The aperture is circular; the outer lip is surrounded by a thickened rib. A thick pad of callus covers the umbilical area. The colour is translucent white.
Size: 5mm.
Range: New South Wales to Victoria, including Tasmania.

129. ***Lodderia lodderae*** (Petterd, 1884)

The shell is minute, flat and umbilicate. The sculpture consists of five strong spiral ribs, with wide interstices. The aperture is circular, oblique and surrounded by a thickened rib. The umbilicus is wide and open. The colour is translucent white.
Size: 2mm.

Range: Southern Queensland to South Australia, including Tasmania.

130. *Pseudoliotia micrans* (A. Adams, 1850)

The shell is thick, flat and umbilicate. The sculpture consists of 5-6 strong spiral ribs on the last whorl, which are crossed by axial ribs, forming nodules at the intersections. The aperture is circular, oblique, surrounded by a thickened rib. The colour is white, covered with a dark brown periostracum in fresh specimens.
Size: 4mm.
Range: Northern Queensland to South Australia, including Tasmania.
Remarks: *P. speciosa* is smaller and has more spiral ribs.

131. *Pseudoliotia speciosa* (Angas, 1877)

The shell is flat and umbilicate. The sculpture consists of 4-5 strong spiral ribs on the last whorl, crossed by fine axial lirae, giving the shell a cancellate appearance. The aperture is circular, oblique, surrounded by a thickened rib. The colour is white (beach specimens).
Size: 2mm.
Range: Northern Queensland to central New South Wales.

Family Caecidae

The family Caecidae consists of a homogeneous group of species with slightly curved, tube-like shells closed off on one side by a cap (septum). Caecidae are related to Rissoidae and have an unusual shell-building process. They have a pelagic larval stage when they possess normal, coiled shells. As growth continues into a tube and the animal settles as a bottom-dweller, the protoconch is shed and the apex of the tube is closed off by a cap. There has been no review of the genera, but Moore (1968) found that the longitudinal microsculpture is useful in separating species. The systematic position of the family is discussed by Moore (1962).
One species was found in shell grit on Sydney's beaches. Another species, *Caecum liluanum* Hedley, 1903 can be found in shell grit in New South Wales and southern Queensland; it has strong concentric ribs.

132. *Caecum amputatum* Hedley, 1893

The shell is very small, smooth and shiny. The apical end of the tube covered by a cap-like plate. The colour is translucent white.
Size: 2.5mm.
Range: Southern Queensland to southern Western Australia.

Superfamily Stromboidea

Family Struthiolariidae

The species belonging to this family have large and heavy shells, with a thickened outer lip. Only one living species occurs in Australian waters; it belongs to the genus *Tylospira*, which also has nine fossil members in Australia (Darragh, 1991). The family is more widespread in New Zealand.
The animals of the Struthiolariidae live in sandy bottoms or mud flats, where they adopt a buried feeding position just below the sand surface. The siphon constructs an inhalant and exhalant siphonal tube lined with mucus. The animal is a not true sand-dweller in that it does not move through the sand.

133. *Tylospira scutulata* (Leach, 1814)

The shell is thick, with shouldered whorls and a blunt appearance. The sculpture consists of fine spiral threads in early whorls, but the last whorl is smooth. A thick callus covers the columella and fades to a translucent glaze covering the rest of the shell. The outer lip is heavy and thickened. The colour is light brown with irregular darker and lighter flames.
Size: 45mm.
Range: Northern to southern New South Wales.

Family Strombidae

A well-known tropical family, the members of which have conical or biconical shells with a stromboid notch in the outer lip, just above the anterior canal. Family references include Wilson (1993) for Australian shells and Abbott (1960) and Kronenberg and Berkhout (1980) for worldwide Strombidae.
The animals are gregarious and live in sandy or muddy habitats, feeding on algae or detritus. They have very conspicuous and colourful eyes on stalks. The animal is very active and possesses a pointy operculum, which it uses in self-defence and to flip itself over when placed on its back.
Although most species live in the tropics, a few species range into New South Wales. Three species can be found in the Sydney region, two of which are figured here; the third is discussed under *S. mutabilis*.

134. *Strombus luhuanus* L., 1758

This species has a heavy and conical shell, with straight sides and a relatively short but sharp apex. The whorls are roundly shouldered; the sutures are incised. The aperture is long and elongate. The outer lip is slightly thickened and possesses a clear stromboid notch. The colour is white mottled with brown; the inside is vivid red and the columella is black. Fresh specimens are covered in a thick, felt-like periostracum.
Size: 50mm.

Habitat: In colonies in seagrass beds.
Range: Northern Queensland to central New South Wales, Indo-Pacific.
Remarks: Some scattered colonies of this tropical species have established in the Sydney region.

135. *Strombus mutabilis* Swainson, 1821

A widely distributed tropical species, characterised by its conical shape and pinkish red inside of the aperture. The columella and inside of the outer lip are finely lirate. The shoulder of the last whorl has a number of large irregular knobs. The shell is white with irregular brown maculations.
Size: 35mm.
Range: Western Australia to central New South Wales, Indo-Pacific.
Remarks: *S. microurceus* Kira, 1959 is a similar species, which can be found as far south as Sydney (Beechey, 1989). It can be separated by having a black rim deep inside the outer lip.

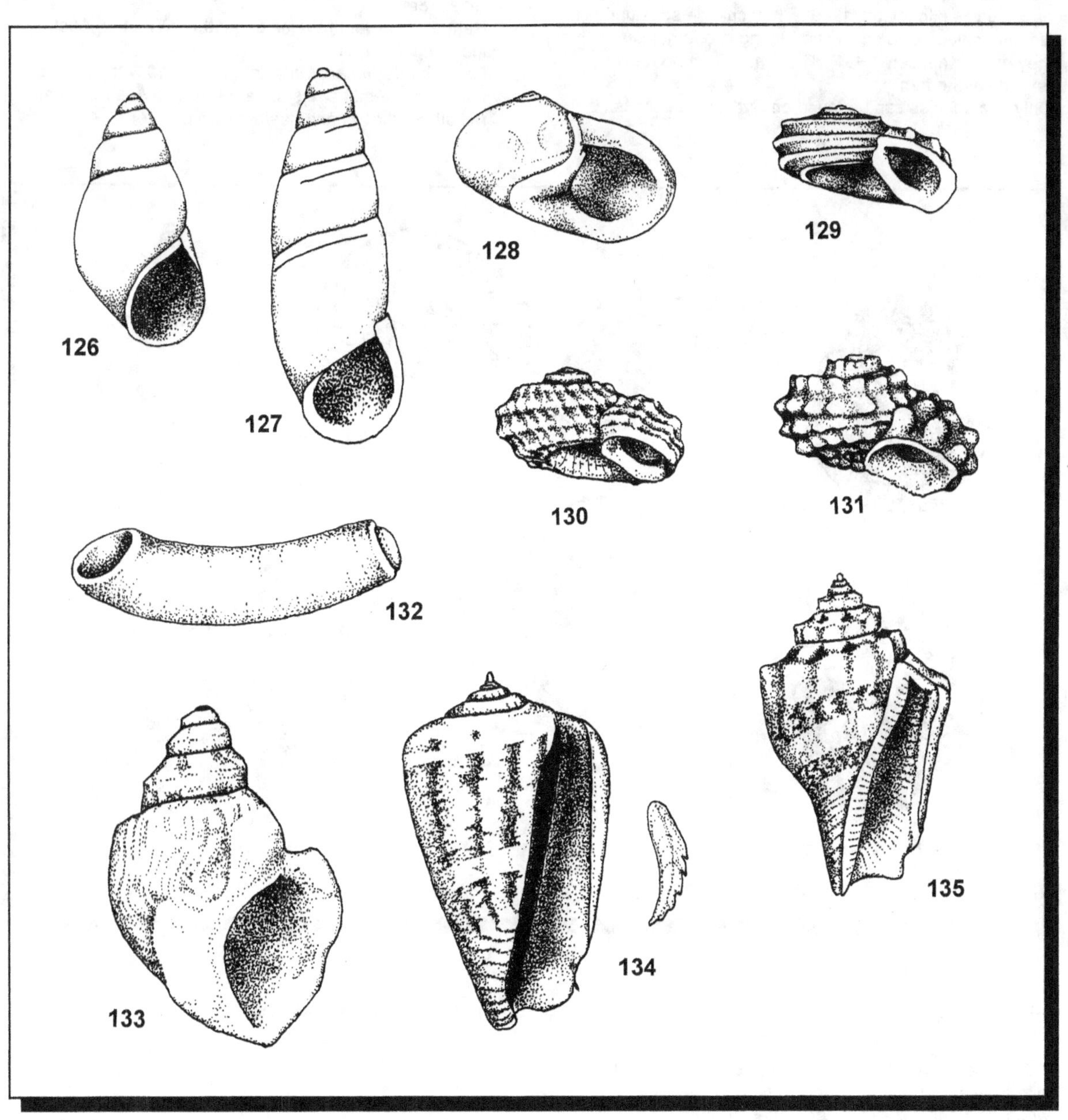

Superfamily Vanikoroidea

Family Hipponicidae

Shells are medium-sized, limpet-shaped, with the apex pointing posteriorly.

The animals live on stones or shells. The females deposit a cluster of egg sacs, containing one to several eggs per sac. Larvae have both direct and planktotrophic development, and both modes can even be found within one species (Hoagland, 1986). They change sex during life, the males being small and turning into females as they grow (Knudsen, 1991). There has been no recent revision of the family.

Only one species can be found on Sydney's beaches.

136. *Antisabia foliacea* (Quoy & Gaimard, 1834)

The shell is limpet-shaped, thick, with irregular margins. The apex is close to the posterior margin of the shell. The sculpture consists of irregular crenulated concentric lamellae. The inner margin is thickened. The colour is white, fresh specimens are covered in a yellow periostracum.
Size: 18mm.
Range: New South Wales to southern Western Australia, including Tasmania.
Remarks: *Sabia australis* Lamarck, 1819, which can be found from Victoria to southern Western Australia, has radiating grooves and has a brown inside.

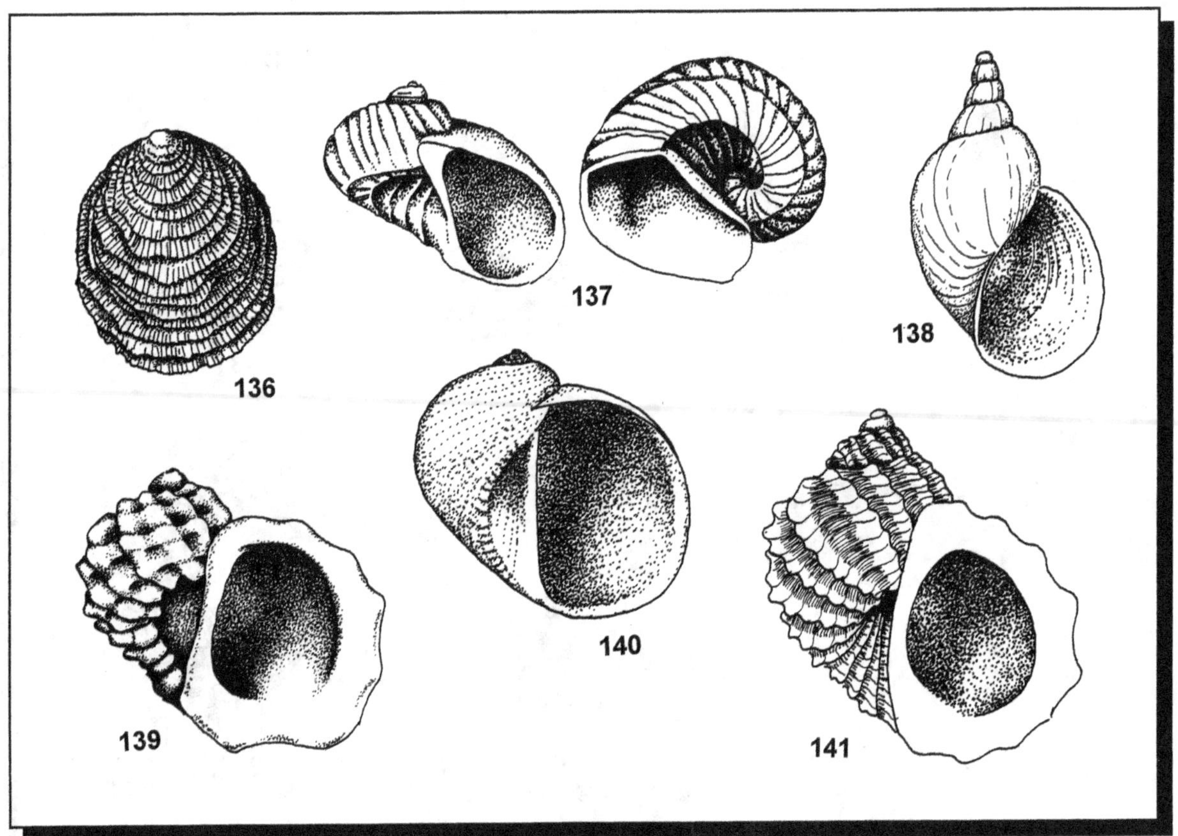

Family Vanikoridae

The shells are mostly very small to medium-sized, white, with axial as well as spiral sculpture, and a large last whorl. The animals live under stones or amongst rubble intertidally or in shallow water. There has been no recent review of the Australian species of this family.

137. *Adeorbis cf. angulata* Hedley, 1905

The shell is fragile. The sculpture consists of irregular axial lamellae, which are crossed by two rounded keels on the base. The protoconch is strongly spirally ribbed. The aperture is large; the columella is reflected. The colour is white.
Size: 3.5mm.
Range: New South Wales.

Remarks: This shell was tentatively identified as Hedley's species. The holotype is larger and only has strong axial folds on earlier whorls, but some smaller shells amongst the paratypes are very similar to the species described here.

138. *Couthouyia gracilis* Henn & Brazier, 1894

The shell is high-spired, very thin and bulbous. The first three whorls are small and narrow, the fourth whorl rapidly expanding. The apertural characteristics are simple. The aperture is large and teardrop-shaped. The shell surface is smooth except for some fine axial growth lines. The colour is transparent white.
Size: 4mm.
Range: New South Wales.
Remarks: The genus *Couthouyia* used to be placed in the Fossariidae, but was placed in the Vanikoridae by Houbrick (1990*b*).

139. *Vanikoro foveolata* Souverbie & Montrouzier, 1866

The shell is thick, rounded and narrowly umbilicate. The spire is almost flat. The sculpture consists of strong axial ribs crossed by spiral ribs of equal size, leaving deep pits in the interstices. The columella is nearly straight and slightly reflected; some callus covers the umbilical area. The outer lip is wide, flaring and simple. The colour is entirely white.
Size: 6mm.
Range: New South Wales.

140. *Vanikoro sigaretiformis* Potiez & Michaud, 1838

The shell is bulbous, thin and widely umbilicate, with a low spire. The sculpture consists of axial ribs crossed by spiral ribs on juvenile whorls; on later whorls only faint spiral striae are left. The outer lip is thin, simple and flaring. The colour is entirely white, slightly translucent in fresh specimens.
Size: 10mm.
Range: Northern Territory to central New South Wales.
Remarks: The fading sculpture with increasing size, thinner shell and higher spire separate this species from *V. cancellata* Lamarck, 1822, another species of similar size that lives in the Sydney area.

141. *Vanikoro orbignyana* Récluz, 1843

The shell is small, turboid and narrowly umbilicate. The last whorl is large. The sculpture consists of axial lamellae, which are crossed by fine spiral striae, forming nodules at the intersections. The aperture is nearly circular; the peristome is entire. The colour is white.
Size: 3.5mm.
Range: New South Wales.
Remarks: *Vanikoro gueriniana* Récluz, 1843 is another small species from the Sydney area. It has weaker axial ribs than *V. orbignyana*.

Superfamily Calyptraeoidea

Family Calyptraeidae

Flat, small to medium-sized, slipper or limpet-shaped shells, which have a plate-like process on the underside of the shell. The animals are protandrous hermaphrodites (they change sex during life). Males are small and are often attached to the shells of much larger females. The female produces egg capsules that are similar for the whole family and are flask-shaped. They contain one to several eggs per capsule.
The egg capsules are brooded for some time in the mantle cavity. At the release of her brood, the female raises and lowers her shell. The Atlantic *Crepidula fornicata* uses the radula to pull the egg capsules free of the mantle cavity (Hoagland, 1986).
Four species were found on Sydney's beaches, three of these species are reasonably common.

142. *Crepidula aculeata* (Gmelin, 1795)

The shell is slipper-shaped, flat; the spire is hardly visible. The aperture occupies the entire underside of the shell; the plate covers almost half the aperture. The sculpture consists of several spiral ribs with sharp spines. The colour is off-white to yellowish brown, sometimes with thin dark brown bands.
Size: 25mm.
Habitat: Under intertidal rocks.
Range: All Australian states, Japan, Lord Howe Island, USA, South Africa.

143. *Sigapatella calyptraeiformis* (Lamarck, 1822)

The shell is limpet-shaped, with a slightly elevate, almost centrally located apex. The plate covers about one third of the aperture. The whorls are rounded; the sutures are impressed. The sculpture consists of fine axial growth lines. The colour is off-white to light brown. The apex is often pink. The underside of the shell is white.
Size: 20mm.
Habitat: Commonly found on sandy beaches.
Range: Northern New South Wales to southern Western Australia, including Tasmania.

144. *Clypeola hedleyi* (Smith, 1915)

The shell is limpet-shaped and thin. The spire whorls are flat; the sutures hardly visible. The growth margin occupies nearly the entire circumference of the shell. The

columella is long, forming a thin plate, which is curved with the whorls of the shell. The shell surface is almost smooth. The colour is white; the apical whorls are often tinged with red.
Size: 13mm.
Range: New South Wales.
Remarks: This species is similar to *Sigapatella calyptraeiformis*, but can be separated by its less rounded whorls, more centrally placed apex and a longer, coiled columella. It is also quite rare.

145. *Zeacrypta immersa* (Angas, 1865)

The shell is slipper-shaped; the shape is variable, twisted and irregular. The underside has a thin plate, covering about one third of the underside. The sculpture consists of fine concentric growth lines. The colour is entirely white or brown.
Size: 28mm.
Habitat: This species lives on dead shells, which accounts for its often irregular shape.
Range: Southern Queensland to southern Western Australia, including Tasmania.
Remarks: Two forms exist in this species: a flat, white, elongate form and a rounded, brown, more elevated form. These have, in the past, been separated into two species, but it is now recognised that the two forms belong to the same species (Macpherson and Gabriel, 1962). The elevated form inhabits the outside of shells, whereas the flat form lives on the inside of dead shells.

Superfamily Vermetoidea

Family Vermetidae

This is a family of sedentary worm-like gastropods that live attached to a substrate. The protoconch has a normal shape and the larvae have a planktonic or crawling life style. They undergo a metamorphosis when they find a suitable place to settle. The shell becomes irregular, without a columella, new growth instead being cemented to a substrate. The foot is no longer used for crawling and turns into a plug sealing the tube; it may or may not retain the operculum. Animals produce mucous feeding nets, which females also use to catch sperm released in the water by males. Hughes (1985) has studied some Vermetidae from Hong Kong, but the Australian species are badly in need of a revision.

146. *Serpulorbis sipho* (Lamarck, 1818)

The shell is irregularly coiled, attached to a substrate, not unlike a large tube-worm. The aperture is irregular. The sculpture consists of fine longitudinal ribs, crossed by axial growth lines. The colour is white, irregularly mottled with light brown.
Size: 50mm.
Range: Queensland to Victoria.

Superfamily Cypraeoidea

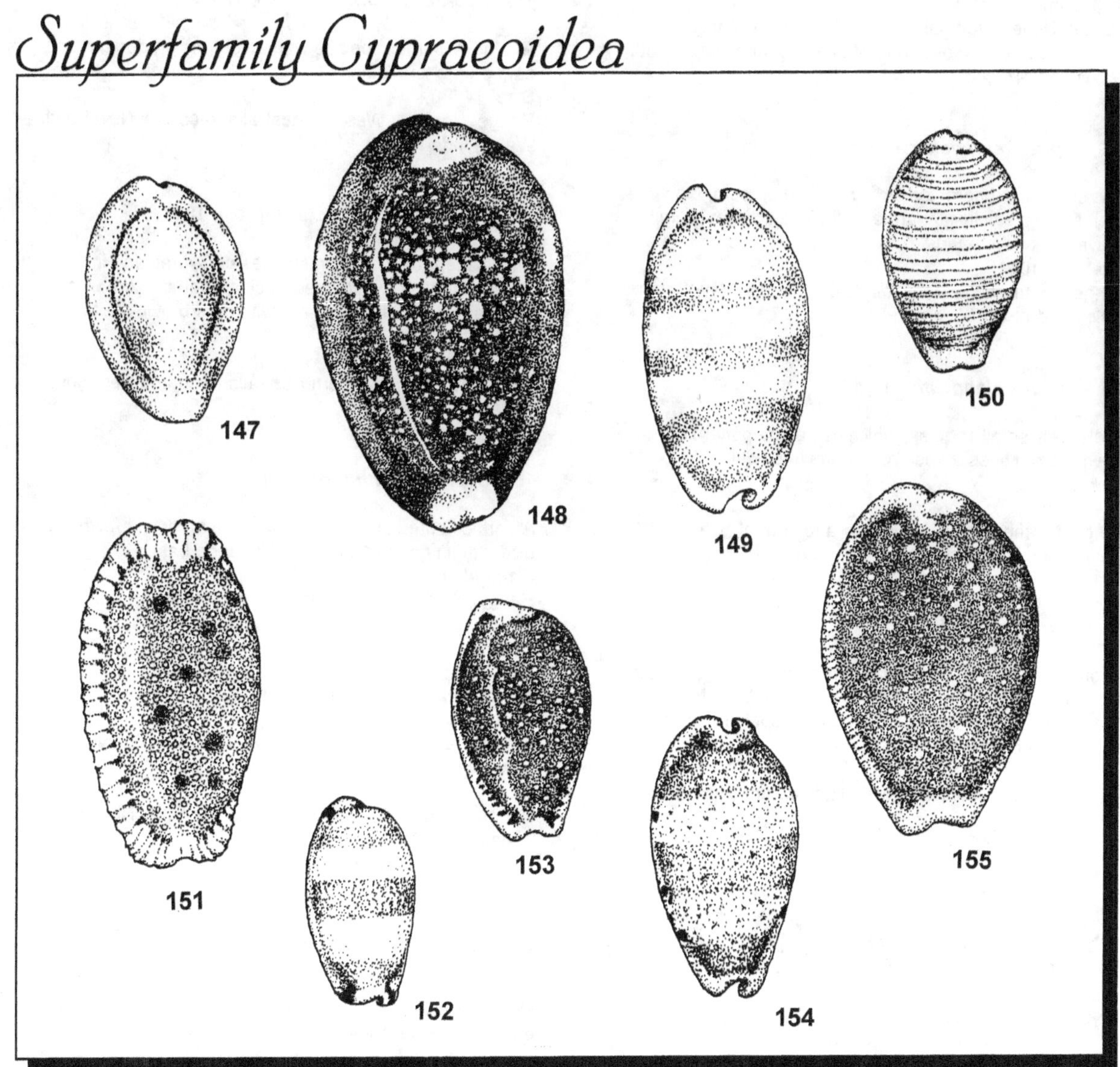

Family Cypraeidae

Nine species from this predominantly tropical family were found in the Sydney area. The Australian members of the family have been described adequately in other books (eg. Wilson and Gillett, 1985; Wilson, 1993) and the species will only be dealt with briefly here. All species, except *C. xanthodon*, which is endemic to the eastern Australian coast, have a wide Indo-Pacific distribution. None of the typical southern Australian species live in Sydney.

The animals of the Cypraeidae are nocturnal and hide in crevices during the day. Most are herbivores, although some feed on sponges and bryozoans. The female produces an egg mass or capsules and stays with them until they hatch as veligers. A characteristic of this family is the mantle, which envelops the shell entirely and often has a very different colour from the shell.

147. *Cypraea annulus* L., 1758

A widely distributed Indo-Pacific species, characterised by two yellow lines on both sides of the dorsum. The area enclosed by the lines is greyish blue; the remainder of the shell is white; the interior is dark purple.
Size: 23mm.
Range: Northern Western Australia to central New South Wales, Indo-Pacific.

148. *Cypraea caputserpentis* L., 1758

This species is quite common in Sydney, and can be found alive intertidally under stones. It is heavy, has a flattened base and is black to dark brown with white spots on the dorsum.

Size: 38mm.
Habitat: Under intertidal stones. The animal is grey.
Range: Southern Western Australia to central New South Wales, Indo-Pacific.

149. *Cypraea carneola* L., 1758

This species is characterised by its high dorsum, elongate shell and especially its purple teeth. The dorsum is light brown with white bands.
Size: 40mm.
Range: Northern Western Australia to central New South Wales, Indo-Pacific.

150. *Cypraea clandestina* L., 1767

A relatively small species, which has a fine pattern of brown zigzag lines across a light brown or white background.
Size: 19mm.
Range: Northern Western Australia to central New South Wales, Indo-Pacific.

151. *Cypraea erosa* L., 1758

A common species, which has a thickened rim around the base, bordered by numerous pits and lirae. The dorsum is light brown, maculated with round white spots enclosed by darker coloured circles.
Size: 38mm.
Range: Northern Western Australia to central New South Wales, Indo-Pacific.

152. *Cypraea fimbriata* Gmelin, 1791

A relatively small species with a light brown dorsum and dark purple terminals.
Size: 14mm.
Range: Northern Western Australia to central New South Wales, Indo-Pacific.

153. *Cypraea labrolineata* Gaskoin, 1848

This is the most common species of Cypraeidae in Sydney. It has a white base, a cinnamon dorsum with white spots and a callous rim with dark brown spots around the base.
Size: 24mm.
Range: Northern Western Australia to central New South Wales, Indo-Pacific.

154. *Cypraea xanthodon* Sowerby, 1832

A dark coloured shell with a blue dorsum with brown spots arranged in bands and a brown/orange base.
Size: 38mm.
Range: Northern Queensland to central New South Wales.

155. *Cypraea vitellus* L., 1758

A rather large, inflated and heavy shell. The dorsum is brown with white spots; the base is white.
Size: 46mm.
Range: Northern Western Australia to central New South Wales, Indo-Pacific.

Superfamily Lamellarioidea

Family Triviidae

The Triviidae have small to very small, *Cypraea*-like shells, which are smooth or with numerous transverse wrinkles, which look like extensions of the teeth on both sides of the aperture. They are much more uniformly coloured than the Cypraeidae.
The Triviidae and the Lamellariidae are placed in a separate superfamily. The reason is the very unusual protoconch of two layers, which is thought to help control buoyancy in the veliger; this type of protoconch is called echinospira. The animals of the Triviidae possess a brightly coloured and pustulose mantle. They live in rocky habitats, from low tide level down.

Subfamily Triviinae

The Triviinae have small, bean-shaped Cypraea-like shells. They usually possess strong ribs, originating from the ventral side of the shell. They are mostly uniformly coloured, with white and pink being the most common colours.
Cate (1979) has revised the worldwide Triviinae based on shell characteristics. Two species can commonly be found on Sydney's beaches.

156. *Ellatrivia merces* Iredale, 1924

A very common species on Sydney's beaches. It has transverse wrinkles, which are strongest on the sides and fade on the dorsum. It has a pale pink colour with three red spots on the dorsum and red terminals.
Size: 13mm.
Range: Northern New South Wales to southern Western Australia, including Tasmania.

157. *Trivirostra oryza* (Lamarck, 1810)

Smaller and less common than *E. merces*. The shell is entirely white. The sculpture of transverse lirae is interrupted by a smooth line in the centre of the dorsum.
Size: 10mm.
Range: Northern Western Australia to central New South Wales, Indo-Pacific.

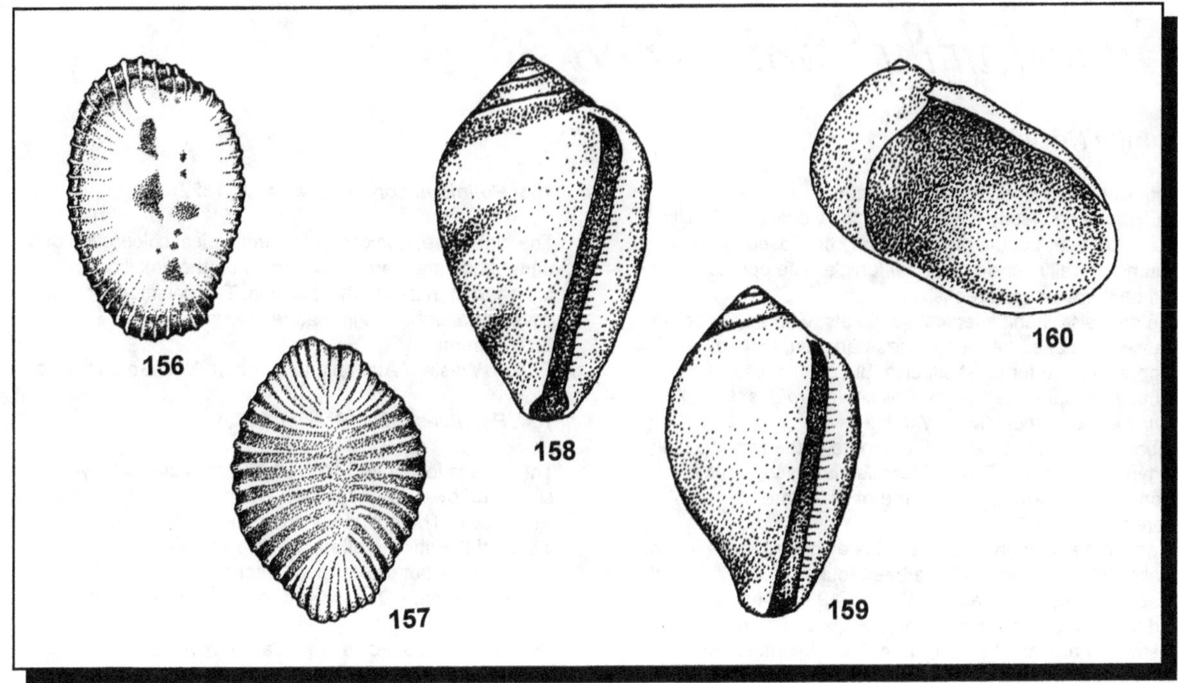

Subfamily Eratoinae

Early workers placed this group near the Marginellidae because of similarities in shell shape. However, Marginellidae have a different aperture shape and are quite different anatomically.

The shells of the Eratoinae have an echinospira protoconch. The animals feed on ascidians. Schilder (1933) and Cate (1977) have revised the Eratoinae based on shell characteristics. Two species can be found on beaches in the Sydney area. The first is quite common in shell grit; the second is much rarer.

158. *Proterato (Sulcerato) lachryma* (Sowerby, 1832)

The shell is thick and smooth; the spire is low. The aperture is slit-shaped; the outer margin is thick, with many small teeth. The columella is straight and simple. The colour is white to greenish in fresh specimens, with three encircling red bands of which the top one is the most prominent.
Size: 7mm.
Range: Southern Queensland to southern Western Australia, including Tasmania.

159. *Proterato (Eratoena) corrugata* (Hinds, 1844)

The shell shape is very similar to that of *P. lachryma*, but slightly more rounded and smaller and with a narrower aperture. The dorsum is covered in small pustules. The colour is uniform light brown or white, with a small purple spot inside the siphonal notch.
Size: 5mm.
Range: Northern Queensland to central New South Wales.

Family Lamellariidae

The shell of species of this family is internal, concealed or fully enveloped in the mantle, which is not retractile. The shell is thin and few-whorled, with a periostracum. The aperture is large; the suture is impressed. There is no operculum. The mantle shape, texture and colour are highly variable within species. The mantle closely resembles the species of ascidian on which the animal feeds. The protoconch is echinospira type (Behrens, 1980). In the Antarctic, Weddell seals have been observed to feed on giant Lamellariids (Numanami and Okutani, 1991).

The Australian species of the family are poorly documented. Allan (1958) has described and illustrated four different species of Lamellariidae from New South Wales, none of which were identified as *Lamellaria innominatus* (Iredale, 1936), the one species described from New South Wales. Behrens (1980) has revised the east Pacific species, placing them in genera based on radula, anatomic features and reproductive type (monoecious or dioecious).

160. *Lamellaria sp.*

The shell is thin, fragile, imperforate and low spired. The last whorl occupies nearly the entire shell height. The shell surface is smooth except for some fine growth lines. The colour is translucent white.
Size: 6mm.
Range: New South Wales.

Superfamily Naticoidea

Family Naticidae

Naticidae have small to medium-sized, round shells, which are completely smooth and highly polished. Shells are umbilicate, but the umbilicus may be closed off by columellar callus or an umbilical funicle. The operculum can be horny or calcareous.
The animals inhabit intertidal sand flats, where their egg-masses can often be found. These are thin, curved ribbons of sand for most species, but gelatinous, sausage-shaped masses for *Polinices sordidus*, *P. conicus* and *P. incei* (Murray, 1962).
Kabat (1991) has reviewed the genera of the family based on type specimens. Four subfamilies are recognised (Ponder and Warén, 1988), three of which are represented here.
The animals prey on other molluscs by drilling holes in the shells. Different species have been found to have different attack strategies (Ansell and Morton, 1987). The radula and the accessory boring organ are used to both chemically and mechanically penetrate the shell. The Naticid borehole is parabolic in shape with irregular edges. It is sometimes confused with the hole made by Muricids, which has straight sides (Kabat, 1990). Naticidae prey on sand-living species, mostly on gastropods and bivalves.
Ten species of Naticidae can be found on Sydney's beaches; all are discussed here.

Subfamily Naticinae

Shells with a calcareous operculum. The foot is large, but can easily be retracted.

161. *Natica pseustes* Watson, 1887

The shell is globose and thick. It has axial folds below the sutures. The umbilicus is closed off by a small, round umbilical funicle. The colour is white usually with two broad brown, sometimes black, spiral bands.
Size: 12mm.
Range: Northern Queensland to central New South Wales.
Synonyms: *N. lavendula* Woolacott, 1956.

162. *Tanea sagittata* (Menke, 1843)

The shell is globose and low-spired. The umbilicus is partly closed off by a small, round funicle, which originates from a spiral rib inside the umbilicus. The colour is white or light brown with a pattern of brown zigzag lines. The columella and the umbilical funicle are white.
Size: 13mm.
Range: All Australian states.

Subfamily Polinicinae

Shells with a horny operculum. The foot is large and may envelop the entire shell. It cannot be retracted quickly.

163. *Polinices conicus* (Lamarck, 1822)

The high spire, conical shape and typical colouration of dark bands and dark brown areas on the umbilical callus are characteristic for this species. The columellar callus covers the umbilicus in mature specimens.
Size: 28mm.
Range: Western Australia to southern New South Wales.

164. *Polinices incei* (Philippi, 1853)

The shell is low-spired. The umbilicus is completely closed off by a round funicle. The colour is off-white to light brown. The columella and funicle are white. The inside of the shell is often dark brown.
Size: 22mm, but grows much larger.
Range: Northern Queensland to central New South Wales.
Remarks: This species is similar to *Neverita didyma* but its large umbilical funicle does not bear a groove.

165. *Polinices sordidus* (Swainson, 1821.)

The shell is relatively high-spired and rounded; the umbilicus is partly closed by callus. The colour is grey with an orange outer lip and columellar callus.
Size: 36mm.
Habitat: Common in intertidal sand in bays.
Range: Northern Queensland to southern New South Wales.

166. *Polinices melastomus* (Swainson, 1821)

The shell is not unlike *P. sordidus*, but smaller and lower-spired, with a round funicle in the umbilicus, completely closing it off. It is usually lighter in colour than *P. sordidus*, being light grey instead of bluish grey.
Size: 19mm.
Range: New South Wales.

167. *Neverita didyma* (Röding, 1798)

The shell is rather thin and low-spired. The aperture is large. The columella is thin. The umbilicus is wide, partially closed off by a grooved funicle. The colour is light brown, with a white band just below the sutures. The apex is often blue. The funicle is brown.
Size: 54mm.
Range: Northern Western Australia to southern New South Wales, Indo-Pacific.
Synonyms: *P. aulacoglossa* (Pilsbry & Vanatta, 1908.)

168. *Mammilla simiae* Deshayes, 1838

The shell is thin and elongate. The aperture is elongate. The columella is long, slightly concave, reflected,

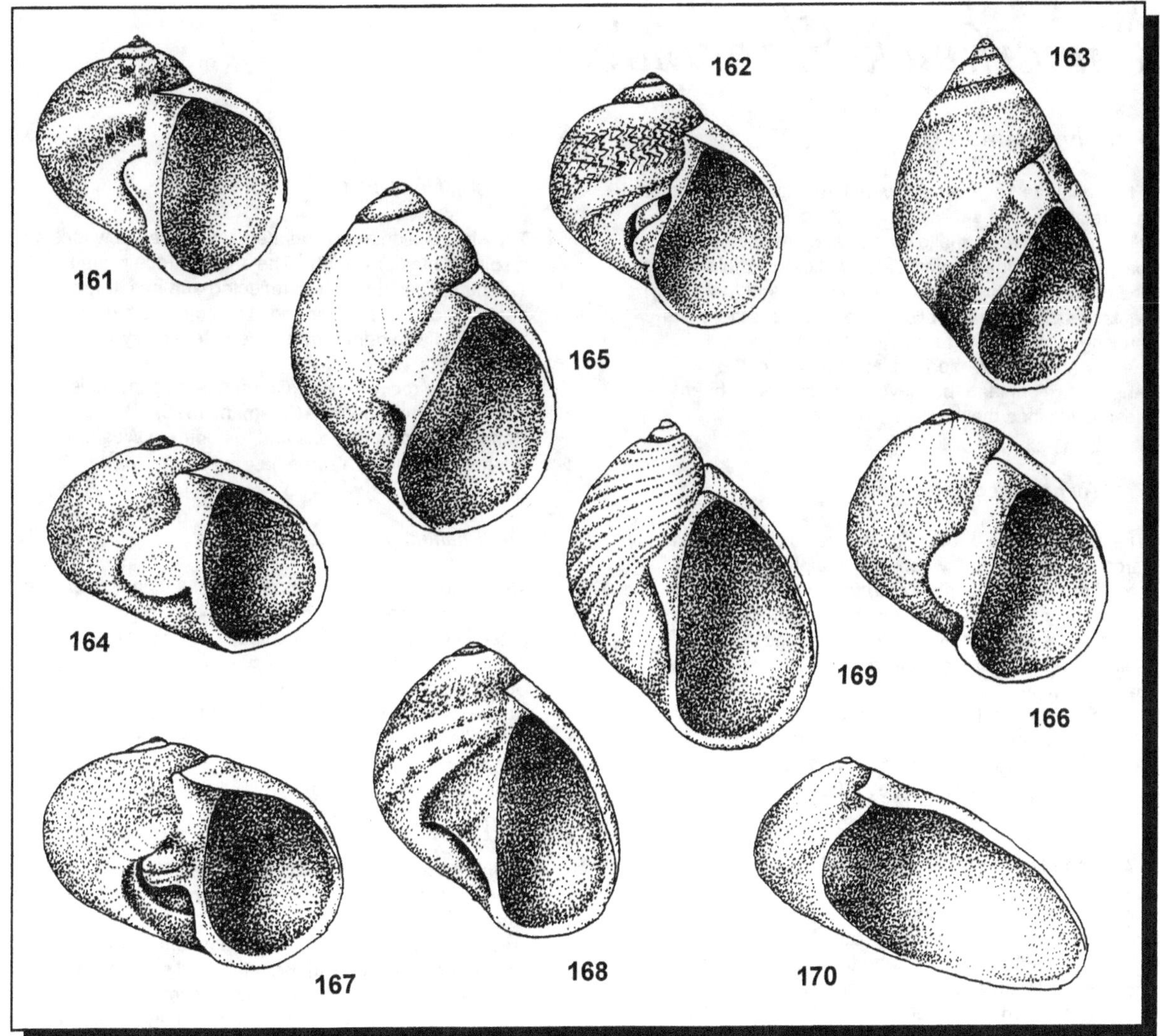

the callus spreading over the umbilicus. The colour is white, maculated with dark brown, often in bands, with a white band in the middle.
Size: 25mm.
Range: Northern Territory to central New South Wales.
Remarks: *M. fibrosa* (Souleyet, 1852) is a tropical species, which is sculptured with fine spiral lines. *M. sebae* Souleyet, 1844 is a related tropical species.

Subfamily Sigaretinae

Low-spired shells, with a large last whorl. The operculum is horny if present.

169. *Eunaticina linneana* (Récluz, 1843)

The shell is thin, low-spired, with a large last whorl. The sculpture consists of spiral grooves; the shell surface is rough, not shiny. The sutures are deeply impressed. The colour is entirely white.

Size: 22mm.
Range: All Australian states.
Synonyms: *E. papilla* of authors.
Remarks: The southern species *N. umbilicata* (Quoy and Gaimard, 1834) has fine spiral grooves, is less elevated and has coloured bands.

170. *Sinum zonale* (Quoy and Gaimard, 1834)

The shell is very low-spired to ear-shaped, imperforate and flat. The shell surface is matt, with many very fine spiral grooves, crossed by axial growth lines. The shell is completely white. The columella is thin, without callus.
Size: 30mm.
Range: Central New South Wales to southern Western Australia.

Superfamily Tonnoidea

Family Tonnidae

The Tonnidae have large to very large, low-spired, inflated and relatively thin shells, with spiral sculpture.
The animals live in shallow water and are nocturnal. They prey on holuthurians, which are swallowed whole through the proboscis. The animals are coloured and have long tentacles. The larval shells are not calcified; there is a prolonged veliger stage (Morton, 1991).
Hedley (1919) published the latest review of the Australian Tonnidae, but several species have been described since then.

171. *Tonna variegata* (Lamarck, 1822)

The shell is large, but thin for its size, low-spired, with a large and inflated last whorl. The sculpture consists of broad rounded spiral ribs, alternating with narrow ribs. The outer lip is only slightly thickened on the inside. The columella is covered by a glaze above and reflected below. The colour is light brown, mottled with white and dark brown.
Size: to 90mm, but beach specimens are often smaller.
Range: Central New South Wales to central Western Australia, including Tasmania, New Zealand
Synonym: *T. cerevisina* Hedley, 1919

172. *Tonna chinensis* (Dillwyn, 1817)

This species is smaller than *T. cerevisina*. Juvenile specimens can be very similar, but always lack the narrow ribs between the broad ribs and the interstices are narrower. Also, they are always smaller for a given number of whorls. The colour is light brown, mottled with white and with sparse dark brown spots.
Size: 60mm.
Range: Southern Western Australia to central New South Wales, Indo-Pacific.

Family Cassidae

Medium-sized to large, thick and often smooth or spirally sculptured shells. A characteristic is the thickened outer lip, which is reflected and often bears three pointed denticles on the anterior end.
Cassidae feed on sea-urchins. Their proboscis is at least as long as the shell and they have large proboscis glands, which contain a strongly acid solution. They feed mostly at night approaching the prey with caution because many urchins can move faster than they can. When a sea-urchin is captured, an area slightly larger than the proboscis is cleared of spines and a circular groove is cut in the skeleton with the aid of the proboscis and the radula (Hughes and Hughes, 1981).
Beu (1981) recognised two subfamilies, the Cassinae and the Phaliinae, based on the structure of the operculum and the shape of the siphonal canal. Only one subfamily is represented here.

173. *Phalium labiatum* (Perry, 1811)

The shell is elongately rounded, with rounded whorls and a spire of medium height. The shell surface is smooth. The outer lip is thickened, reflected and has three denticles on the anterior end. The colour is bluish, maculated with dark brown. The outer lip is yellow.
Size: 65mm.
Habitat: On rocky shores. Communal egg-laying is common in this species (Coleman, 1975)
Range: Southern Queensland to southern Western Australia, including Tasmania.

174. *Phalium pyrum* Lamarck, 1822

This species has a much broader shell than *P. labiatum* and is shouldered; the shoulder may bear knobs. The outer lip is smooth and reflected. The colour is light pinkish brown with darker maculations.
Size: 55mm, but grows larger.
Range: Central New South Wales to southern Western Australia, including Tasmania, South Africa.

Family Ranellidae

Formerly called the Cymatiidae, this family comprises mainly medium-sized to very large species, which have a varix around the aperture and often at regular intervals on previous whorls. They have a prominent anterior canal; a posterior canal is very indistinct if at all present. All species have a thick, hairy periostracum.
The females produce eggs in capsules attached to a substrate. The larvae hatch as veligers and have a prolonged planktonic stage. The larval shell of some genera is not calcified.
Ranellidae feed on bivalves, gastropods, echinoderms, starfish and ascidians. They detect their prey by chemoreception of substances carried downstream by current. Some are active predators, while others are scavengers. Some Ranellidae feed only at night, while others were observed to be active throughout the day (Laxton, 1971).
Beu (eg. 1970a, 1970b, 1971a, 1985, 1988) in cooperation with other workers (eg. Beu and Cernohorsky (1986) and Beu and Knudsen (1987)) has worked extensively on the taxonomy of this family.
Six species can be found on Sydney's beaches, more species live in deep water off the NSW coast.

175. *Sassia parkinsonia* (Perry, 1811)

The shell is high-spired and medium-sized. The sculpture consists of fine spiral ribs, which cross large nodules on the shoulder. The outer lip is thickened and there are varices every 2/3rd whorl. The colour is uniform light brown or orange; the interior is porcellaneous white.

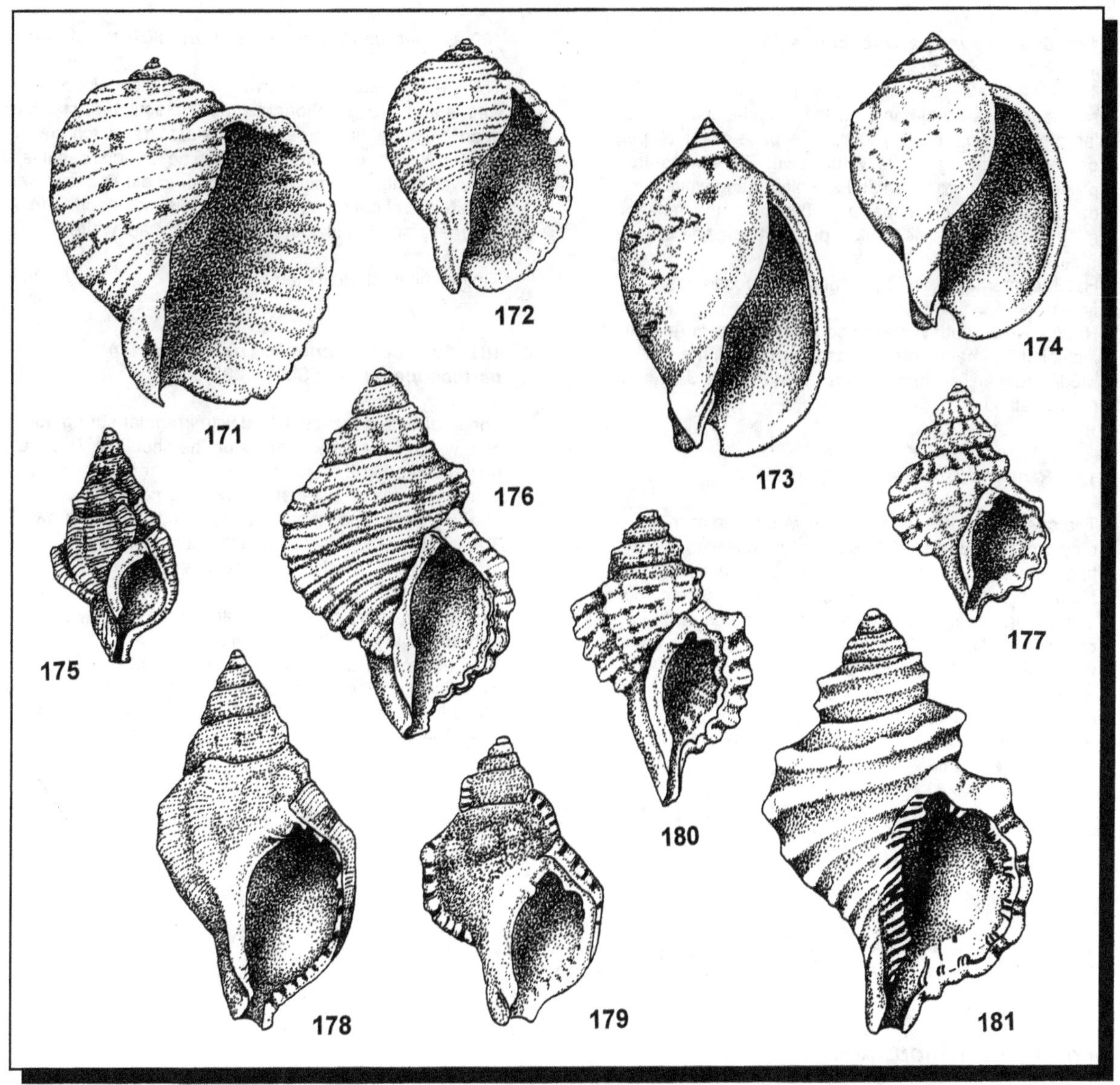

Size: 40mm.
Habitat: Subtidally on rocks.
Range: New South Wales to Victoria, including Tasmania; New Zealand.

176. *Cabestana spengleri* Perry, 1811

A heavy shell, sculptured with double spiral ribs crossing rounded nodules on the shoulder. The sculpture on early whorls is a reticulate pattern of spiral and axial ribs. The outer lip is thickened, expanded and flaring in large specimens. There are varices every 1/3rd whorl. The colour is light brown; the interstices between the ribs are dark reddish brown.
Size: 150mm.
Habitat: Common between intertidal stones on rock flats. Often, there are groups of animals in the same crevice. Sydney specimens live almost entirely on cunjevoi (Laxton, 1971). The animal is red.

Range: Southern Queensland to South Australia, including Tasmania.

177. *Cymatium (Turritriton) labiosa* Wood, 1828

The shell is medium-sized and thin for the family; the whorls are strongly shouldered. The sculpture consists of four spiral ribs below the shoulder, which are crossed by axial ribs. The anterior canal is short. The outer lip is marked by a varix; there is another varix halfway the last whorl. The colour is light reddish brown; the varices, the columella and the inside of the shell are white.
Size: 23mm.
Range: All Australian states; southern and eastern Africa, Indo-Pacific, Japan, New Zealand, western Atlantic, eastern Pacific.
Remarks: The short anterior canal, differences in sculpture and smaller size separate this species from *Cymatium exaratum*. This species is uncommon.

178. *Charonia lampas rubecunda* (Perry, 1811)

The shell is relatively thin for its very large size. The sculpture consists of fine crowded irregular spiral ribs and large nodules on the shoulders. The base colour is purple or pink, heavily maculated with brown. The varices are present every third whorl and are alternating white and dark brown; this is is especially obvious for the varix forming the outer lip. The apex is purple; the inside is white.
Size: 150mm.
Habitat: Intertidally and subtidally on exposed rock surfaces.
Range: New South Wales to southern Western Australia, including Tasmania; other subspecies live in the Mediterranean, eastern Atlantic, South Africa, Japan and New Zealand.

179. *Ranella australasia* (Perry, 1811)

The shell is heavy and large. The whorls are rounded, only slightly shouldered. The sculpture consists of very fine spiral ribs and small nodules on the rounded shoulder. There are varices every 1/2 whorl. The colour is uniform dark brown; the varices are alternating white and dark brown. The inside is white. Fresh specimens have a very resilient yellowish, velvet-like periostracum.
Size: 90mm.
Habitat: Intertidal rock flats.
Range: New South Wales to southern Western Australia, including Tasmania.

180. *Cymatium (Monoplex) exaratum* (Reeve, 1844)

The shell is medium-sized, with strongly shouldered whorls and a long siphonal canal. The sculpture consists of strong spiral ribs, crossed by axial folds, which are especially strong on the shoulder. The anterior canal is relatively long. The colour is reddish or bluish brown with a white spiral band in the middle of the last whorl. The columella and the inside of the aperture are white.
Size: 50mm.
Range: All Australian states.

181. *Cymatium (Monoplex) parthenopeum parthenopeum* (von Salis, 1793)

The shell is heavy, sculptured with irregular strong spiral ribs, which bear large nodules on the shoulder. There are no varices other than the thickened outer lip, which bears paired nodules on the inside. The columella callus is strongly lirate. The colour is almost uniform light brown. The inside of the outer lip and the columella are maculated with black; the inside is white.
Size: 100mm.
Habitat: On rocky shores. The animal has a very pretty pattern of black, yellow and white.
Range: New South Wales to southern Western Australia, including Tasmania, western and eastern Atlantic, Mediterranean, South Africa, Japan, eastern Pacific and New Zealand.

Suborder Ptenoglossa

Superfamily Triphoroidea

Family Cerithiopsidae

A family of small to minute high-spired shells, characterised by their cancellate sculpture and tilted first whorl of the protoconch. They feed on sponges. The larvae hatch as veligers.
Members of this family from New South Wales and tropical Australia were reviewed by Laseron (1951a; 1956b), who used the protoconch as a characteristic for identification. South Australian Cerithiopsidae were reviewed by Cotton (1951).
The species belonging to the genus *Ataxocerithium* are larger than other species in this family. The genus has previously been placed in the Cerithiidae (Loch, 1992) and Triforidae (Cunningham-Vaught, 1989), but Houbrick (1987c) has placed it in the Cerithiopsidae. Loch (1992) has discussed the southern Australian species belonging to this genus.
Cerithiopsidae are quite common in shell grit on Sydney's beaches. However, most are in poor condition and the protoconch is usually lacking, so identification is virtually impossible.

182. *Ataxocerithium serotinum* (A. Adams, 1855)

The shell is thin and high-spired. The whorls are slightly rounded; the sutures are impressed. The sculpture consists of many axial ribs crossed by fine spiral ribs, the axial sculpture becoming weaker on the base. The columella is reflected below. The outer lip is slightly flaring and thin. The colour is light brown to purplish, maculated with darker brown areas, especially on the base, the columella and below the sutures.
Size: 13mm.
Habitat: Under stones subtidally.
Range: Southern Queensland to northern Western Australia, including Tasmania.

183. *Ataxocerithium applenum* Iredale, 1936

The shell is rather broad. The spire whorls are rounded with impressed sutures. The sculpture consists of fine spiral ribs crossed by irregular axial ribs. The outer lip is flaring; the columella is reflected. The colour is dirty white.

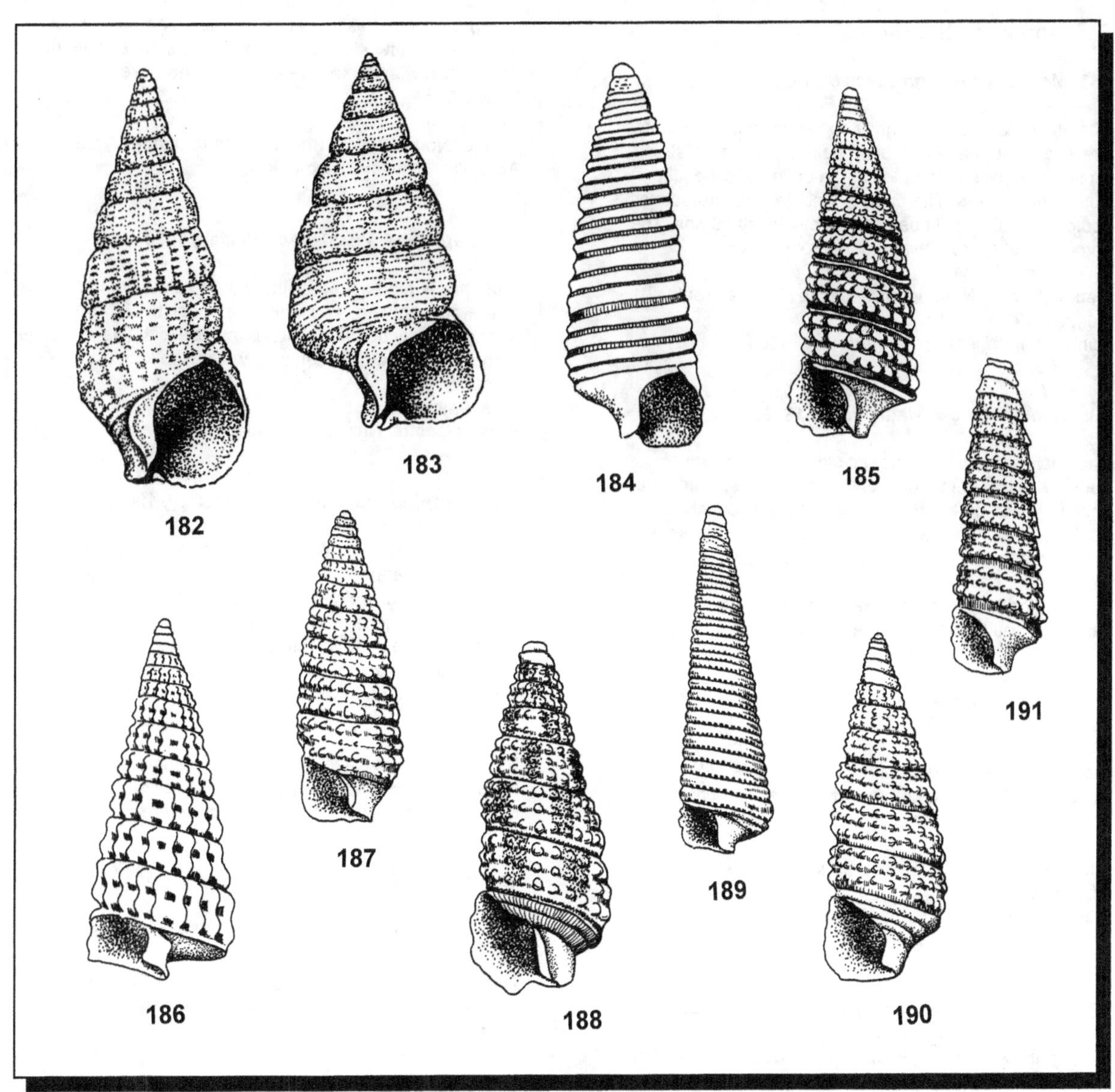

Size: 12mm.
Range: Central New South Wales to eastern Victoria.

184. *Seila nigrofusca* Laseron, 1951

The shell is high-spired and needle-shaped, with straight sides. The spire whorls are flat; the sutures are hardly visible. The sculpture consists of four spiral ribs on each whorl, which are narrower than the interstices between them. The interstices are finely axially striated. The colour is dark brown; the spiral ribs are somewhat lighter in colour.
Size: 9mm.
Range: Central New South Wales.

Family Triphoridae

The most obvious characteristic of this family is that many species are sinistral. Shells are small to minute, high-spired and sculptured with spiral cords with nodules. The protoconch of the Triphoridae has up to five whorls and bears a distinct sculpture, which is useful in identification. They feed on sponges and have a long proboscis. They live worldwide from tropical to arctic seas to depths of 1000m. Shell characters, including colour, are usually sufficient to separate species.
Marshall (1983) has revised the southern Australian Triphoridae, recognising three subfamilies, one of which (Adelacerithiinae) does not live in Australia. The subfamily Metaxinae contains dextral species. Marshall recorded twenty-nine species from New South Wales. Six identified and one unidentified species are described here. All belong to the sinistral subfamily Triphorinae.

Subfamily Triphorinae

185. *Monophorus nigrofusca* (A. Adams, 1851)

The shell is small with slightly convex sides. The sutures
are incised but hardly visible. The sculpture consists of
three spiral rows of nodules and a plain spiral rib just
above the sutures. The base is smooth. The protoconch is
sculptured with axial ribs crossed by two spiral ribs. The
colour is light brown with a dark brown base.
Size: 10mm.
Range: Central New South Wales to Victoria; South
Australia (?).
Synonyms: *Triphora cinerea* Hedley, 1903.

186. *Hedleytriphora elata* (Thiele, 1930)

The shell is broad with straight sides. The sculpture
consists of two spiral rows of strong nodules, which are
linked to each other by axial ribs. The protoconch is
sculptured with fine axial ribs crossed by a spiral keel.
The colour is white; the interstices are brown.
Size: 7mm.
Range: Northern to central New South Wales, South
Australia, southern Western Australia.

187. *Hedleytriphora fasciata* Tenison-Woods, 1879

The shell is very small with convex sides; the base is
tapering. The sculpture consists of two rows of large
nodules, with one smaller row of nodules in between. The
protoconch is sculptured with a spiral keel, below which
there are some indistinct axial ribs, the area above the
spiral keel is smooth. The colour is light brown.
Size: 5mm.
Range: Central New South Wales to southern Western
Australia, including Tasmania.

188. *Tetraphora granifera* (Brazier, 1894)

The shell is very small, with convex sides. The sculpture
consists of three spiral rows of closely-packed nodules

The protoconch has axial ribs crossed by a spiral keel.
The base has two flat spiral ribs. The colour is white or
light brown with darker maculations. The base is dark
brown.
Size: 6mm.
Range: Northern New South Wales to central Western
Australia, including Tasmania.

189. *Latitriphora kesteveni* (Hedley, 1093)

The shell is high-spired; with straight sides; the periphery
is sharply angulate. The sculpture consists of three
strong, weakly nodulose, ribs per whorl with fine axial ribs
in the interstices. The colour is white with light brown
maculations.
Size: 9mm.
Range: Central New South Wales.

190. *Aclophoropsis maculosa* (Hedley, 1903)

The shell is thick and has convex sides. The sutures are
incised; the periphery is roundly angulate. The sculpture
consists of three spiral rows of granules on each whorl.
The base has spiral ribs. The protoconch is smaller than
in other species and indistinctly sculptured. The colour is
white or light brown with darker maculations. The
columella and the base are dark brown. The protoconch is
white.
Size: 8 mm.
Range: Northern New South Wales to eastern Victoria.
Remarks: This species resembles *T. granifera*, but is
larger and has fewer whorls and a coarser sculpture.

191. *Triphora sp.*

The shell is high-spired; the sides of the spire are straight.
The sculpture consists of three spiral rows of nodules, the
bottom one of which is larger than the others. The
protoconch is missing. The colour is uniform brown.
Size: 6mm.
Range: New South Wales.

Superfamily Janthinoidea

Family Epitoniidae

Epitoniidae live on or near sea anemones, on which they
feed. Robertson (1983*a*) has studied the life history of the
American species *Epitonium albidum*. The animals
secrete a purple fluid when disturbed. They possess very
small to medium-sized high-spired, many-whorled shells,
which often have axial lamellae. Identification of Epitoniid
species has often been based on axial rib counts, but
Robertson (1983*b*) has shown that this is variable within
species.
Iredale (1936) has described and figured the New South
Wales Epitoniidae. Eleven species are dealt with here; it
is possible that some additional species could be found
on Sydney's beaches.

192. *Opalia australis* Lamarck, 1822

The shell is medium-sized, thick and imperforate. The
whorls are flatly rounded; the sutures are impressed.
There are nine axial ribs per whorl, which are strong and
continuous over the whorls of the spire, with a small knob
just below the suture of each whorl. The ribs fuse into a
spiral rib just below the periphery. Below this, the base is
smooth. The aperture is almost circular. The outer lip is
thickened and incomplete. The shell surface has a rough
appearance. The columella is slightly reflected. The colour
is white.
Size: 30mm.

Range: Northern New South Wales to southern Western Australia, including Tasmania.

193. *Granuliscala ballinensis* Smith, 1891

The shell is medium-sized, thin and imperforate. The whorls are flatly rounded; the sutures are impressed. The sculpture consists of weak axial ribs, which fuse into a basal rib as in *Opalia australis*, only much weaker. The shell surface has a rough appearance. The aperture is nearly circular. The outer lip is slightly thickened and incomplete. The columella is covered with a very thin layer of callus. The colour is white.
Size: 22mm.
Range: Southern Queensland to southern New South Wales.
Remarks: The Victorian *Granuliscala granosus* Quoy & Gaimard, 1834 has a broader shell and less rounded whorls.

194. *Epitonium perplexum* Pease, 1860

The shell is broad, thick and imperforate. The whorls are rounded; the sutures are impressed. The sculpture consists of 13 sharp, reflected axial ribs, which are almost continuous over the whorls and continue on the base. On the last whorl, there is a weak spiral rib just below the periphery. The colour is usually off-white; the ribs are white. Many shells have one or more encircling dark bands, often just below the suture.
Size: 21mm.
Range: Southern Western Australia to southern New South Wales, Indo-Pacific.
Synonyms: *Pomiscala perplicata* Iredale, 1936.

195. *Epitonium jukesianum* Forbes, 1852

The shell is small, thin, fragile and imperforate. The whorls are rounded; the sutures are deeply incised. The sculpture consists of about 11 thin axial lamellae on the last whorl, which are not reflected, nor continuous over the whorls. The interstices are smooth and polished. The outer lip is only slightly thickened. The number of lamellae and the spire height is extremely variable in this species. The colour is white.
Size: 9mm.
Range: Central Queensland to southern Western Australia, including Tasmania.
Synonyms: *Acutiscala ampacta* Iredale, 1936.

196. *Epitonium minora* (Iredale, 1936)

The shell is thick and imperforate. The whorls are rounded and the sutures are deeply channelled; the whorls are joined only by about eight large continuous axial lamellae. The lamellae are strong, not reflected or hooked. The peristome is entire. The shell surface is matt, the interstices are smooth, but not polished. The colour is off-white.
Size: 19mm.
Range: Northern to southern New South Wales.

197. *Cirsotrema (Plastiscala) morchi* (Angas, 1871)

The shell is thick, needle-like and imperforate. The whorls are rounded; the sutures are impressed. The shell surface has a fine, net-like sculpture of spiral ribs crossed by axial growth lines. The colour is yellowish.
Size: 13mm.
Range: Central New South Wales to eastern Victoria, Tasmania.

198. *Epitonium fabia* (Iredale, 1936)

The shell is small, thin, fragile and imperforate. The aperture is circular. The whorls are rounded; the sutures are impressed. The general appearance of the shell is not unlike *E. jukesianum*, but with many more axial lamellae. The colour is white.
Size: 7mm.
Range: Northern New South Wales to eastern Victoria, Tasmania.
Remarks: Macpherson and Gabriel (1962) synonymise *E. fabia* with *E. jukesianum*. The name *E. fabia* has been maintained here to indicate the group of shells which has consistently many more and finer lamellae than a typical *E. jukesianum*.

199. *Epitonium christyi* (Iredale, 1936)

The shell is thick and imperforate. The whorls are rounded; the sutures are deeply channelled, linked only by axial lamellae. There are nine lamellae on the last whorl, which are reflected and hooked on the shoulder. The interstices are smooth; the shell surface is rough. The colour is white.
Size: 8mm.
Range: Central New South Wales.

200. *Epitonium (Foliaceiscala) carchedon* Iredale, 1936

The shell is thin and imperforate. The aperture is circular. The whorls are rounded; the sutures are deeply impressed. There are about 20 lamellae on the last whorl, which are not continuous and of unequal strength; most are strongly reflected. The colour is white.
Size: 4mm.
Range: Central New South Wales.

201. *Cycloscala jacobiscala* (Iredale, 1936)

The shell is thin and fragile. The spire is loosely coiled; the whorls are not joined. There are about eight lamellae on the last whorl, which are thin and slightly reflected. The shell surface is smooth and polished in fresh specimens; the interstices are smooth. The aperture is circular. The colour is white.
Size: 4mm (Iredale recorded up to 13mm).
Range: Central New South Wales.
Remarks: There are several similar species described from tropical Queensland and adjacent oceans. They may be synonymous with this species, but this remains yet to be established.

202. *Epitonium tenellum* Hutton, 1885

The shell is thin, broad and narrowly umbilicate. The whorls are rounded; the sutures are impressed. The sculpture consists of irregular fine axial ribs, which are not continuous over the whorls. The colour is off-white with three dark brown bands.
Size: 8mm, but grows larger.
Range: Northern Queensland to eastern Victoria.
Synonyms: *Limiscala helicornua* Iredale, 1936

Family *Janthinidae*

Shells are very small to medium-sized, thin, short-spired and purple. A characteristic for this family is the sinus in the outer lip, which is more obvious in some species than in others. The animals are pelagic (surface-living) and construct a float of air bubbles. This mode of life results in a large distribution for most species. They are often found in summer after inshore winds. The animals change sex during life and feed on the pelagic *Velella*. They secrete a purple fluid when disturbed.

Two species are described here, only the first one is common in New South Wales.

203. *Janthina janthina* (L., 1758)

The shell is turboid, thin and fragile. It is characterised by its broad shape and purple underside and light purplish-grey top. The sinus in the outer lip is below the periphery, but is very shallow.
Size: 25mm.
Range: All Australian states, worldwide tropical and subtropical seas.

204. *Janthina exigua* (Lamarck, 1816)

This shell can be separated from *J. janthina* by its more globulose shape and uniform deep purple colour. The sinus is at the periphery and is very deep.
Size: 13mm.
Range: All Australian states, Indo-Pacific.

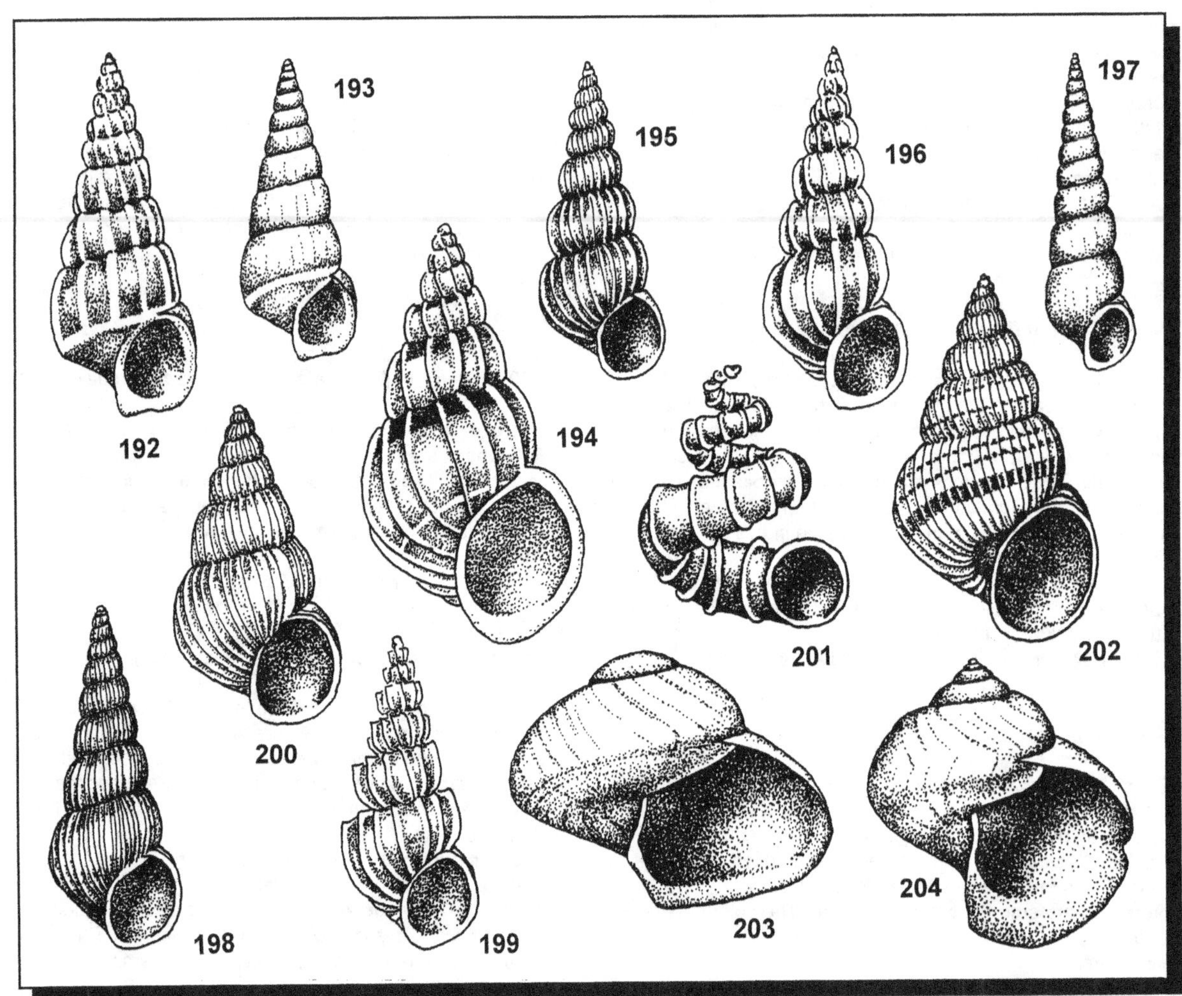

Superfamily Eulimoidea

Family Eulimidae

The Eulimidae is a diverse family with a range of shell shapes and anatomical features. Some species have no shell at all, others have a limpet-shaped shell, but most have small to minute, high-spired, smooth, shiny and mostly white featureless shells. In some species, the axis of coiling is bent, giving the shell a distorted appearance. Laseron (1955a) has used the sinus in the outer lip, which is present in most species, as recognition mark, together with the texture of the shell.

The animals of the Eulimidae are parasitic on other marine creatures, mainly echinoderms and are associated with a particular host. Many genera have no radula and they penetrate the calcareous skeleton of their host by chemical means with their proboscis (Warén and Crossland, 1991). Sexual dimorphism is common in the Eulimidae, the males being smaller than the females.

So far, only Laseron (1955a) has worked on the Eulimidae of New South Wales. Warén (1984) has revised the genera of the Eulimidae based on type specimens. Eulimidae are found in shell grit on sandy beaches, but are not common. Six species are described and figured here; additional species could probably be found on Sydney's beaches.

205. *Curveulima cornuta* Laseron, 1955

The shell is high-spired; the axis of coiling is curved over its entire length. The whorls are flat; the sutures are slightly impressed. The aperture is small. The shell surface is smooth and polished. The colour is entirely transparent white.
Size: 5mm.
Range: Central New South Wales to southern Western Australia.

206. *Eulima acutissima* Sowerby, 1866

The shell is large for the family and needle-shaped. The apex is blunt; the sides of the spire are slightly convex; the periphery is weakly rounded. The individual whorls are slightly rounded; the sutures are somewhat impressed. The aperture is high and narrow, teardrop-shaped. The columella is slightly reflected below. The outer lip is thin. The shell is entirely white and translucent; some specimens are almost transparent.
Size: 17mm.
Range: New South Wales.

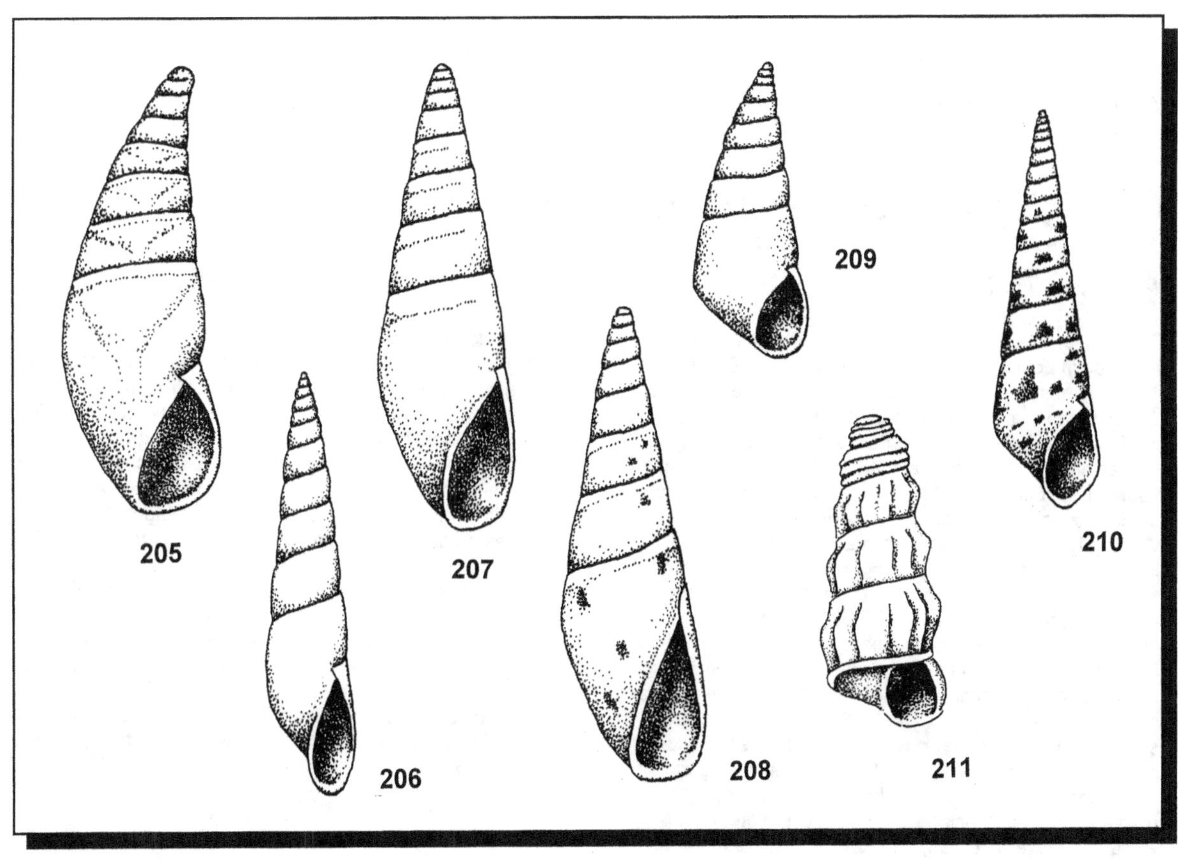

207. *Eulima iredalei* (Laseron, 1955)

The shell is needle-shaped and thin. The whorls are flat; the sutures are hardly impressed. The aperture is elongate and teardrop-shaped. The columella is nearly straight and reflected. The outer lip is thin. The colour is translucent yellow.
Size: 5 mm.
Range: New South Wales.

208. *Eulima sobrina* (Laseron, 1955)

The shell is high-spired and needle-shaped. The whorls are flat; the sutures are hardly visible. The shell surface is smooth and polished. The aperture is elongate; the columella is reflected over its entire length. The colour is yellowish with darker spots.
Size: 7mm.
Range: New South Wales.
Remarks: The longer aperture and the fewer number of whorls separate this species from *C. iredalei*.

209. *Parvioris lata* (Laseron, 1955)

The shell is broad and thick. The axis of coiling is slightly curved; the periphery is roundly angulate. The whorls are slightly rounded. The aperture is relatively small and teardrop-shaped. The columella is situated slightly to the right of the centre of the last whorl. The apex is blunt. The shell is completely white.

Size: 3mm.
Range: New South Wales.

210. *Pictobalcis articulata* (Sowerby, 1834)

The shell is large for the family, straight-sided, with a roundly angled periphery. The whorls are slightly rounded. The aperture is somewhat elongate and teardrop-shaped. The columella is simple; the outer lip has a slight sinus below the suture. The shell surface is highly polished. The colour is white, irregularly marked with brown, with a white band around the periphery.
Size: 16mm.
Range: Central Queensland to central New South Wales.

Family Aclididae

The following species was tentatively placed in this family by Ponder (1985*b*).

211. *Coenaculum minuta* Tate & May, 1900

The shell is high-spired and fragile. The whorls are slightly shouldered. The periphery is sharply angulate. The sculpture on the last whorl and the two previous whorls consists of broad axial folds. There is a spiral keel at the periphery. The apical whorls have spiral ribs. The base is smooth. The colour is translucent yellow.
Size: 2.3mm.
Range: New South Wales.

Order Neogastropoda

Superfamily Muricoidea

Family Muricidae

This is a large family, which has received considerable attention in popular literature (eg. Radwin and D'Attilio, 1976). The family comprises several subfamilies (Ponder, 1972), but the taxonomy of the subfamilies remains confused. Several authors (eg. Wilson, 1994) have used characteristics of the central tooth of the radula to identify subfamilies, but Kool (1993) has shown that this results in subfamilies consisting of two or more groups. Ponder and Warén (1988) recognised only three recent subfamilies, lumping several previously recognised subfamilies into the Muricinae and reducing the Coralliophilidae to subfamilial rank within the Muricidae. Kool (1993) has revised the group formerly known as Thaididae or Thaidinae. He found that Thaididae is synonymous with Rapaninae, the former being the junior synonym, and that several genera were sufficiently different to keep them in a separate subfamily, Ocenebrinae. However, the affinities of a large group formerly included in the Thaidinae, including many Australian genera, remains unknown and thus the taxonomy of the Muricidae is far from complete. Here Ponder and Warén (1988) and Kool (1993) are followed as much as possible.

Muricidae are carnivorous. They live on a wide range of prey. Many bore holes in the shells of their prey, with the aid of the radula, and chemical dissolution, with the aid of an additional boring organ (ABO). The Naticidae also have an ABO, but its presence in the Muricidae is merely a result of convergence and does not indicate a close relationship between the two families (Kabat, 1990). The holes made by the Muricidae can be separated from those made by the Naticidae by being straight-sided.

The shells of the Muricidae are small to very large, variable in shape and sculpture, but many possess varices and spines or frills. A siphonal canal is present, and ranges in length from short to much longer than the last whorl.

Several species were found on Sydney's beaches, some additional species occur in deep water off the New South Wales coast.

Subfamily Muricinae

According to Ponder and Warén (1988), this subfamily includes previously recognised subfamilies such as the Typhinae, Trophoninae, Ergalataxinae and Muricopsinae, but this group needs further clarification through biochemical and anatomical study (Dr. Winston Ponder, personal communication).

212. *Chicoreus damicornis* (Hedley, 1903)

This species normally lives in deeper water, but one dead shell was found on the beach at Narrabeen. It has long, flat spines on the shoulder and a long siphonal canal. The spines are situated on axial varices of which there are three per whorl. The sculpture between the varices consists of fine spiral ribs and usually one or two knobs on the shoulder between each set of varices. The colour is light to dark brown.
Size: 36mm.
Range: Northern Queensland to South Australia.

213. *Chicoreus denudatus* (Perry, 1811)

This species has a biconical shell, with a siphonal canal of moderate length. The shell has three varices per whorl, which have a delicate sculpture of frills, which are usually worn in beach specimens. The sculpture between the varices consists of lamellose spiral ribs, alternating with deep interstices. There are two knobs on the shoulder between each set of varices. The colour is uniform pink or light orange.
Size: 42mm.
Habitat: Below low tide level on rocks, common around Sydney.
Range: Southern Queensland to South Australia, including Tasmania.

214. *Favartia brazieri* Angas, 1877

The shell is biconical and small for the family; the whorls are shouldered. The sculpture consists of rough spiral cords, which are crossed by seven varices on the last whorl; the varices are not continuous over the whorls. The columella is reflected. The outer lip coincides with the last varix. The siphonal canal is curved and of moderate length. The colour is pink with dark brown spiral bands.
Size: 12mm.
Range: Southern Queensland to southern Western Australia, including Tasmania.

215. *Prototyphis angasi* (Crosse, 1863)

This species is easily recognised by its smooth surface and three strong, plate-like varices per whorl; the varices are continuous over the whorls. Each varix possesses a spine on the shoulder, which points upwards and forms a tube-like process. The area between the varices is smooth, except for one or two knobs on the shoulder in some shells. Most shells are white, but coloured or banded forms exist.
Size: 20mm.
Habitat: Under stones from low tide level down.

Range: New South Wales to southern Western Australia, including Tasmania.

216. *Phyllocoma speciosa* Angas, 1871

The shell is small for the family, high-spired and delicate. The whorls are rounded. The sculpture is a cancellate pattern of many fine spiral and axial cords, crossed by about five varices on the last whorl. The varices are almost continuous over the whorls, the last one coinciding with the outer lip. The siphonal canal is short. The colour is white, irregularly mottled with brown.
Size: 16mm.
Habitat: Rare under rocks.
Range: New South Wales to Victoria.
Remarks: Victorian specimens have fewer or even no varices.

217. *Bedeva paivae* (Crosse, 1864)

This common species has a biconical shell, with a siphonal canal of moderate length. The whorls are strongly shouldered and the shoulder bears large axial folds. There are no axial varices. The shell is sculptured with fine irregular spiral cords. The outer lip is slightly crenulated, but not thickened. The colour ranges from yellow to light brown to bluish grey and dark brown.
Size: 28mm.
Habitat: In mud in shallow bays and mangrove areas, where it feeds by drilling holes in oyster shells.
Range: Northern Queensland to Western Australia, Indo-Pacific region and the east coast of South Africa. It was recently discovered in the Canaries, a group of Islands west of the north African coast. Distribution through a seagoing vessel seems the most likely explanation for this occurrence (Poppe and Goto, 1991).
Remarks: *B. hanleyi* (Angas, 1867) is a similar species from central Western Australia to southern Queensland. These two species have been considered synonymous, but they have different eggs (Dr. Winston Ponder, personal communication).

Subfamily Rapaninae

This subfamily includes many genera previously placed in the Thaidinae, which is now a synonym of the Rapaninae (Kool, 1993).

218. *Agnewia tritoniformis* Blainville, 1832

The shell is thick and high-spired, with a short siphonal canal. The sculpture consists of axial folds crossed by broad spiral ribs. There are no varices. The outer lip is thickened and lirate within. The columella is reflected and simple. The colour is off-white. The interstices between the axial and spiral ribs are dark in colour, giving the shell a typical checked appearance.
Size: 34mm.
Habitat: On rocks from low tide level down.
Range: New South Wales to Victoria, including Tasmania, New Zealand.

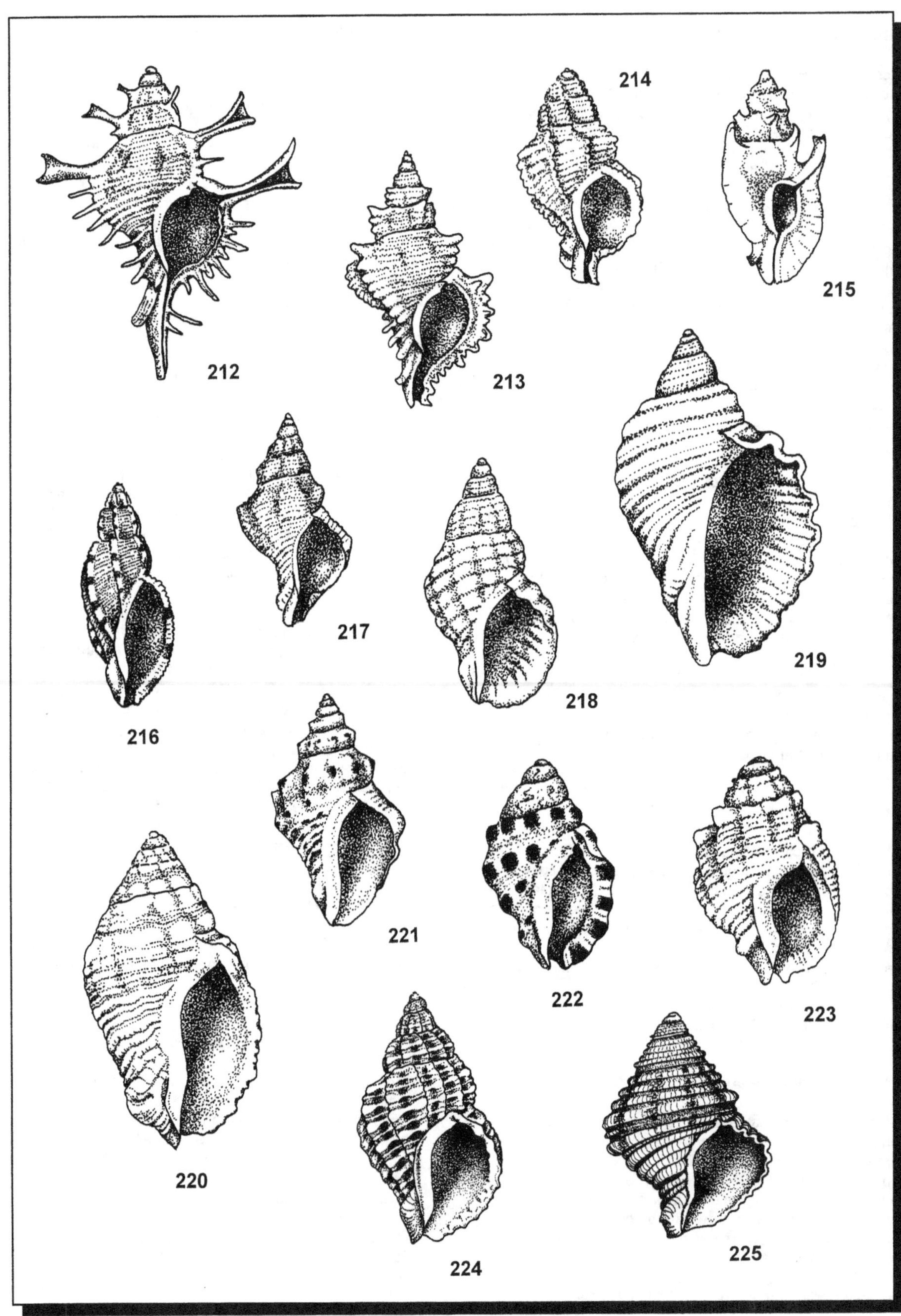

219. ***Dicathais orbita*** (Gmelin, 1791)

This common species has a thick, rounded shell with a very short siphonal canal. The sculpture is variable, but in New South Wales specimens consists of strong square spiral ribs, which may be equal or alternating larger and smaller. There are no varices and the outer lip is not thickened. The colour is white; the inside is yellow.
Size: 46mm.
Habitat: Between intertidal and subtidal rocks.
Range: New South Wales to central Western Australia, New Zealand.
Synonyms: *D. textilosa* Lamarck, 1822, *D. aegrota* Reeve, 1846.
Remarks: Shells from Western Australia are less high-spired and have a weaker spiral sculpture and often axial sculpture.

220. ***Cronia aurantiaca*** (Hombron & Jacquinot, 1853)

The shell is thick, biconical, with a short siphonal canal. The whorls are shouldered. The sculpture consists of lamellose spiral ribs crossed by axial folds. There are no varices and the outer lip is not thickened. The colour is black, with white and brown bands. The columella and the inside are light orange.
Size: 34mm.
Habitat: Between stones intertidally and subtidally.
Range: Queensland to central New South Wales.
Synonyms: *Purpura pseudamygdala* Hedley, 1903.

221. ***Lepsiella reticulata*** Blainville, 1832

The shell is small, biconical, with shouldered whorls and a short siphonal canal. The sculpture consists of irregular spiral cords, of which the one at the shoulder is the most prominent. The spiral sculpture is crossed by weak axial folds, forming sharp knobs on the shoulder. There are no varices. The columella is simple and reflected. The outer lip is thin and simple and slightly flaring. The colour is light grey, irregularly mottled with darker or lighter spots.
Size: 22mm.
Habitat: On algae and stones subtidally.

222. ***Morula marginalba*** (Blainville, 1832)

The shell is thick, biconical, with a short siphonal canal. The sculpture consists of large squarish nodules arranged in spiral bands and fine spiral ribs. The outer lip is somewhat thickened, with denticles and notches. The colour is white; the nodules are black. The outer lip has alternating black and yellow spots.
Size: 26mm.
Habitat: Common on exposed intertidal rocks.
Range: Queensland to New South Wales.

223. ***Morula nodiliferus*** Menke, 1829

The shell is thick and short-spired, with a short siphonal canal. The sculpture consists of strong axial folds, which fade towards the base of the shell, crossed by fine spiral cords, and a spiral groove about 2mm below the suture. The columella is reflected. The colour is entirely white.
Size: 17mm.
Habitat: Between intertidal rocks.

Range: Queensland to New South Wales.
Synonyms: *M. chaidea* Duclos, 1832.

Subfamily Coralliophilinae

A subfamily with heavy and strongly shouldered shells, which are mostly white, pink or orange.

224. ***Coralliophila squamosissima*** Smith, 1876

The shell is thick and biconical, with a short siphonal canal. The whorls are roundly shouldered. The sculpture consists of about 11 axial ribs on the last whorl, which are crossed by fine narrow spiral ribs. The outer lip is slightly thickened and bears some small denticles on the inside. The columella is reflected and covered by a thin, smooth callus. The outer lip is crenulate. The colour is uniform white or pink.
Size: 22mm.
Range: Central New South Wales, Indo-Pacific.

225. ***Mipus arbutum*** (Woolacott, 1954)

The shell is small but thick, with a square appearance. The sides of the spire are flat; the last whorl is roundly shouldered. The sculpture consists of irregular fine lamellose spiral ribs crossing weak and irregular axial folds. The columella is covered by a thin, smooth callus. The outer lip is thin. The colour is uniform orange or yellow.
Size: 7mm.
Range: Northern to central New South Wales.

Family Buccinidae

The family Buccinidae consists of many species of small to very large, high-spired, biconical shells. They posses a siphonal canal, the length of which ranges from very short (subfamily Nassariinae) to many times longer than the last whorl (subfamily Fasciolariinae).
The animals live worldwide, they are carnivorous and are mainly scavengers, although some are predators.
The taxonomy of the family has recently undergone some changes. Ponder and Warén (1988) reduced several families to subfamilies of the Buccinidae, because there was insufficient anatomical evidence to separate them.

Subfamily Buccininae

High-spired shells with a short siphonal canal. This subfamily now includes the group previously known as Colubrariidae (Ponder and Warén, 1988).

226. ***Cominella eburnea filiacea*** Fischer, 1864

The shell is thin and high-spired. The whorls are roundly shouldered. The shell surface is smooth and matt with about ten rounded axial folds per whorl. The columella is reflected. The outer lip is slightly thickened. The colour is white, maculated with brown bands and characteristically a pattern of fine dark spiral lines, about 1mm apart, dotted with small squares.

Size: 26mm.
Habitat: On rocky reefs subtidally.
Range: New South Wales.
Remarks: The nominal subspecies *C. eburnea eburnea* does not live in Sydney, but further to the south and has a sculpture of spiral grooves and often a bluish colour. *C. lineolata* is another species, which occurs further to the south. It has more rounded whorls and broad spiral ribs.

227. *Colubraria brazieri* Angas, 1869

The shell is high-spired, with a short siphonal canal. The whorls are rounded; the sutures are impressed. The sculpture consists of fine axial ribs crossed by spiral ribs of equal size. Every 2/3rd whorl there is a varix, the last coinciding with the outer lip. The columella is reflected and callus forms a shield over part of the parietal area. The colour is light brown, with some white spots on the varices.

Size: 49mm.
Range: New South Wales.

228. *Engina australis* Reeve, 1872

The shell is small, thick and high-spired. The whorls are rounded. The sculpture consists of many finely crenulated spiral ribs, crossed by weak axial ribs. The outer lip is crenulated; the inside is lirate. The columella is reflected. The colour is white, heavily maculated with dark brown especially near the sutures and the base of the shell.
Size: 14mm.
Habitat: Under stones intertidally and subtidally.
Range: New South Wales to Victoria.
Remarks: This species has been placed in the genus *Maculotriton*, which is placed in the Muricidae. However, Ponder (1972) has shown that it is a Buccinid and is best placed in the genus *Engina*.

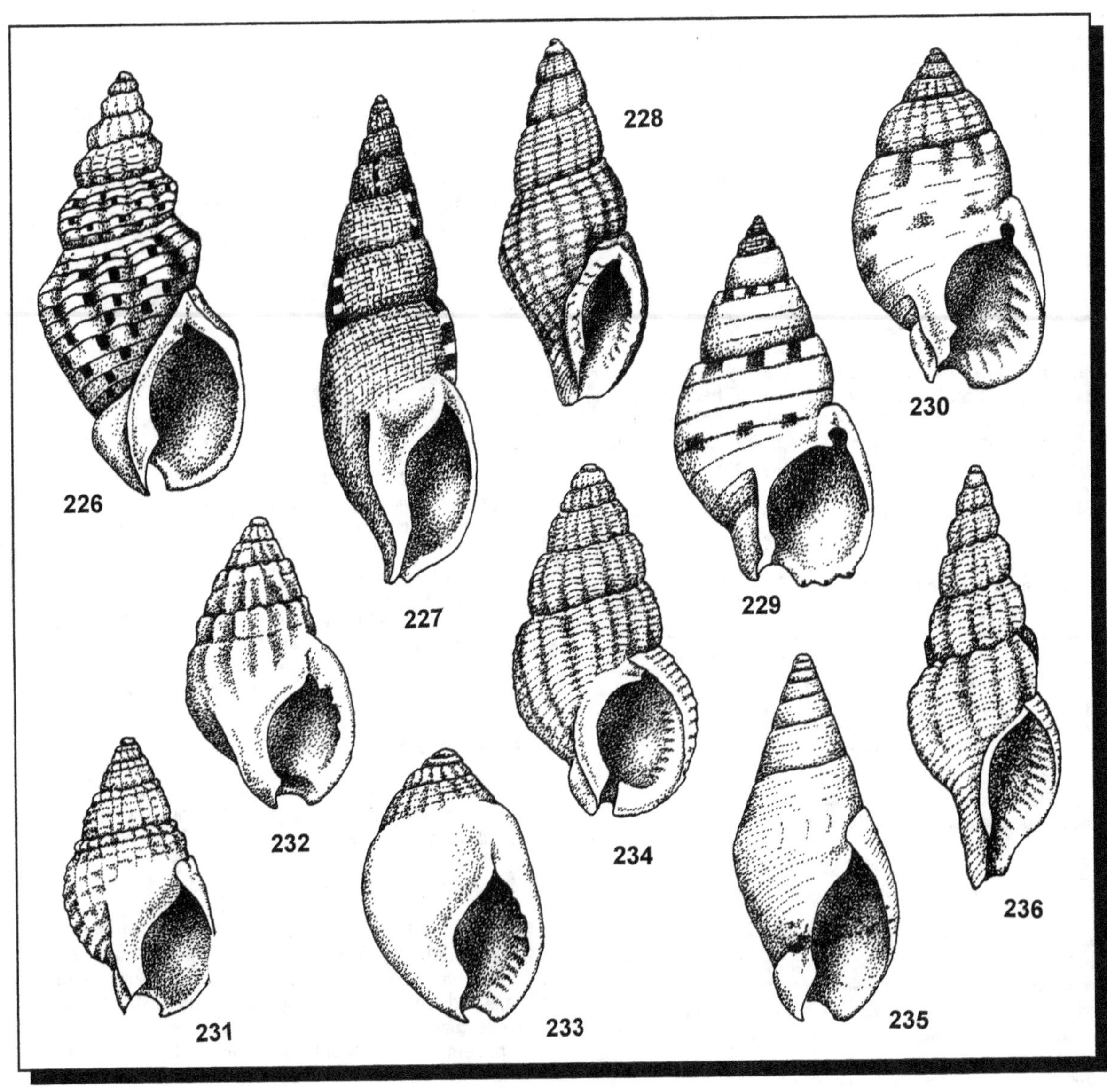

Subfamily Nassariinae

The shells of the Nassariinae are small to medium-sized, biconical to high-spired, with the siphonal canal just a notch in the outer lip. They usually possess reticulate sculpture, although sometimes only on earlier whorls. The columella is covered in a callus, which may cover the whole parietal area of the shell.
The shell shape and sculpture are extremely variable within species. Also, the size and thickness of the parietal callus are variable, and so is the size of the operculum. Most of the species live intertidally in lagoons in sand or on reefs and often live in colonies. The animals feed on carrion and are extremely bold and agile. In Sydney, live animals can be observed on the intertidal sand flats in Botany Bay.
The Indo-Pacific Nassariinae were reviewed by Cernohorsky (1972).

229. *Nassarius (Alectrion) glans particeps* (Hedley, 1915)

The nominate subspecies is common the Indo-Pacific region; this subspecies is restricted to Australia. Both it and *N. glans glans* L., 1758 have thin, almost smooth shells, with rounded whorls. The early whorls are faintly sculptured with a reticulate pattern of spiral and axial ribs. The columella is simple, with only a thin callus. The outer lip is only slightly thickened and has three denticles near the base. The colour is light brown, with a characteristic pattern of fine dark brown lines and squares. Early whorls are blue. This subspecies varies from *N. glans glans* by being smaller, narrower and not having nodules on the shoulders of the last two whorls.
Habitat: On rocky reefs. The animal is yellow, spotted with black.
Size: 26mm.
Range: New South Wales to South Australia.

230. *Nassarius (Telasco) gaudiosus* (Hinds, 1844)

The shell is similar to the previous species, but has a somewhat depressed spire, with convex sides; the spire whorls are rounded. Early whorls are sculptured with axial folds crossed by spiral ribs. Later whorls are almost smooth. The parietal callus is only very thin. The colour is white, heavily maculated with brown. The apex is purple. The columella and the outer lip are white.
Size: 17mm.
Range: Western Australia to central New South Wales, Indo-Pacific.

231. *Nassarius (Niotha) nigellus* Reeve, 1854

The shell is thin and semi-translucent. The sculpture consists of axial folds, which are often nodulose, and sometimes crossed by spiral grooves and a spiral rib of larger nodules just below the suture. The parietal callus is thin. The colour is white with some brown bands. Some shells are uniform white or brown.
Size: 12mm.
Range: Northern New South Wales to Western Australia.

232. *Nassarius (Plicarcularia) burchardi* (Dunker in Philippi, 1849)

The shell is thick and low-spired. The sculpture consists of axial folds crossed by a few spiral ribs at the base of the shell. The parietal callus is not very thick and overridden by axial ribs. The outer lip is thickened; the inside is lirate. The colour is brown or yellow with two dark brown bands, one just below the suture and one at the base of the last whorl. The columella and the outer lip are white. The parietal callus is white maculated with brown.
Size: 12mm.
Range: All Australian states, Indo-Pacific.

233. *Nassarius (Plicarcularia) jonasii* (Dunker, 1846)

The shell is thick and low-spired for the family. The sculpture consists of axial folds, crossed by much finer spiral ribs, which are strongest on the base. The axial folds fade on the last half of the last whorl. A characteristic of this species is the large area of parietal callus, which is white, thick and highly polished. The inside of the outer lip is dentate. The colour is yellowish with dark brown bands at the sutures and at the base of the shell.
Size: 10mm.
Habitat: On intertidal sand bars. The animal is yellow.
Range: Queensland to southern New South Wales.

234. *Nassarius.(Hima) pauperus* Gould, 1850

The shell is small but thick. The whorls are rounded; the sutures are impressed. The sculpture consists of broad axial ribs, crossed by fine spiral ribs. The columella callus is very small, parietal callus is absent. The outer lip is thickened but sharp; the inside is dentate. The colour is usually light brown, often with darker bands. Some specimens are uniform white or brown. The columella and the outer lip are white.
Size: 14mm.
Range: All Australian states, Indo-Pacific.
Remarks: The name of this species is often confused with *N. (Niotha) pauperatus* Lamarck, 1822, a southern Australian species, which does not live in Sydney.

235. *Cyllene royana* Iredale, 1924

The shell is slender and thin. The sides of the spire are straight; the sutures are slightly incised. The sculpture consists of fine spiral grooves sometimes crossed by weak axial folds The last whorl is weakly shouldered. The columella and the parietal area are without callus. The colour is light brown with an irregular pattern of darker and lighter spots. The apex has a tinge of purple. The columella and the outer lip are white.
Size: 14mm.
Range: New South Wales and Victoria.
Remarks: The relationship between this species and *Cyllene lactea* A. Adams and Angas, 1864 is unclear; they may be synonymous.

Subfamily Fasciolariinae

Slender and high-spired shells, which often have a long siphonal canal, but this feature is less obvious in the species described here. They are mainly tropical, only one species lives in the Sydney region; it is rare.

236. *Fractolatirus normalis* Iredale, 1936

The shell is thick and high-spired; the siphonal canal is of moderate length. The whorls are shouldered, giving the shell a turreted appearance. The sculpture consists of broad axial folds, which fade on the lower part of the last whorl. The entire surface has fine spiral ribs. The colour is uniform brown.
Size: 25mm.
Range: Central New South Wales.

Family Columbellidae

Minute to small shells, which have a high spire and narrow aperture. A wide range of shell shapes exists and many species resemble species from other families, such as Turridae or Terebridae. The inside of the outer lip is usually dentate.
The animals live in a variety of habitats, ranging from soft bottoms to rocky and coral reefs. Many of them are carnivores, but some are herbivores.
There has been no revision of the Australian species and their classification remains confused. Radwin (1977; 1978) has reviewed the American species and has figured the radula of many genera. Two subfamilies are recognised within the Columbellidae; all species described here belong to one subfamily.
Columbellidae are plentiful on Sydney's beaches, with several species commonly found in shell grit. Eighteen species are described here.

Subfamily Pyreninae

237. *Pyrene scripta* (Lamarck, 1822)

The shell is thick, biconical and rather low-spired for the family. The whorls are roundly shouldered. The shell surface is smooth except for some spiral cords around the base of the shell. The outer lip is thickened but sharp and dentate within. The colour is white, with a pattern of brown triangles arranged in broad spiral bands.
Size: 14mm.
Range: Northern Western Australia to central New South Wales, Indo-Pacific.

238. *Pyrene opulens* Woolacott, 1957

The shell is thick with convex sides; the sutures are impressed. The shell surface is smooth but not polished. The outer lip is sharp, with a faint thickened rib just behind the lip. The colour is white, maculated with brown.
Size: 17mm.
Range: New South Wales.
Remarks: *Dentimitrella semiconvexa* (see below) is similar but narrower, with flatter whorls and without the thickened rib behind the lip.

239. *Dentimitrella semiconvexa* Lamarck, 1822

The shell is thick and high-spired. The whorls are slightly rounded. The shell surface is smooth and polished except for some spiral cords at the base. The outer lip is sharp and dentate within. The colour consists of spiral bands of brown or black blotches on a background of purple, pink or red. Fresh specimens are covered in a green periostracum.
Size: 14mm for Sydney specimens, but grows larger.
Range: New South Wales to southern Western Australia, including Tasmania.

240. *Dentimitrella tayloriana* Reeve, 1859

The shell is high-spired; the sides of the spire are slightly convex. The whorls are flat and smooth; the sutures are visible, but barely impressed. The shell surface is smooth and polished, covered in a thin periostracum. The outer lip is sharp and dentate within. The colour consists of patterns of brown on a white background. A row of sharply defined brown circles just below the sutures is characteristic for this species.
Size: 11mm.
Range: Central New South Wales to Victoria, including Tasmania.
Remarks: This is one of the most common species of Columbellidae on Sydney's beaches.

241. *Dentimitrella lincolnensis* Reeve, 1859

The shell is thin and high-spired, with straight sides. The whorls are flat; the sutures are barely impressed. The shell surface is smooth. The aperture is narrow. The outer lip is sharp and weakly dentate within. The colour is white or light brown, with patterns of darker brown.
Size: 12mm.
Range: Central New South Wales to southern Western Australia, including Tasmania.

242. *Dentimitrella peroniana* Hedley, 1913

The shell is thick and smooth. The sides of the spire are straight. The whorls are rounded, more so than in any previous species. The outer lip is sharp and curved at the base, forming a distinct but short anterior canal. The colour is brown, sometimes with white encircling bands.
Size: 9mm.
Range: New South Wales.

243. *Pseudamycla dermestoidea* Lamarck, 1822

The shell is rather short-spired, with convex sides. The spire whorls are slightly rounded. The shell surface is smooth but not polished; a shiny surface develops only in worn shells. The outer lip is slightly thickened and weakly dentate within. The colour is very characteristic, consisting of a fine pattern of dark brown lines, forming rectangles on a lighter brown background. There are two encircling bands of alternating dark brown and white rectangles at the periphery and below the suture.
Size: 9mm.
Range: Central New South Wales to southern Western Australia, including Tasmania.

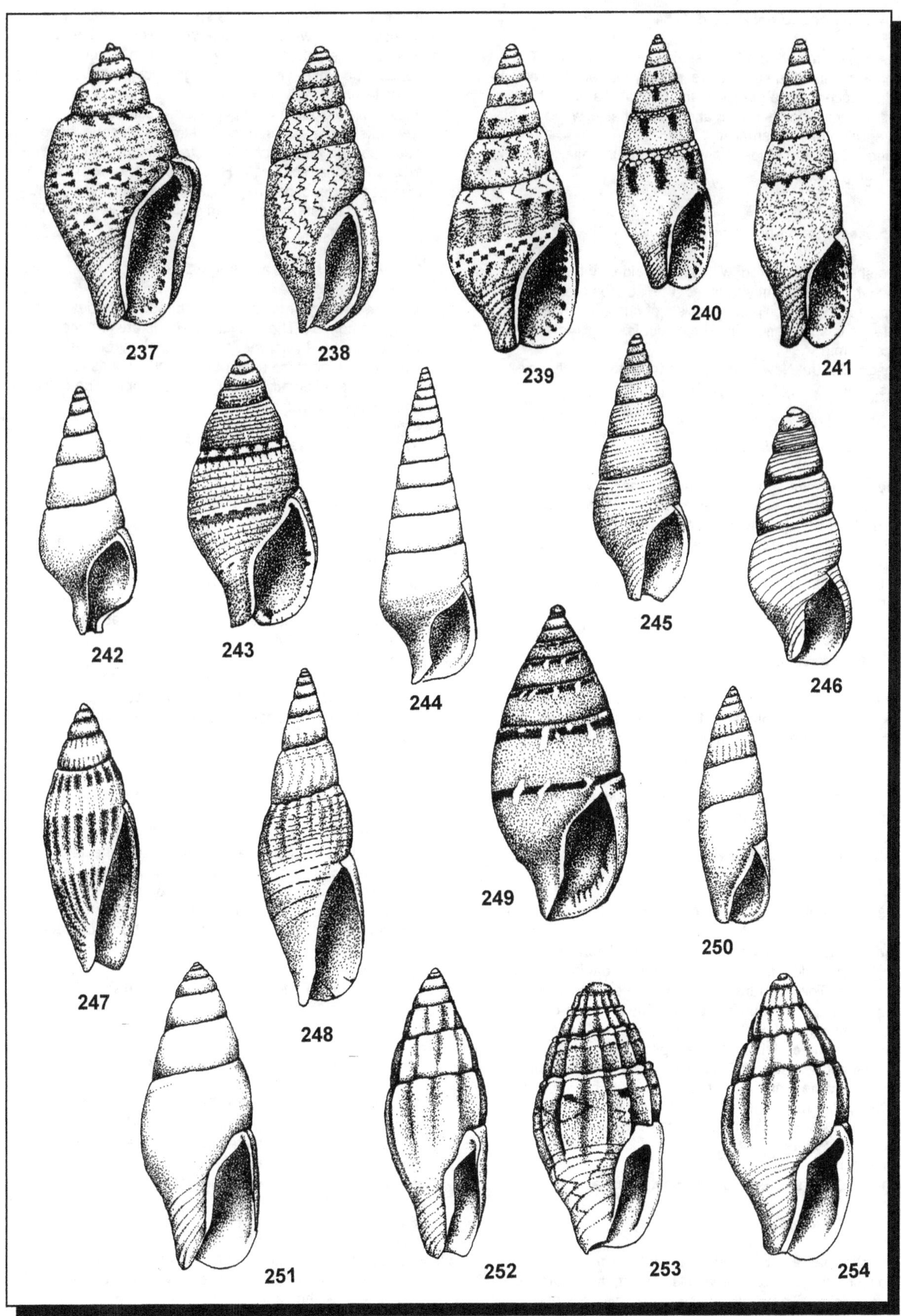

237 238 239 240 241 242 243 244 245 246 247 248 249 250 251 252 253 254

244. *Zella beddomei* Petterd, 1884

The shell is many-whorled, needle-like and smooth. The whorls are flat; the sutures are slightly incised. The colour is translucent white or brown. In some shells the bottom half of each whorl is brown and the top half is white.
Size: 9mm, mostly smaller.
Range: Southern Queensland to South Australia, including Tasmania.

245. *Aesopus pleurisulcatus* Reeve, 1859

The shell is high-spired, with straight sides of the spire. The whorls are slightly rounded; the sutures are impressed. The sculpture consists of fine spiral ribs. The outer lip is sharp and thin. The colour is completely white.
Size: 12mm.
Range: Central New South Wales to Victoria, including Tasmania.

246. *Aesopus pallidulus* Hedley, 1906

The shell is minute and high-spired. The individual whorls are rounded; the sutures are impressed. The sculpture consists of very fine spiral grooves. The outer lip and columella are simple. The colour is translucent white.
Size: 4mm.
Range: Central New South Wales to Victoria, including Tasmania.

247. *Parviterebra brazieri* Angas, 1875

The shell is thin and narrow, with the last whorl occupying about 4/5th of the total shell height. The sides of the shell are convex. The whorls are slightly rounded. The sculpture consists of weak longitudinal folds, which may be absent on the last whorl. The outer lip is thin and fragile. The colour is translucent white, with one or more broad light brown bands encircling the last whorl.
Size: 9mm.
Range: All Australian states.

248. *Parviterebra trilineata* A. Adams and Angas, 1863

The shell is high-spired and thin. The sculpture consists of longitudinal folds, fading on the bottom two-thirds of the last whorl. The aperture is narrow. The columella is nearly straight; the outer lip is thin. The colour is off-white and slightly translucent in fresh specimens. The last whorl has encircling dark brown lines, spaced equally apart. Adams and Angas (1863) have figured a shell with only three dark lines, but shells may have more brown lines. Other brown markings are present on the shell, often just below the sutures. Worn specimens are usually completely white.
Size: 12mm.
Range: Central Queensland to South Australia.

249. *Metanachis* sp.

The shell has a depressed spire and is thick. The sides of the spire are convex. The whorls are flat; the sutures are barely visible. The shell surface is completely smooth and polished. The outer lip is sharp but thickened and weakly dentate within. The colour is very variable. Usually there are fine patterns of brown lines arranged in broad bands on a white, yellow or orange background.
Size: 11mm.
Range: New South Wales, Western Australia.
Remarks: Several lots in the Australian Museum have been labelled *Metanachis bicincta* Sowerby, but the type location for that species is Hong Kong. The distribution of the species described here is unknown, only New South Wales and Western Australian specimens were found.

250. *Truncaria australis* Angas, 1877

The shell is very small and high-spired. The sides of the spire are convex. The individual whorls are flat; the sutures are hardly impressed. The shell surface is smooth, but for some axial ribs on early whorls. The columella is reflected; the outer lip is simple. The colour is uniform light brown.
Size: 6mm.
Range: Central New South Wales to Victoria.

251. *Macrozafra lurida* Hedley, 1907

The shell is thin and narrow. The whorls are rounded. The shell surface is smooth and polished, with a few spiral grooves at the base of the last whorl. The outer lip is slightly flaring. The columella is reflected. The colour is white or light brown, usually with two or three darker encircling bands. The apex is frequently purple.
Size: 4mm.
Habitat: This species can be extremely common in shell grit on both ocean and estuarine beaches.
Range: Southern Queensland to Victoria, including Tasmania.

252. *Macrozafra atkinsoni* Tenison-Woods, 1875

The shell is narrow and high-spired. The sides of the spire are convex. The sculpture consists of strong axial folds, which are not always obvious because of the patterns on the shell. There are several spiral grooves on the base. The aperture is narrow and somewhat contracted in the middle. The colour is white with dark patterns of black or dark brown.
Size: 5mm.
Range: Southern Queensland to southern Western Australia, including Tasmania.

253. *Macrozafra succinea* Hervier, 1899

The shell is broad and thick. The sculpture consists of very strong axial ribs, with knobs just under the suture. The base has several spiral grooves. The aperture is narrow. The outer lip is slightly thickened. The colour is white with a broad darker encircling band, often with patterns of dark blotches.
Size: 3mm
Range: New South Wales.
Remarks: This species can be separated from the similar *Z. avicennia* (see below) by its narrower aperture and much stronger sculpture.

254. *Zafra avicennia* Hedley, 1915

The shell is broad and thick. The sides of the spire are convex. The sculpture consists of strong axial folds, which fade towards the base, and several spiral grooves around the base. The aperture is rather broad. The outer lip has a denticle just below the suture. The columella is reflected. The colour is brown, often with a white encircling band at the periphery.
Size: 5mm.
Range: New South Wales.

Family Volutidae

A well-known family, which has received considerable attention from collectors. The species of the worldwide Volutidae have been figured by Weaver and Dupont (1970).
The Volutidae have medium-sized to very large, thick, smooth and often highly polished shells. The last whorl occupies most of the shell height, and may be narrow or inflated. Most species have very little sculpture, but a few have spines or knobs on the shoulder, or axial folds. Nearly all species have four columella folds.
There is great variation in shell shape and colour within species. This is most likely the result of direct development in the Volutidae. The animals are carnivorous predators and live in sand. The radula may have three (rachiglossate) or one tooth per row. The animal possesses a long siphon and a large foot, which may be even more colourful than the shell.

255. *Amoria undulata* (Lamarck, 1804)

The shell is large, thick and elevate. The last whorl is slightly shouldered. The outer lip is thickened. The colour is white or light brown, with a pattern of dark brown zigzag lines and often some irregular dark brown maculations.
Size: 73mm.
Range: Southern Queensland to South Australia, including Tasmania.

256. *Amoria zebra* (Leach, 1814)

The shell is broad, medium-sized and thick. The spire is short and its sides are slightly concave. The last whorl is roundly shouldered. The outer lip is thickened. The colour is light brown with a pattern of longitudinal dark brown stripes. Colour variations include plain (without stripes), golden and very dark specimens.
Size: 46mm.
Range: Northern Queensland to central New South Wales.

257. *Cymbiola magnifica* (Gebauer 1802)

The shell is relatively thin and very large, with a large and inflated last whorl. The shell surface is smooth, but usually not as highly polished as in most species. The whorls are slightly shouldered and may bear some very weak knobs. The colour is light brown, irregularly maculated with grey.
Size: to 350mm.
Habitat: Observed live at 7m in sand; the animal is grey.
Range: Southern Queensland to eastern Victoria.

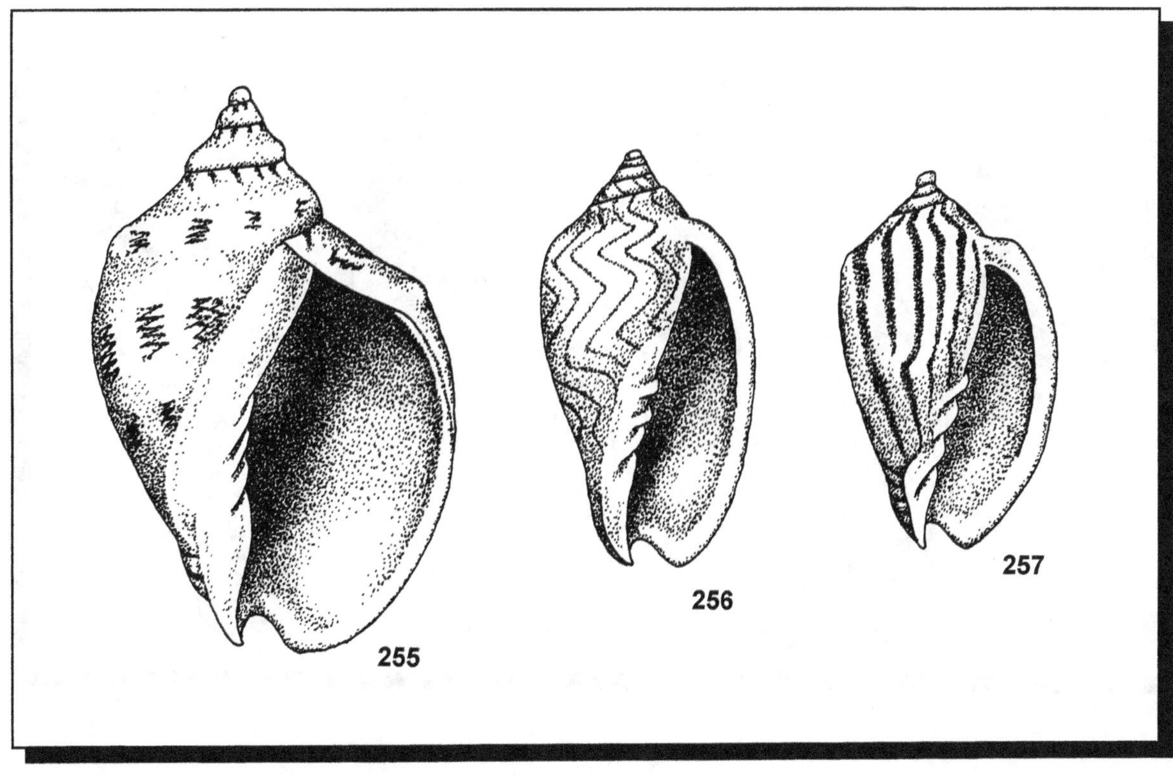

Family Olividae

Kantor (1991) has recently revised the family, splitting it up into four families, of which the family Olividae, as presented here, probably still contains more than one family. The shell shape is elongate, but the spire is low; the last whorl occupying a large proportion of the shell height.

The shells are small to medium-sized, smooth and polished, sometimes with sparse spiral sculpture at the extremities. The animals are true sand-dwellers and live and feed under the sand surface. They are scavengers or predators and use their large foot to hold their prey. The front end of the foot is enlarged and it is used to plough through the sand. The radula has a central tooth and lateral teeth; there are no marginal teeth.

The subfamily Olivinae is tropical; two species of the subfamily Ancillinae live in the Sydney area.

Subfamily Ancillinae

The shells are relatively high-spired and have some spiral sculpture, including an Ancillid groove around the base of the shell. An operculum is present.

258. *Alocospira marginata* (Sowerby, 1830)

The shell is low-spired for the subfamily, with strongly convex sides and a rounded last whorl. The last whorl is smooth, except for one spiral groove 2mm under the suture and four spiral grooves at its base. The spire whorls are spirally grooved. The columella is strongly S-shaped and covered with callus. The colour is pinkish-brown with a band of red brown blotches just below the sutures and sometimes another band at the base.

Size: 40mm.
Range: Central New South Wales to southern Western Australia, including Tasmania.
Remarks: Several similar species occur in Victoria (Macpherson and Gabriel, 1962; May, 1923).

259. *Alocospira oblonga* (Sowerby, 1830)

The shell is much narrower and higher spired than the previous species. The spire whorls are flat; the sutures are covered with callus and barely discernible. The shell surface is smooth, with some weak spiral grooves at the top and base of the last whorl. The columella is slightly S-shaped. The colour is pink to off-white with a band of dark brown blotches just below the sutures and another band at the base of the last whorl.
Size: 40mm.
Range: Central New South Wales to southern Western Australia, including Tasmania.

Family Olivellidae

This family, formerly a subfamily of the Olividae, is characterised by very small to small, relatively high-spired shells, which differ from those of the Olividae in the absorption of the inner walls of earlier whorls. The animals have marginal teeth in the radula.
Four species live in the Sydney area.

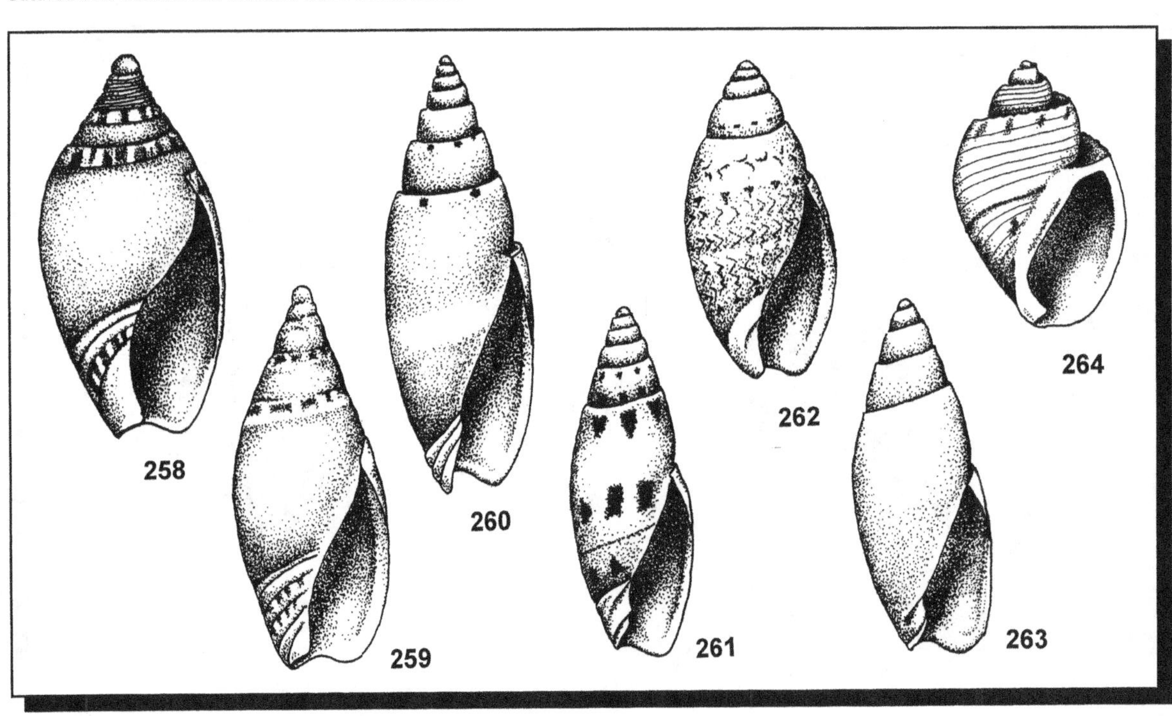

260. *Olivella leucozona* A. Adams and Angas, 1864

The shell is thin and high-spired. The whorls are rounded; the sutures are slightly indented, deep and very clearly visible. The shell surface is completely smooth and polished. The colour is yellowish with some very weak rows of darker spots, especially just below the sutures, and a white band around the periphery.
Size: 15mm.
Range: Southern Queensland to Victoria, including Tasmania.

261. *Belloliva triticea* (Duclos, 1835)

The shell is narrow and high-spired. The whorls are slightly rounded. The shell surface is completely smooth. The colour is white with three spiral rows of brown spots. Sometimes there is a black encircling line between the second and the third row of spots.
Size: 9mm.
Range: Central New South Wales to southern Western Australia, including Tasmania.

262. *Belloliva exquisita* (Angas, 1871)

The shell is short-spired and blunt compared with the previous species. The sutures are incised; the whorls are rounded. The colour is yellowish, with weak patterns of dark brown zigzag lines organised in broad spiral bands. The base of the last whorl and the outer lip are white.
Size: 8mm.
Range: New South Wales.
Remarks: The Columbellid, *Pseudamycla dermestoidea* Lamarck, 1822, which is extremely common on ocean beaches, has a similar appearance.

263. *Cupidoliva nympha* (A. Adams and Angas, 1864)

The shell is thin and high-spired. The sutures are slightly incised; the sides of the whorls are almost straight. The shell is completely smooth. The colour is white, translucent in fresh specimens.
Size: 9mm.
Range: Central New South Wales to South Australia, including Tasmania.

Family Pseudolividae

Shells of various shape with a spiral groove on the last whorl. The operculum is present. The animal has head tentacles of short or medium length, with eye-lobes. The radula has a broad central tooth with three large cusps or numerous smaller ones and bi- or unicuspidate laterals. Only two species live in Australia, one of which can be found on beaches in the Sydney area.

264. *Zemira australis* Sowerby, 1841

The shell is broad and heavy, with rounded whorls and deeply and widely incised sutures. The whorls are shouldered, with the shoulders bearing small knobs. The sculpture consists of fine spiral grooves, with a deeper spiral groove below the periphery on the last whorl. The columella ends abruptly in a tooth-like projection below. The colour is light brown, maculated with darker brown, especially just below the sutures.
Size: 20mm, but grows larger.
Range: Northern New South Wales to Victoria, including Tasmania.

Family Marginellidae

Over 100 recent species of Marginellidae have been described from Australia; some 50 species of Marginellidae have been described from New South Wales. These were put together in one publication by Laseron (1948). Most shells are small, few species reach a length of 10mm or more, and most are completely white. They have blunt, short-spired shells, with a glossy surface, lacking any sculpture. Most have a thickened outer margin and four collumella plaits.
Laseron described all species of New South Wales Marginellidae under one genus, *Marginella*, but he later reviewed the Australian members of the family based on shell shape (Laseron, 1957), dividing them into many new genera. This classification is largely still in use today. The family was revised badly by Coan (1965), but a complete revision has been submitted by Gary Coovert (Dean Hewish, personal communication).
Marginellidae live intertidally and in deep water, most live in sandy bottoms, although a few species live on rocky shores. The animal is very similar to that of *Cypraea*. It has a mantle covering both sides of the shell, long tentacles and a long siphon. However, there are large differences in animals, especially in their colour. The animals are very active, as many carnivores. The diet of the Marginellidae is varied. *Austroginella muscaria* and *A. johnstoni* drill holes in small bivalve shells to insert a poison, relaxing and killing the prey. A similar method of attack may yet be found in other species (Ponder and Taylor, 1992). A species of *Hydroginella*, a genus also present in Australian waters, was found to parasitise on sleeping fishes (Bouchet, 1989).
Several species can be found regularly in shell grit on Sydney's beaches. Seventeen species are described here; additional species may be found (Laseron, 1948).

265. *Mesoginella turbinata* (Sowerby, 1846)

The shell is thick. The spire is moderately elevate, with straight sides, forming an angle of about 90°. The sutures are visible, but not impressed. The sculpture consists of a single row of longitudinal knobs on the body whorl just below the suture. The columella is nearly straight, plaits occupying one third of its length. The outer lip is straight, slightly thicker in the middle than at both ends. The colour is white, in fresh specimens the colour is off-white with a very faint yellow band visible just below the sutures.
Size: 10mm.
Range: Central New South Wales to southern Western Australia, including Tasmania.

266. *Mesoginella translucida* (Sowerby, 1846)

The shell is thick. The spire is moderately elevate, with straight sides. The columella is straight, with plaits occupying half its length. The outer lip is straight and more thickened in the middle than on both ends. The aperture is narrow. The colour is yellow and translucent in fresh specimens, with a darker yellow subsutural band.
Size: 6mm.
Range: Southern Queensland to South Australia.

267. *Mesoginella infelix* (Jousseaume, 1875)

The shell is egg-shaped. The spire is visible, but barely elevate. The last whorl is rounded, with the greatest width above the middle of the shell. The columella is nearly straight, with plaits occupying 1/4th of its length. The outer lip is straight. The colour is white.
Size: 8mm.
Range: Central New South Wales to Victoria, including Tasmania.

268. *Mesoginella inconspicua* (Sowerby, 1846)

The shell is narrow and low-spired. The columella and outer lip are nearly straight. Columella plaits occupy 2/5th of the columella. The outer lip is thin. The colour is yellowish, with a darker band below the suture.
Size: 4mm.
Range: Central New South Wales to eastern Victoria, including Tasmania.

269. *Mesoginella sinuata* (Laseron, 1948)

The shell is thick and low spired. The columella and the outer lip are nearly straight. Plaits occupy the bottom half of the columella. The outer lip is thick, with a sinus above and a thickened area in the middle. The colour is white.
Size: 5mm.
Range: New South Wales to Victoria, Tasmania.
Synonyms: *Marginella strangei* Angas, 1877 may be synonymous.
Remarks: The broad shell, thickened outer lip and posterior sinus are characteristic for this species.

270. *Mesoginella olivella* (Reeve, 1865)

The shell is short-spired and narrow. The sides of the whorls are nearly straight; the last whorl is slightly shouldered. The columella and the outer lip are nearly straight; plaits occupy the bottom 2/5th of the columella. The aperture is narrow above, widening below. The outer lip is slightly thickened. The colour is white.
Size: 8mm.
Range: Central New South Wales to eastern Victoria, including Tasmania.
Remarks: This species is similar to *S. infelix*, from which it can be separated by being narrower, having straight, instead of rounded sides and a more prominent shoulder.

271. *Mesoginella binivitta* (Laseron, 1848)

The shell is rounded and short-spired. The aperture is broad, widening below. The columella plaits are not very strong and occupy the bottom 2/5th of the columella. The outer lip is thickened, especially in the middle, and rounded. The colour is translucent white, with two yellowish encircling bands on the last whorl.
Size: 7mm.
Range: Central New South Wales to Victoria.

272. *Ovaginella ovulum* (Sowerby, 1846)

The shell is egg-shaped, not unlike some species of the tropical family Ovulidae. The spire and the apex are completely enveloped by the last whorl, which is evenly rounded. The columella is convex, with plaits occupying only 1/5th of its length. The outer lip is relatively thin and curved. The anterior sinus is almost nonexistent. The colour is white.
Size: 9mm.
Range: Central New South Wales to Victoria.

273. *Austroginella muscaria* (Lamarck, 1822)

The shell is large and high-spired for the family. The whorls are shouldered, with a single knob on the dorsal side of the last whorl. The columella is concave, with plaits occupying half its length. A callus covers the ventral side of the last whorl. The outer lip is thickened, becoming thinner towards the base of the shell. The colour is light yellow or white.
Size: 11mm.
Range: Central New South Wales to Victoria, including Tasmania.

274. *Austroginella johnstoni* (Petterd, 1884)

The shell is similar to that of *A. muscaria* but smaller, with thicker callus on the ventral side of the body whorl and thicker outer lip. Its colour is white or yellow.
Size: 8mm.
Habitat: Rocky shores.
Range: Northern New South Wales to South Australia, including Tasmania.

275. *Austroginella tasmanica* (Tenison-Woods, 1876)

The shell is high-spired for the family, even more so than the previous two species, and rounded. The whorls are rounded. A callus covers the ventral side of the last whorl. The columella is concave with plaits occupying its bottom half. The colour is yellow with a white subsutural band.
Size: 7mm.
Range: Central New South Wales to Victoria, including Tasmania.

276. *Haloginella mustelina* (Angas, 1871)

The shell is cylindrical, narrow and thin. The aperture is narrow, widening anteriorly. The outer lip is nearly straight and thin. The columella is convex; the columella plaits are small and inconspicuous, occupying one third of its length. The colour is light brown with patterns of interrupted dark brown, light brown and white bands.

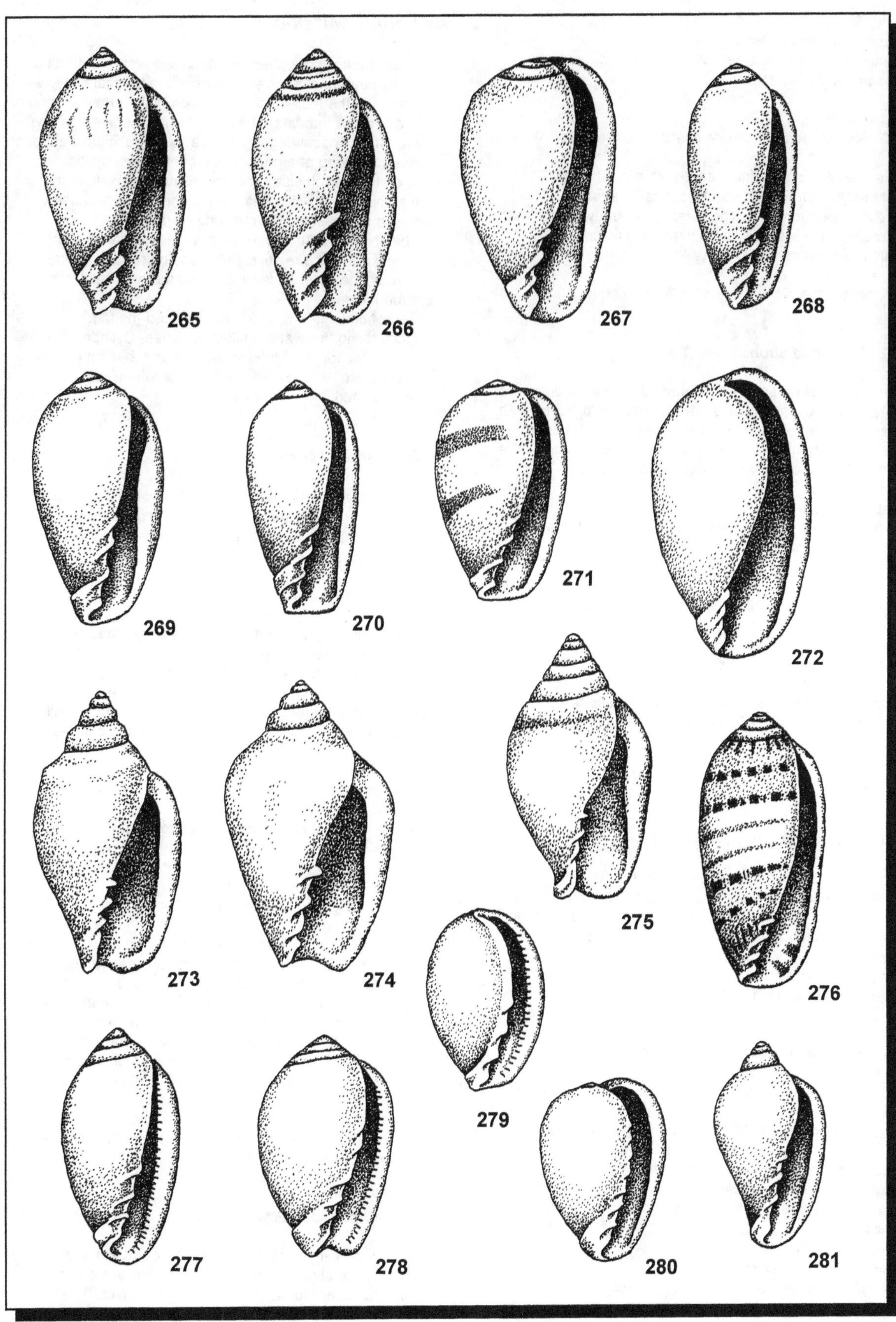

265
266
267
268
269
270
271
272
273
274
275
276
277
278
279
280
281

Size: 6mm.
Habitat: Under intertidal stones.
Range: Central New South Wales to Victoria, including Tasmania, New Zealand.

277. *Mesoginella victoriae* (Gatliff & Gabriel, 1908)

The shell has a prominent spire with a blunt apex. The columella is straight to slightly concave, strong plaits occupy its bottom half. The outer lip is nearly straight and thickened; the inside is finely dentate. The colour is translucent white to slightly yellowish.
Size: 5mm.
Range: Northern New South Wales to Victoria.

278. *Gibberula subbulbosa* (Tate, 1878)

The shell is short-spired and rounded. The aperture is narrow. The columella is nearly straight, multiplicate, with the plications becoming smaller at greater distance from the base. The outer lip is only slightly thickened and lirate within. The colour is white, slightly translucent.
Size: 4mm.
Habitat: Rocky shores.
Range: Queensland to southern Western Australia, including Tasmania.

279. *Granulina nympha* (Henn & Brazier, 1894)

The shell is minute and rounded. The last whorl completely envelops the spire. The aperture is narrow. The columella is convex, covered with callus; plaits occupy its bottom half. The outer lip is thickened and dentate within. The colour is white.
Size: 2mm.
Habitat: Rocky shores.
Range: Central New South Wales to South Australia.

280. *Cysticus angasi* (Crosse, 1870)

The shell is broad; the last whorl nearly envelops the spire. The columella is convex, multiplicate, the plications become smaller towards the posterior end. The outer lip is slightly thickened, flaring above. The colour is white.
Size: 3mm.
Habitat: Rocky shores.
Range: All Australian states.

281. *Alaginella ochracea* (Angas, 1871)

The shell is thin; the spire is prominent. The whorls are slightly rounded; the sutures are impressed. The last whorl is roundly shouldered above and contracted below the periphery. The columella is almost straight, with plaits occupying more than half its length. The outer lip is slightly thickened and flaring. The colour is translucent to almost transparent yellow in fresh specimens, fading to dull white.
Size: 4mm.
Habitat: Rocky shores.
Range: Southern Queensland to Victoria.

Family Mitridae

A large family, members of which live worldwide, but a concentration of species occurs in the tropical shallow waters of the Indo-Pacific. Species may burrow in sand or live in rocky habitats. They are carnivores, and may be predators or scavengers. The radula is rachiglossan, each row consisting of a multicuspid central with multicuspid laterals on each side. The proboscis may be longer than the shell. The larvae hatch as veligers and because of this, many species have a wide distribution.
The shells are narrow, often many times higher than broad, and have relatively little sculpture. The aperture is narrow, the outer lip is simple and the columella has four strong folds.
Cernohorsky (1976; 1991) has revised the family, recognising three subfamilies: Mitrinae, Cylindromitrinae and Imbricariinae. Mitridae are present, but not common in southern Australia and only one subfamily is represented in the Sydney area.

Subfamily Mitrinae

This subfamily is represented in Australia by only one genus. The shells have a relatively smooth surface. The radula has a small central tooth. Most species live in rocky habitats.

282. *Mitra carbonaria* Swainson, 1822

The shell is high-spired, with a relatively broad last whorl. The whorls are straight; the sutures are only very slightly incised. The shell surface is smooth but not polished. The columella is straight and reflected. The outer lip is slightly flaring. The colour is uniform dark brown; some shells have some small white spots just below the sutures. The columella is lighter in colour.
Size: 48mm.
Habitat: Under intertidal stones at rocky shores; the animal is white.
Range: Central New South Wales to southern Western Australia.

283. *Mitra glabra* Swainson, 1822

The shell is large, high-spired, heavy and thick. The sides of the spire are slightly convex; the whorls are nearly straight; the sutures are slightly impressed. The shell surface is almost smooth except for some weak spiral grooves, especially at the base of the last whorl. The colour is light brown with a dark brown periostracum, which is flaky and worn in large specimens. The base is lighter in colour; the spiral grooves are darker brown.
Size: 60mm.
Habitat: Under intertidal stones; the animal is white.
Range: Central New South Wales to southern Western Australia, including Tasmania.

284. *Mitra cookii* Sowerby, 1874

The shell is small for the family and narrow in shape. The sutures are slightly impressed. The shell surface is smooth except for some weak spiral grooves. The

aperture is narrow. The colour is light brown, marked by a white band at the periphery.
Size: 28mm.
Range: Southern Queensland to South Australia.
Remarks: The tropical *M. variabilis* Reeve, 1844 is similar but has a much stronger spiral sculpture.

285. *Mitra badia* Reeve, 1845

The shell is small for the family and narrow in shape. The whorls are slightly convex; the sutures are impressed. The shell surface is smooth but not polished. The aperture is narrow. The colour is uniform dark brown.
Size: 23mm.
Range: Central New South Wales to southern Western Australia.

Remarks: This species can be separated from *M. carbonaria* by being smaller, narrower and having more rounded whorls.

286. *Mitra solida* Verco, 1896

The shell is broad and thick. The sides of the spire are convex; the sides of individual whorls are convex; the sutures are impressed. The shell surface is smooth except for some spiral grooves at the base. The columella is covered with a transparent callus. The colour is cream or salmon, with some alternating white and brown spots just below the sutures.
Size: 48mm.
Range: Southern Queensland to central New South Wales.

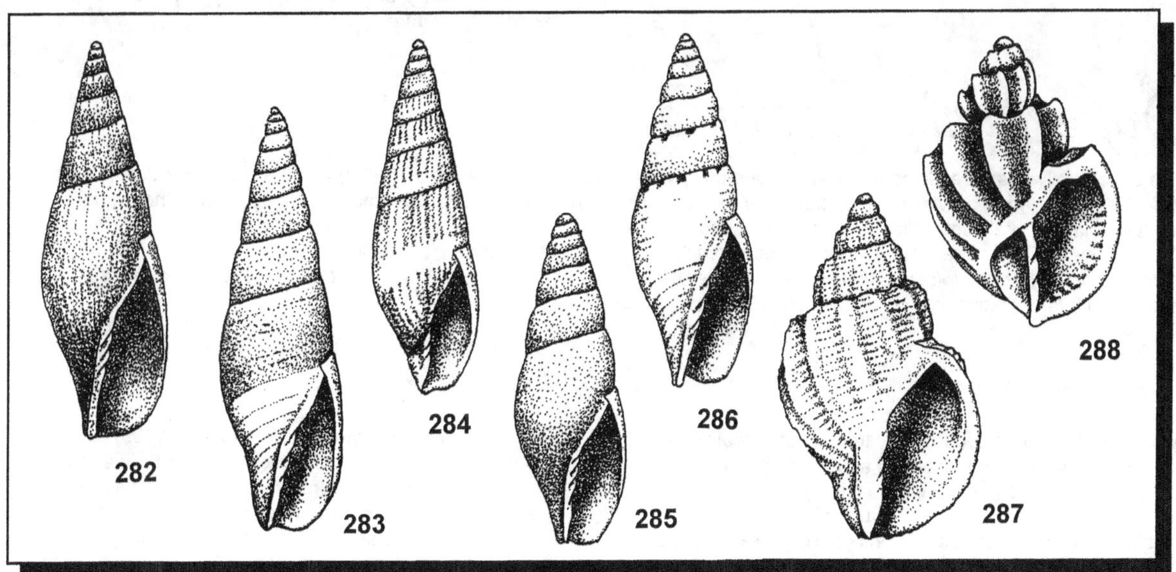

Superfamily Cancellarioidea

Family Cancellariidae

Most members of this family live on rocks in deeper water. Very few species wash up on beaches and when they do, it is mostly in eroded condition. The shells have a turreted spire and cancellate sculpture. Many species are umbilicate and most have columella plaits. Three subfamilies are currently recognised (Ponder and Warén, 1988).
Cancellariidae have either planktotrophic or direct development. The egg capsules often have very long stalks in the subfamily Cancellariinae (Pawlik *et al.*, 1988). Adult shells do not have an operculum, but the larvae of at least some species do have an operculum in the late larval stage.
The New South Wales Cancellariidae were revised by Laseron (1955*b*), but he described several species that are no longer considered valid. Garrard (1975) revised the Australian Cancellariidae.
Two species can be found on Sydney's beaches. One is relatively common; the other is rare. Both belong in the same subfamily.

Subfamily Cancellariinae

Shells thick, with strong columella folds.

287. *Cancellaria (Sydaphera) undulata* Sowerby, 1848

The shell is heavy. The whorls are shouldered; the sutures are indented, giving the shell a turreted appearance. The sculpture consists of about 14 strong axial ribs, crossed by fine spiral ribs. The columella is

concave, a callus covers the umbilicus. There are two strong and one weaker (lowest) columella plaits, which are hardly visible from the front in fully mature specimens. The colour is uniform off-white to salmon or yellowish.
Habitat: Sandy bays, commonly found on beaches around Botany Bay.
Size: 38mm.
Range: Southern Queensland to southern Western Australia, including Tasmania.
Synonyms: *S. renovata* Iredale, 1929, *S. obnixa* Iredale, 1936 and *S. deliciosa* Laseron, 1955.
Remarks: *C. granosa* Sowerby, 1832 from Victoria and South Australia is similar but has a stronger spiral sculpture, especially in early whorls.

288. *Trigonostoma bicolor* (Hinds, 1843)

The shell has a turreted spire and is narrowly umbilicate. The whorls are sharply shouldered. The sculpture consists of about nine strong axial ribs on the last whorl, which fuse into a spiral rib surrounding the umbilicus; the interstices are nearly smooth but may have some very weak spiral sculpture. The columella is reflected, with three plaits. The outer lip is thickened and weakly lirate within. The colour is white, heavily maculated with brown, often in spiral bands; the axial ribs, the columella and outer lip are white.
Size: 27mm.
Range: Northern Western Australia to central New South Wales, Indonesia, Philippines, Japan.
Synonyms: *Trigonaphera interlaevis* Laseron, 1955 and *Cancellaria septemcostata* Ohdner, 1917.
Remarks: The tropical *T. scalarina* Lamarck, 1822 is similar, but has a stronger spiral sculpture and strong lirae inside the aperture.

Superfamily Conoidea

This superfamily has recently been revised based on foregut anatomy by Taylor *et al.* (1993) and the resulting classification is radically different from previous classifications. The division between Conidae and Turridae has changed, with the Conidae now including several subfamilies previously included in the Turridae.
The revision by Taylor *et al.* (1993) has not been complete. More than 300 genera are included in their new classification, but many genera have been left out, including some genera of Sydney species. In their treatment here, these genera have been retained with their original classification; this is indicated in the text.

Family Terebridae

A family of medium-sized to very large, mostly tropical species. Shells are many-whorled and high-spired. The sculpture, when present, mainly consists of weak axial ribs or spiral grooves. The shell surface is smooth and polished. The radula is absent or has solid, sickle-shaped teeth or harpoon-like teeth. The proboscis or a venom gland may be present or absent (Taylor *et al.*, 1993).
The animals are common in sand in shallow water near coral reefs. A few species live in southern waters. Bratcher and Cernohorsky (1987) reviewed the species of Terebridae.
Only one species is common in the Sydney area.

Subfamily Terebrinae

Shells medium-sized to very large, mostly smooth. The radula is absent in many species, but when present, consists of long, harpoon-like marginal teeth.

289. *Hastula brazieri* (Angas, 1871)

The shell is thick and small for the family. The whorls are flat; the sutures are only slightly incised. The sculpture consists of weak axial folds, which are strongest just below the sutures, where they form nodules. The colour is light brown, maculated with white and fine dark brown axial bands.
Size: 31mm.
Range: New South Wales to Victoria, including Tasmania.

Family Turridae

This family was redefined by Taylor *et al.* (1993) based on radula and anatomical characteristics. The radula always has a radular membrane (to which teeth are attached) and has either three teeth per row (the central tooth small), four teeth per row (no central tooth) or only marginal teeth. A venom gland is always present. The animal has an operculum.
The shells are high-spired to biconical and possess an anal (posterior) sinus above the shoulder on the outer lip. Works on Australian Turridae include those by Hedley (1922), Laseron (1954*b*) and Wells (1990, 1991).

Subfamily Clavatulinae

Shells small to medium-sized and variable in form. The anterior canal is moderately long, but sometimes short. The whorls are usually depressed below the shoulder. The anal (posterior) sinus is on the shoulder slope and is rather deep. The protoconch is smooth and has one and a half to three whorls. The sculpture, if present, is predominantly axial.

290. *Austrodrillia angasi* (Crosse, 1863)

The shell is thick and high spired. The spire whorls are sharply shouldered; the sutures are indented. The sculpture consists of broad ribs, which start just above the periphery and fade towards the base of the shell and become overridden by fine spiral ribs. The outer lip has a thickened rib and a deep sinus just above the shoulder.

The colour is beige; the axial ribs are white; the interstices are chocolate brown.
Size: 13mm.
Range: Central New South Wales to Victoria.

291. *Austrodrillia beraudiana* (Crosse, 1863)

The shell is broad and thick. The whorls are shouldered; the sutures are indented. The sculpture consists of strong axial ribs. The interstices and the rest of the shell are smooth. The outer lip has a raised rib and almost no sinus. The colour is cinnamon brown, irregularly maculated with darker brown and white. The ribs are usually lighter in colour.
Size: 13mm.
Range: Central New South Wales to Victoria, including Tasmania.

Subfamily Crassispirinae

The shells are medium-sized to large, with a short anterior canal. The anal sinus is situated on the shoulder, with a pad of callus above. Sculpture can be spiral or axial and may be quite strong. The protoconch has few whorls, and is initially smooth, but later sometimes with axial sculpture.

292. *Epideira hedleyi* (Iredale, 1931)

The shell is medium-sized and thick. The sutures are hardly impressed. The sculpture consists of two bands of weak nodules below the suture, followed by a pattern of thin spiral ribs crossed by axial, slightly curved ribs. The sinus is at the top of the outer lip, below a pad of callus. The colour is uniform salmon pink.

Size: 27mm.
Range: New South Wales.
Synonyms: *Epidorona striata* Hedley, 1922 (non Gray, 1827).

293. *Paradrillia coxi* (Angas, 1867)

The shell is narrow and high-spired. The whorls are sharply shouldered; the sutures are indented. The sculpture consists of strong axial folds crossed by fine sharp spiral ribs forming two rows of sharp nodules at the periphery. The axial sculpture fades towards the base of the shell. The sinus is above the shoulder below a pad of callus, and is rather deep. The colour is uniform light brown.
Size: 15mm.
Range: Central New South Wales to Victoria, including Tasmania.

294. *Paradrillia metcalfei* (Angas, 1867)

The shell is thick and high-spired. The whorls are roundly shouldered; the sutures are impressed. The sculpture consists of two spiral rows of nodules just below the suture and at the periphery. Below the lowest spiral there is a net-like pattern of fine axial ribs crossed by fine spiral ribs, forming small nodules at the intersections. The outer lip is sharp; the sinus is between the shoulder and a pad of callus at the top of the outer lip. The columella is covered with a thin callus. The colour is rust-brown.
Size: 18mm.
Range: New South Wales.

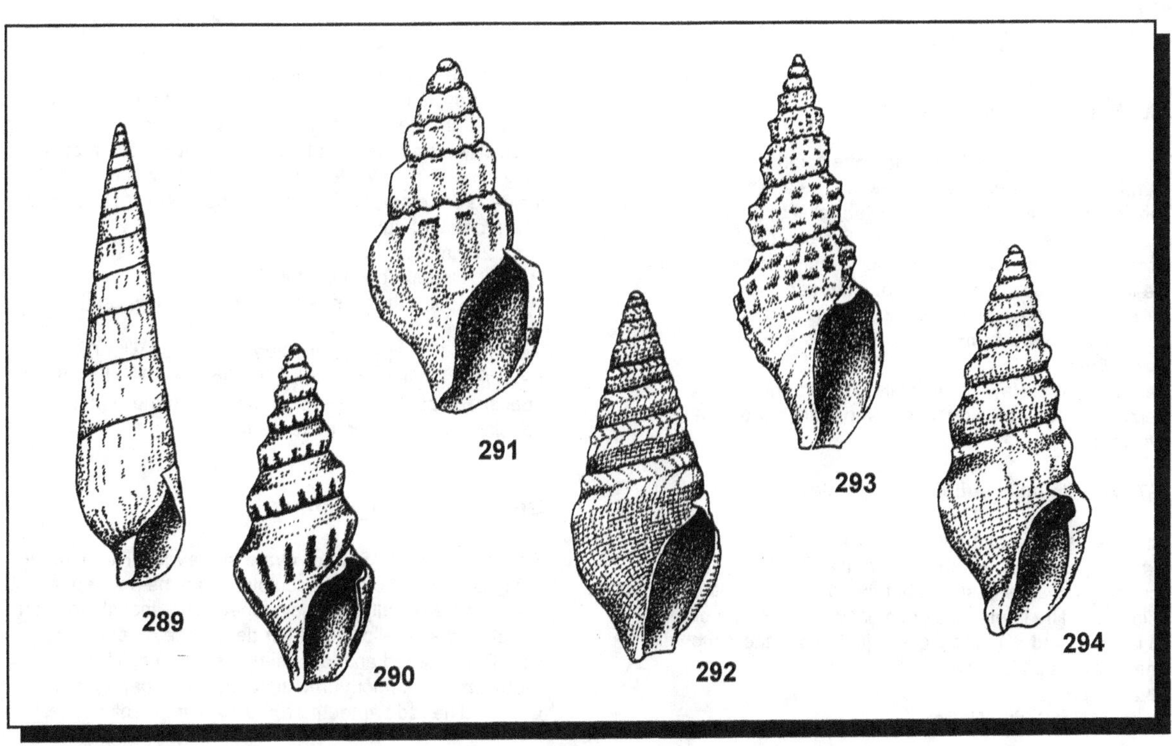

Family Conidae

This family now includes several subfamilies and genera formerly included in the Turridae, with the Conidae in the old sense of the name reduced to subfamilial rank. Thus, the family contains species with a wide range of shell shapes, from narrow to conical. The radula, if present, has no radular membrane and consists of hollow marginal teeth only. A venom gland is commonly associated with this group, but may be absent. The operculum is absent or present.

The subfamily Coninae is well-documented (e.g. Walls, 1978). Hedley (1922) and Laseron (1954*b*) have described Australian species from other subfamilies.

Subfamily Clathurellinae

Shells very small to large, elevate to biconical. Anterior canal short or indistinct to moderately elongate. The sculpture is spiral in most genera. The anal sinus is deep to very shallow, on the shoulder slope or the periphery. The protoconch is usually few-whorled and smooth. The radula consists of harpoon-like marginal teeth without a solid base.

295. *Etrema alliterata* (Hedley, 1915)

The shell is very small, high spired and thin. The spire whorls are rounded. The sutures are impressed. The sculpture consists of fine axial folds crossed by spiral striae; the axial sculpture fades towards the base of the shell. The outer lip has a strong rib; the sinus is shallow and right at the top of the lip. The colour is yellowish brown with a chocolate brown band encircling the last whorl, visible in previous whorls in some shells. The columella is chocolate brown.
Size: 6mm.
Range: New South Wales.

296. *Etrema bicolor* (Angas, 1871)

The shell is small but thick. The spire whorls are flatly rounded; the sutures are impressed. The sculpture consists of axial folds crossed by spiral ribs; the axial sculpture fades towards the base. The outer lip has a strong rib, forming a small anterior canal. The sinus is at the top of the outer lip. The colour is creamy with dark brown spiral bands just below the suture and below the periphery. The base and the columella are brown.
Size: 10mm.
Range: Central New South Wales to Victoria.
Remarks: Less common, larger and more sturdy than *E. alliterata*.

297. *Maoritomella subtilineata* (Hedley, 1922)

The shell is small and thick. The sides of the spire are extremely straight; the sutures are hardly visible. The sculpture consists of strong but thin and sharp raised spiral ribs. The interstices are axially striated. The outer lip is sharp and thin; the sinus is just above the periphery. The colour is uniform white.
Size: 19mm.
Range: New South Wales.

Subfamily Coninae

Shells small to large, conical or biconical. The inner shell walls are partially resorbed. The anterior canal is short. The aperture is usually parallel-sided. The sculpture, if present, is spiral, but mostly absent. Sometimes there are weak knobs on the shoulder. The anal sinus is on the upper shoulder, and is shallow to relatively deep. The operculum is small. The radular teeth are harpoon-shaped, sometimes with hooked tips, without solid base, usually open at the base.

298. *Conus anemone* Lamarck, 1810

The shell is narrow and thin. A recognition mark for this species is the sculpture of spiral ribs. The colour is white with chocolate brown maculations, often tinged with blue.
Size: 41mm.
Range: Central New South Wales to southern Western Australia, including Tasmania.

299. *Conus papilliferus* Sowerby, 1834

The shell is broad, with variable spire height and thin. It is slightly lower spired than *C. anemone*, but differs mainly in lacking spiral sculpture. The colouring can be very similar to that of *C. anemone*, but it is often more bluish and with a pattern of brown-white dotted lines. The inside is dark brown.
Size: 33mm.
Habitat: In rock pools under intertidal stones.
Range: Northern Queensland to eastern Victoria.

300. *Conus aplustre* Reeve, 1843

The shell is small for the family, and heavy. The spire is low. The sculpture consists of some spiral grooves around the base of the shell. It differs from *C. papilliferus* in being thicker and smaller and in colour pattern, which consists of broad bluish grey bands, alternating with pink, overlaid with a pattern of black and white spots in spiral lines. The spire is white with chocolate brown flames; the inside is deep purple. Fresh specimens have a thick olive-green periostracum.
Size: 20mm.
Habitat: Under stones intertidally.
Range: Southern Queensland to central New South Wales.
Remarks: This species has been confused with *C. papilliferus*; Wilson and Gillett (1985) have illustrated two specimens of *C. papilliferus* under this name. The two species are, however, quite distinct.

Subfamily Mangeliinae

Shells very small to small, ovate or elevate. The anterior canal is rather short. The sculpture may be both spiral and axial, and is usually well-developed. The anal sinus is on the shoulder, shallow to rather deep. The outer lip is usually thickened and is sometimes dentate. The protoconch is smooth or sculptured. The operculum is absent. The radular teeth are hollow with a solid base.

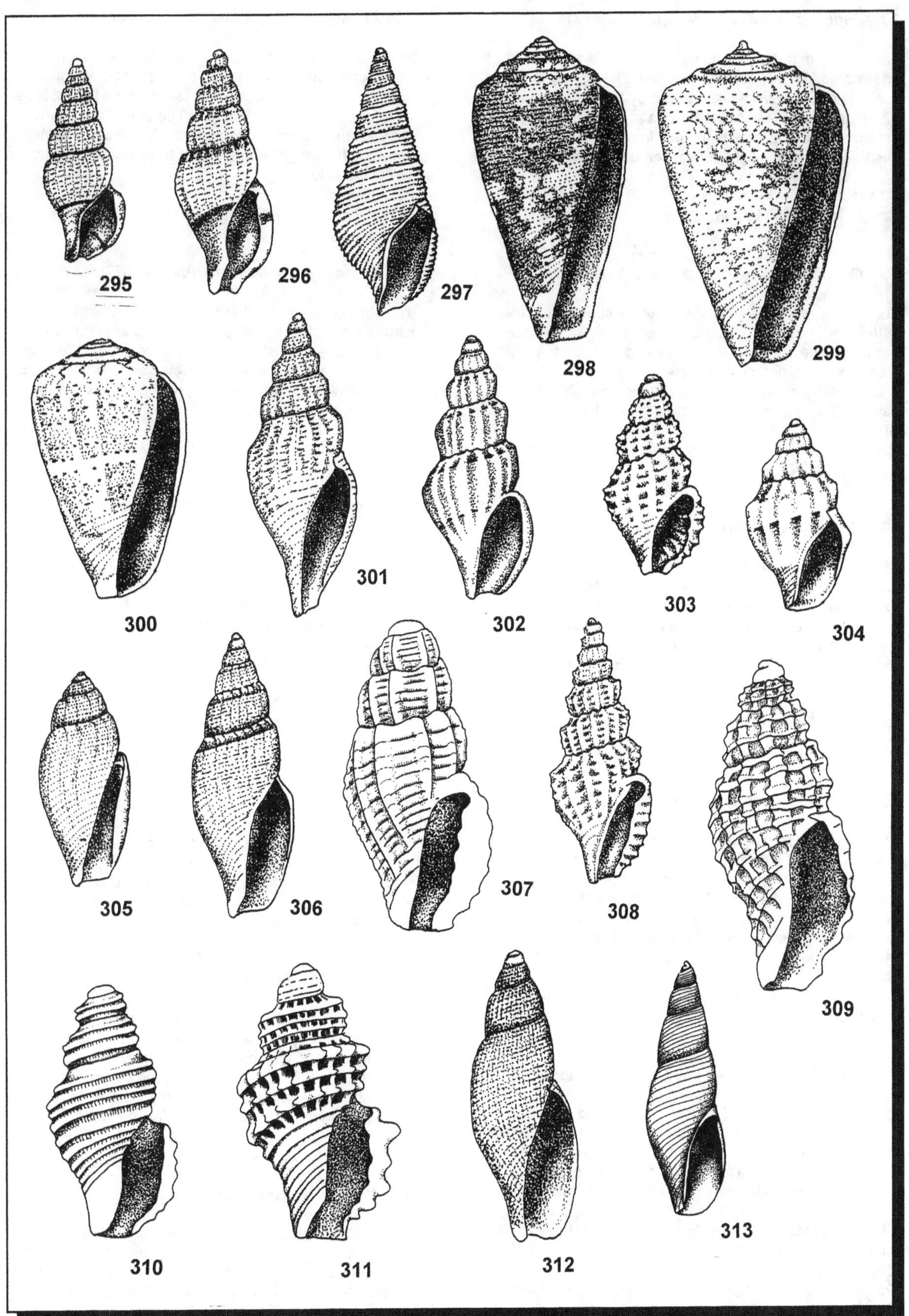

301. *Euguraleus jacksonensis* (Angas, 1877)

The shell is high-spired and thin. The whorls are weakly
shouldered; the sutures are indented. The sculpture
consists of broad axial ribs crossed by fine spiral striae.
The outer lip has a very small sinus at the top. The
anterior end of the shell is narrow, forming an anterior
canal. The colour is light brown, sometimes with very fine
spiral dark brown lines.
Size: 13mm.
Range: New South Wales.

302. *Guraleus pictus* (A. Adams and Angas, 1864)

The shell is thin. The whorls are roundly shouldered; the
sutures are indented. The sculpture consists of rounded
axial ribs. The shell surface is polished. The outer lip has
a small smooth rib; the sinus is almost absent. The colour
is white with usually one or more brown spiral bands,
usually at the top and bottom of each whorl.
Size: 11mm.
Range: Central New South Wales to southern Western
Australia, including Tasmania.

303. *Heterocithara bilineata* (Angas, 1871)

The shell is thick, with roundly shouldered whorls; the
sutures are indented. The sculpture consists of sharp
axial folds crossed by thin spiral ribs forming sharp
nodules at the intersections. The axial sculpture fades
towards the base of the shell. The outer lip is thickened;
the sinus is at the top of the outer lip. The inside of the
outer lip is dentate. The colour is uniform white.
Size: 7mm.
Range: Central New South Wales to Victoria, including
Tasmania.

304. *Macteola anomala* (Angas, 1877)

The shell is thick; its general appearance is not unlike a
juvenile Muricid. The sculpture consists of strong axial
folds, which fade towards the base and several spiral
cords encircling the base. The outer lip is without sinus or
rib. The colour is white with a chocolate spiral band below
the periphery and an area of salmon pink or light brown at
the base. The axial ribs are white.
Size: 9mm.
Range: Central New South Wales to Victoria, including
Tasmania.

305. *Marita compta* (A. Adams and Angas, 1864)

The shell has a high and narrow aperture and a relatively
low spire. The whorls are rounded; the sutures are slightly
impressed. The last whorl is very large, occupying 3/4th of
the total spire height. The sculpture consists of some
irregular, curved axial folds crossed by faint spiral striae.
The outer lip is thickened; the sinus is at the top of the
whorl. The columella is nearly straight. The colour is white
with irregular brown streaks.
Size: 12mm.
Range: Central New South Wales to Victoria, including
Tasmania.

306. *Mitraguraleus mitralis* (A. Adams and Angas, 1864)

The shell is narrow and thick. The whorls are slightly
shouldered; the sutures are impressed. The sculpture
consists of a net-like pattern of fine axial and spiral lines
overridden by larger axial folds. The outer lip is sharp and
not thickened; the sinus is absent. The colour is salmon
pink to light orange, with a brown to dark orange band just
below the suture.
Size: 16mm.
Range: Central New South Wales to Victoria.

307. *Paramontana modesta* (Angas, 1877)

The shell is very small, thick, blunt and high-spired. The
whorls are slightly rounded; the sutures are impressed.
The sculpture consists of axial folds crossed by fine spiral
ribs. The aperture is elongate; the outer lip is thickened,
slightly dentate within, the sinus is at a small distance
from the suture. The colour is white.
Size: 6mm.
Range: Central New South Wales to Victoria.

308. *Turella letourneauxiana* (Crosse and Fischer,
1865)

The shell is thick but delicately sculptured. The whorls are
sharply shouldered, with indented sutures. The sculpture
consists of sharp axial folds crossed by fine spiral ribs
which form sharp nodules at the intersections. The
aperture is narrow. The outer lip has a thickened varix; the
sinus is almost at the suture. The colour is uniform brown.
Size: 14mm.
Range: New South Wales.

Subfamily Daphnellinae

The shells are very small to large. The anal sinus is
subsutural or on the upper shoulder and varies in depth.
The sculpture is variable, but often cancellate and often
with a smooth shoulder. The protoconch has several
whorls and is diagonally cancellate. The operculum is
absent. The radular teeth are sometimes hooked and
have a large solid base. Some species have no radula.

309. *Asperdaphne hayesiana* (Angas, 1871)

The shell is small and thin. The spire whorls are rounded;
the sutures are impressed. The sculpture consists of
spiral ribs, about nine on the last whorl and four on the
previous whorl. These ribs are crossed by axial ribs of
equal strength forming nodules at the intersections. The
outer lip is without sinus. The colour is off-white.
Size: 6mm.
Range: New South Wales.

310. *Microgenia edwini* (Brazier, 1894)

The shell is very small. The whorls are shouldered; the
sutures are indented. The sculpture consists of 10 spiral
ribs on the last whorl and three on previous whorls. The
interstices are finely axially striated. The outer lip has a

deep sinus just below the suture. The colour is brown.
Size: 4mm.
Range: Central New South Wales to Victoria, including
Tasmania.

311. *Nepotilla excavata* (Gatliff, 1906)

The shell is small; the whorls are shouldered; the sutures
are indented. The sculpture consists of large spiral ribs,
five on the last whorl and three on the previous whorl.
These ribs are crossed by axial ribs forming spines at the
intersections and deep pits in the interstices. The base
has several fine spiral ribs. The outer lip is sharp, with a
sinus just below the suture. The colour is light brown.
Size: 3mm.
Range: Central New South Wales to Victoria, including
Tasmania.

312. *Paradaphne botanica* (Hedley, 1918)

The shell is elongate and thin. The whorls are rounded;
the sutures are impressed. The sculpture consists of a
uniform pattern of spiral striae crossed by fine axial striae

forming a net-like pattern. The outer lip is without sinus or
thickened rib. The colour is light brown with dark brown
spots below the sutures.
Size: 19mm.
Range: Northern New South Wales to Victoria.
Remarks: This genus was not investigated by Taylor *et al.*
(1993), but its original placing in the Daphnellinae is
retained here, because of similarities to other species in
the subfamily.

Conidae, subfamily placing uncertain

313. *Austropusilla hilum* (Hedley, 1908)

The shell is minute, thin and narrow. The last whorl
occupies nearly half the shell height. The sculpture
consists of irregular spiral grooves crossed by fine growth
lines. The aperture is simple; the outer lip has a sinus just
below the suture. The colour is uniform transparent light
brown.
Size: 4mm.
Range: New South Wales.

Subclass Heterobranchia

Order Heterostropha

Superfamily Architectonicoidea

Family Architectonicidae

The Architectonicidae have conical to depressed conical
shells, which vary in size from minute to 50mm or larger.
All are umbilicate, but the width of the umbilicus varies.
The protoconch of the Architectonicidae is said to be
coiled sinistrally, with a dextrally organised animal. Bieler
(1993) points out that this is not true, and that the
protoconch only appears to be sinistral because it grows
upside down, with the umbilicus facing upwards.
The animals have a prolonged veliger stage and larvae
can cover great distances. Plankton samples from the
middle of the ocean often contain architectonicid larvae.
The animals live in shallow to very deep water and are
thought to feed on sponges and coral polyps.
Species are relatively constant over their often large
range. Ranges of several architectonicid species have in
the past appeared disjunct, but this is often a result of
limited numbers of specimens studied, especially in deep
water species.
Garrard (1977) has revised the Australian recent and
tertiary Architectonicidae based on shell characteristics.
He divided the family into three subfamilies: Ar-
chitectonicinae, Heliacinae and Pseudomalaxinae. Only
the first two subfamilies are dealt with here.
Several Architectonicidae can be found on Sydney's
beaches, only one of which is common. Six species are
described here. Bieler (1993) and Garrard (1977) mention
a number of additional species from the New South Wales
coastline.

Subfamily Architectonicinae

314. *Adelphotectonica reevei* (Hanley, 1862)

The shell is medium-sized, depressed conical and widely
umbilicate. The whorls are flat; the sutures are hardly
visible. The sculpture consists of a broad rib, a groove, a
flat area and two ribs, separated by a groove, the bottom
one of which forms a sharp keel. The base has two ribs
(including the keel), a groove, a flat area, a groove and a
wrinkled rib surrounding the umbilicus. The shell surface
is crossed by fine oblique axial grooves. The colour is off-
white to salmon pink, with irregular brown flames near the
sutures and on the rib around the umbilicus.
Size: 26mm.
Range: Southern Queensland to Western Australia, it may
be absent from Victoria, North Island, New Zealand.
Synonyms: *Architectonica offlexa* Iredale, 1931 and *A.
relata* Iredale, 1936.
Remarks: This species was placed in this genus by Bieler
(1993), but used to be placed in the genus *Architectonica*.
The suture joins at the centre of the peripheral keel,
instead of in the centre of the groove above it, as in
Architectonica perspectiva L., 1758, which has also been
recorded from Port Jackson (Garrard, 1977).
Architectonica grandiosa Iredale, 1931 is another species
that has been recorded from central New South Wales. It
resembles *A. perspectiva* in shape, but does

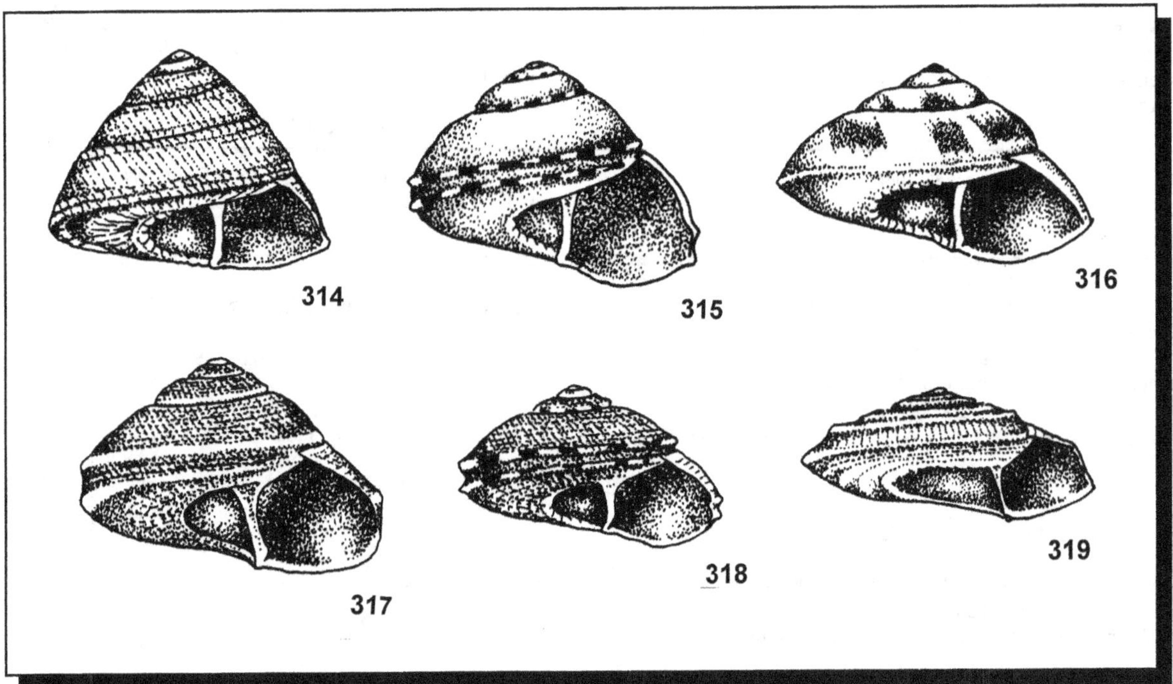

314
315
316
317
318
319

not have any continuous coloured bands, and has white instead of brown nodules around the umbilicus.

315. *Philippia lutea* (Lamarck, 1822)

The shell is depressed conical, with slightly convex sides. The whorls are rounded; the sutures are slightly impressed. The periphery is keeled; the base is convex. The shell surface is almost smooth apart from two strong peripheral keels, separated by a wide groove, and an irregularly wrinkled rib around the umbilicus. The colour is light to olive brown; the peripheral keels are dark brown spotted with white. The columella and the rib around the umbilicus are white.
Size: 11mm.
Habitat: Intertidally and subtidally under rocks. Common on beaches. The animal is red.
Range: Northern New South Wales to Western Australia, North Island, New Zealand.
Remarks: WA specimens are much flatter than NSW specimens and are nearly black in colour.

316. *Psilaxis oxytropis* (A. Adams, 1855)

The shell is depressed conical. The whorls are rounded. The periphery is keeled; the base is convex. The shell surface is polished and almost smooth except for a peripheral keel preceded by a groove and a double nodulose rib surrounding the umbilicus. The colour is light to reddish brown, maculated with white on the peripheral keel. The cord surrounding the umbilicus is white.
Size: 14mm.
Range: Western Australia, Queensland to central New South Wales, New Zealand, Lord Howe Island, New Caledonia, Cook Islands, Hawaii, Japan, Red Sea.

Synonyms: *P. manifesta* Iredale, 1931.
Remarks: *P. radiatus* (Röding, 1798), which has also been reported from Port Jackson, is similar but has colour markings on the keel, is more widely umbilicate and has a white protoconch spotted with brown (in *P. radiatus* the protoconch is entirely white).

Subfamily Heliacinae

317. *Heliacus (Torinista) ponderi* Garrard, 1977

The shell is depressed conical. The whorls are flat; the sutures are incised. The sculpture consists of four spiral nodulose ribs, an enlarged rib, two small granulose ribs, another enlarged rib, the latter four ribs on the periphery; the base has another 5-6 nodulose ribs, the middle two much broader than the others. The colour is light brown, sometimes with irregular darker or lighter maculations especially at the top of the whorls.
Size: 9mm.
Range: Western Australia, New South Wales.
Remarks: *H. enoshimensis* (Melvill, 1893), which also lives in New South Wales, does not have the two granulose ribs between the peripheral keels.

318. *Heliacus (Torinista) implexus* (Mighels, 1845)

The shell is depressed conical and widely umbilicate. The whorls are flat; the sutures are hardly visible. The sculpture consists of four nodulose spiral cords followed by two strong peripheral keels, separated by a groove. The base has five spiral nodulose cords and a wrinkled cord around the umbilicus. The colour is light brown with darker spots on the peripheral keels.

Size: 11mm.
Range: Western Australia, Queensland to New South Wales.
Synonyms: *T. popula* Iredale, 1936.
Remarks: The strong peripheral keels separate this species from *H. ponderi* Garrard, 1977.

Superfamily Pyramidelloidea

Family Pyramidellidae

The family Pyramidellidae has many species worldwide. Most are very small to minute, although a few larger species, up to 30 or 40mm, exist in tropical waters. It is not known how many species live in Australia. Work on the Australian Pyramidellidae is limited to that by Laseron on the New South Wales Pyramidellidae (Laseron, 1951*b*) and the Pyramidellidae from Queensland and the Northern Territory (Laseron, 1959). This work is far from complete and many new species are probably yet to be discovered. There has been no recent review of the family. Høisæter (1989) has reviewed the biology of a few European species.

Pyramidellidae have high-spired shells, which may or may not have sculpture. They may have up to three columella plaits, which are often hidden deep inside the aperture. The aperture is simple, without varices or sinuses. Most shells are white. A recognition mark for the family is the sinistrally coiled protoconch, the axis of coiling of which is set at an angle of up to 90° compared to the axis of coiling of the teleoconch.

The animals live at a great variety of depths and habitats, but few species are found in the intertidal zone. They have no jaws or radula and are parasites, often of species of economic importance (Høisæter, 1989).

The Pyramidellidae from the Sydney region are plentiful. Iredale and McMichael (1962) include 80 species in their checklist of NSW shells, many of which are found only in deep water. Pyramidellidae are commonly found in shell grit on Sydney's beaches. Twenty-five species are described and figured here. They represent the species most commonly found.

Subfamily Pyramidellinae

320. *Charilda rosae* (Hedley, 1901)

The shell is high-spired and umbilicate. The sides of the spire are slightly concave; the individual whorls are flat; the sutures are incised. The sculpture consists of about six sharp narrow spiral ribs on the last whorl. The lowest rib surrounding the keel is enlarged. The base is flat and smooth. The aperture is quadrate. The colour is translucent white.
Size: 5mm.
Range: New South Wales.

319. *Pseudotorinia delectabilis* (Melvill, 1893)

The shell is very small and flat and widely umbilicate; the sutures are slightly incised. The sculpture consists of four narrow, sharply nodulose cords, followed by a wide excavated area and a peripheral keel. The base has five or six spiral cords of varying strength. The base is v-shaped. The colour is translucent white.
Size: 5mm.
Range: Queensland to South Australia.
Synonyms: *Claraxis foveolatus* Tate, 1893.

321. *Eucharilda elegantula* (Angas, 1871)

The shell is thin and needle-like, with straight sides. The sculpture consists of three spiral ribs on each whorl, the interstices between which are obliquely striated. The colour is translucent white.
Size: 5mm.
Range: New South Wales.
Remarks: *Cingulina spina* has a similar appearance, but is not sculptured in the interstices.

322. *Eulimella hasta* Laseron, 1951

The shell is thin and needle-shaped. The whorls are rounded; the sutures are impressed. The shell surface is smooth but not polished. The columella is reflected and simple. The colour is translucent white with two faint brown encircling bands on the last whorl; there is one band on previous whorls.
Size: 7mm.
Range: New South Wales.

323. *Eullimella turrita* (Petterd, 1884)

The shell is high-spired, thin and fragile. The whorls are rounded; the sutures are impressed. The shell surface is smooth and polished. The columella is without a fold. The colour is translucent white.
Size: 2.3mm.
Range: New South Wales.
Remarks: Laseron (1951) records this species from 111 fathoms off Cape Byron, but also from Balmoral Beach.

324. *Cinctiuga diaphana* (Verco, 1906)

The shell is high-spired, thin and fragile. The whorls are keeled; the sutures are indented. The sculpture on the last whorl consists of two strong keels and one weaker keel below and one keel on the previous whorls. The rest of the shell is finely spirally striated. The columella has a prominent tooth. The colour is translucent white.
Size: 1.9mm.
Range: New South Wales.

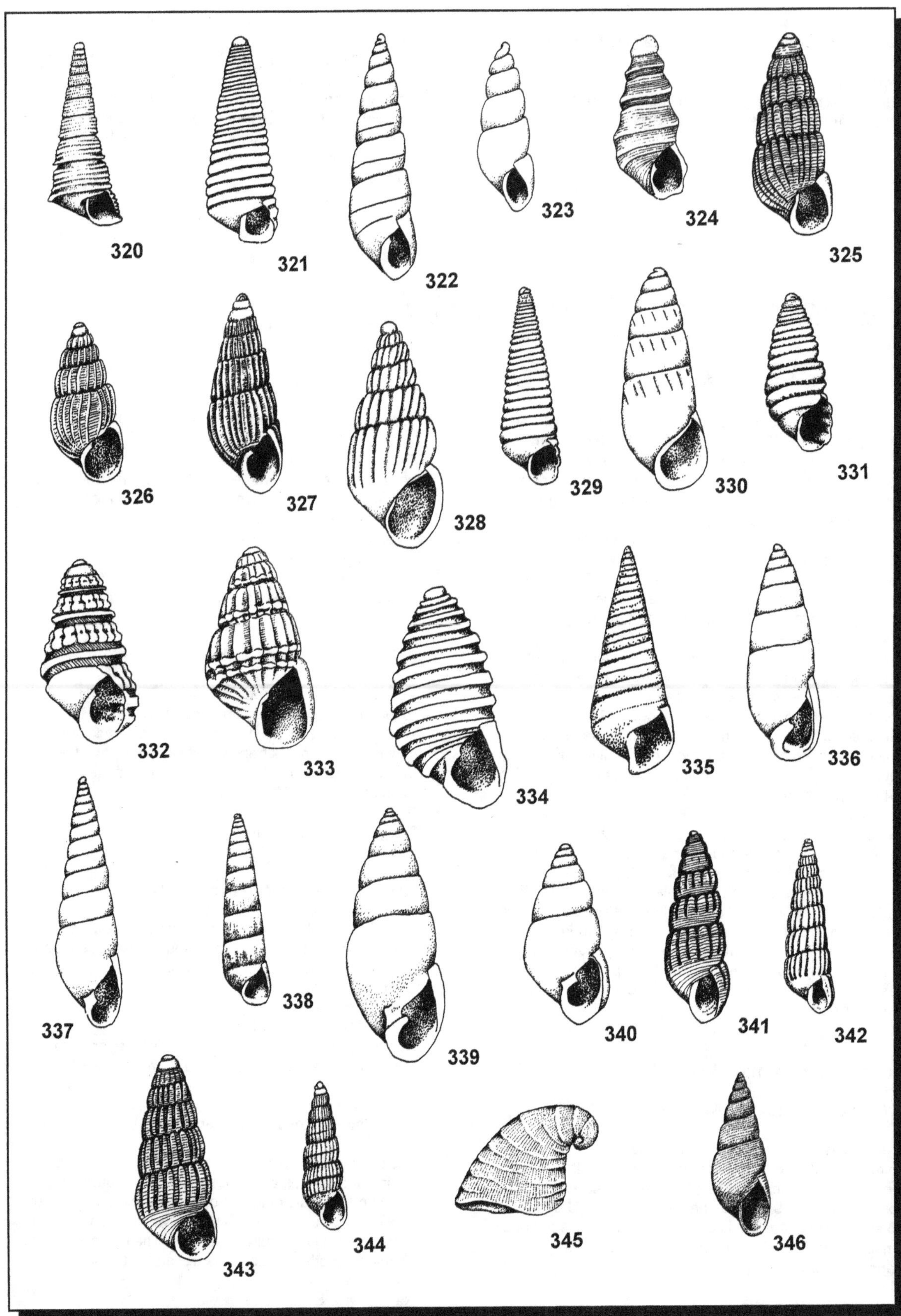

Subfamily Odostomiinae

325. *Linopyrga brevis* (Pritchard & Gatliff, 1900)

The shell is narrow, the whorls are slightly rounded; the sutures are impressed. The sculpture consists of axial ribs crossed by very fine spiral striae. The columella has a very small fold, which is hardly visible from in front. The colour is translucent white.
Size: 4mm.
Range: Central New South Wales to Victoria.
Remarks: The small columella fold separates this species from other species of *Linopyrga*.

326. *Linopyrga ceria* Laseron, 1951

The shell is narrow and thin. The sculpture consists of thin oblique axial ribs, crossed by fine spiral striae. The columella fold is prominent. The colour is translucent white.
Size: 5mm.
Range: New South Wales.
Remarks: Separated from the other species of *Linopyrga* by its narrow ribs, spaced further apart than in the other species.

327. *Linopyrga pascoei* (Angas, 1867)

The shell is large for the genus. The sides of the spire are convex; the periphery and the base are rounded. The whorls are slightly rounded; the sutures are impressed. The sculpture consists of fine axial ribs; the interstices are crossed by microscopic spiral striae. The aperture is elongate; the columella has one fold. The colour is translucent white.
Size: 8mm.
Habitat: Common under stones on intertidal rock platforms. Hedley (1916) has illustrated a living animal.
Range: New South Wales.

328. *Chrysallida caelatura* Laseron, 1951

The shell is elongate-conical. The whorls are rounded; the sutures are impressed. The sculpture consists of oblique axial folds. There is no spiral sculpture. The columella and outer lip are simple; there are no columella folds. The colour is translucent white.
Size: 4mm.
Range: New South Wales.

329. *Cingulina spina* (Crosse & Fischer, 1864)

The shell is thick and high-spired. The sides of the spire are straight to slightly convex; the periphery and the base are rounded. The whorls are flat; the sutures are incised. The sculpture consists of three deep spiral grooves on each whorl. The base is smooth. The aperture is elongate and simple. The colour is white.
Size: 8mm.
Range: Central New South Wales to Victoria, including Tasmania.

330. *Herviera ignava* (Hedley, 1908)

The shell is thick, with slightly convex sides. The whorls are flat; the sutures are only very slightly incised. The shell surface is smooth except for some weak axial folds below the sutures. The columella is simple and slightly reflected over its entire length. The colour is white.
Size: 5mm.
Range: New South Wales.

331. *Latavia pulchra* (Henn & Brazier, 1894)

The shell is narrow and high-spired. The whorls are rounded; the sutures are impressed. The sculpture on the last whorl consists of five broad spiral ribs, the top one of which is about half the width of the others. The ribs are separated by narrow axially ribbed channels. The aperture is narrow and simple. The colour is white.
Size: 4mm.
Habitat: Under stones intertidally.
Range: New South Wales.

332. *Miralda suprasculpta* (Tenison-Woods, 1877)

The shell is thin and fragile. The whorls are straight; the sutures are slightly impressed. The sculpture on the last whorl consists of four spiral ribs; the top two are separated into nodules, the bottom two are smooth and thin. The interstices are obliquely striated. The colour is translucent white.
Size: 3mm.
Range: Central New South Wales to Victoria, including Tasmania.

333. *Paregila henni* (Brazier, 1894)

The shell is conical. The whorls are flat; the sutures are slightly impressed. The sculpture consists of broad axial folds, fading on the base; the interstices are crossed by fine spiral ribs. There are two broad spiral ribs at the periphery, forming nodules at the intersections with the axial ribs. The columella has an insignificant fold. The colour is translucent white.
Size: 2.8mm.
Range: New South Wales.

334. *Oscilla tasmanica* (Tenison-Woods, 1877)

The shell is minute, with convex sides; the spire whorls are flat; the sutures are hardly visible. The sculpture consists of strong, well-defined flat ribs, which are slightly narrower than the interstices; there are four ribs on the last whorl and two on the previous whorls. The columella has a small tooth. The colour is pinkish white.
Size: 2.5mm.
Range: Central New South Wales to Victoria, including Tasmania.

335. *Syrnola bifasciata* Tenison-Woods, 1876

The shell is thick. The sides of the spire are flat; the sutures are incised; the periphery and the base are

rounded. The shell surface is smooth and polished. The columella has a prominent fold. The colour is white with two encircling brown bands on each whorl.
Size: 5mm.
Range: Central New South Wales to Victoria, including Tasmania.

336. *Syrnola convexa* Laseron, 1951

The shell is thick. The sides of the spire are slightly convex; the whorls are flat; the sutures are barely impressed. The shell surface is smooth. The columella has a large and prominent fold. The colour is white.
Size: 7mm.
Range: New South Wales.

337. *Syrnola manifesta* Hedley, 1912

The shell is large for the genus, elongate and thick. The whorls are slightly rounded; the sutures are slightly impressed. The shell surface is smooth. The columella fold is large. The colour is white.
Size: 12mm.
Range: Central New South Wales to Victoria.

338. *Syrnola tincta* (Angas, 1871)

The shell is narrow and needle-like. The whorls are flat; the sutures are only slightly incised. The shell surface is smooth and polished. The columella fold is hardly visible from in front. The colour is off-white to yellowish, often irregularly maculated with brown.
Size: 6mm.
Range: Central New South Wales to Victoria, including Tasmania.

339. *Agatha australis* (Angas, 1871)

The shell is thick, with convex sides. The whorls are rounded; the sutures are impressed. The shell surface is smooth but not polished. The columella fold is prominent and large. The colour is white.
Size: 8mm.
Range: Central New South Wales to Victoria.

340. *Agatha simplex* (Angas, 1871)

The shell is thick and broad. The whorls are rounded; the sutures are impressed. The shell surface is smooth but not polished. The columella has a prominent fold. The colour is white.
Size: 5mm.
Range: Central New South Wales to Victoria, including Tasmania.

Subfamily Turbonillinae

341. *Turbonilla scalarina* Henn & Brazier, 1894

The shell is narrow and high-spired. The whorls are rounded; the sutures are impressed. The sculpture consists of axial ribs, which stop at the periphery, and are crossed by very fine spiral striae. The columella is slightly reflected; there is no columella fold. The colour is translucent white.
Size: 5mm.
Range: Central New South Wales to Victoria, including Tasmania.

342. *Chemnitzia hofmani* Angas, 1877

The shell is high-spired and needle-like. The whorls are rounded; the sutures are impressed. The sculpture consists of about 16 axial ribs on the last whorl, which stop abruptly below the periphery. The colour is white.
Size: 5mm.
Range: Central New South Wales to Victoria, including Tasmania.

343. *Pyrgiscus gravicosta* Laseron, 1951

The shell is elongate, but short for the genus. The whorls are flatly rounded; the sutures are slightly impressed. The sculpture consists of axial ribs, which stop at the periphery, and are crossed by fine spiral striae. The columella is without a fold. The colour is white.
Size: 4mm.
Range: New South Wales.

344. *Pyrgiscus varicifera* (Tate, 1898)

The shell is high-spired, thin and needle-like. The whorls are rounded; the sutures are impressed. The sculpture consists of fine axial ribs; the interstices are crossed by microscopic striae. The axial ribs fade on the base. The colour is translucent off-white to yellowish brown, with two darker brown encircling bands on each whorl.
Size: 5mm, but grows larger.
Range: Central New South Wales to Victoria, including Tasmania.

Family Amathinidae

This family was recently created by Ponder (1987) based on anatomical features. Shells vary from elevate to limpet-like, with predominantly spiral sculpture. An operculum may be present or absent. The animals have no jaws or radula.

345. *Amathina violacea* (Angas, 1867)

The shell is cap-like, with a tiny coiled spire. The sculpture consists of fine spiral ribs, crossed by axial growth lines. The margin is slightly thickened, irregular and concave. The colour is pink; the apical whorls are light brown.
Size:12mm.
Range: New South Wales to Western Australia, including Tasmania.
Remarks: This species was previously placed in the family Capulidae. According to Ponder (1987) the concave base suggests that the animal lives on gastropods.

346. *Leucotina concinna* A. Adams, 1854

The shell is high-spired. The whorls are rounded; the sutures are impressed. The sculpture consists of many fine spiral grooves. The columella is straight; the lower part is reflected. The aperture is elongate. The colour is entirely milky white.
Size: 11mm.
Range: Southern Queensland to South Australia.

Subclass Opisthobranchia

Order Cephalaspidea

Superfamily Philinoidea

Family Acteonidae

The shells of this family are thick and are usually spirally sculptured. The aperture is elongate. The columella has several characteristic folds at its base. The radula has no central tooth and there are five or six laterals on each side. The teeth are very similar in shape and size across the radula, which is specialised for a diet of worms (Rudman, 1972a). Rudman (1971a) studied the animal of *Pupa*. It has a large headshield with a deep median slit, separating it into two posteriorly projecting lobes.
Two species are described here. Iredale (1936) has described several additional species from New South Wales, but their status is unclear.

347. *Pupa fumata* (Reeve, 1865)

The shell is thick. The sides of the shell are convex; the spire whorls are flat; the sutures are incised. The sculpture consists of irregular flat ribs separated by narrow grooves. The aperture is narrow above, widening below. The columella is covered with callus and has a double fold at its base, preceded by a small fold and a notch. The colour is white, heavily spotted with brown or black, often in spiral or axial bands.
Size: 19mm.
Range: Central New South Wales to Victoria.
Remarks: The tropical species *P. solidula* L., 1758 is much heavier and has a shorter spire.

348. *Pupa nivea* (Angas, 1871)

The shell is high-spired for the genus, and thick. The sides of the shell are convex. The whorls are flat; the sutures are incised. The sculpture consists of fine spiral ribs. The columella is covered with a thin callus and has a double fold preceded by a small fold and a notch. The outer lip is often slightly contracted in the middle. The colour is entirely white.
Size: 14mm.
Range: Northern New South Wales to Victoria.

Family Ringiculidae

Shells thick and white, with a short spire. They possess rounded whorls and a thickened outer lip and two columella plaits. They have no operculum. Three species have been reported from the Sydney region, but their status is unclear. There has been no recent review of the family. Pelseneer (1924) illustrates the internal anatomy of the animal, a hermaphrodite like all opisthobranchs.

349. *Ringicula doliaris* Gould, 1850

The shell is thick. The whorls are rounded, sometimes weakly shouldered; the sutures are impressed. The shell surface is smooth and polished. The outer lip is thickened, the bottom half more so than the top half. The columella has two strong teeth and a smaller nodule, and is covered in heavy callus. The colour is white.
Size: 6mm.
Range: New South Wales.
Remarks: *R. denticulata* Gould, 1850 has also been reported from Sydney (Hedley, 1915). *R. semisculpta* Hedley, 1911 is a deep water species.

Family Hydatinidae

The shells are thin, with an inflated last whorl and a flat spire. The shell surface is smooth, usually with spiral patterns. There is no operculum. The animal has a large radula with the central tooth absent or present and the laterals consisting of an incurved flange with a denticulate posterior edge. It feeds on worms. Rudman (1972b) has studied the anatomy of *Hydatina physis*.

350. *Hydatina physis* (L., 1758)

This species has a thin, bulbous shell, which is white with fine black spiral lines.
Size: 25mm.
Habitat: On subtidal reefs. The animal has a frilly mantle, which is pink with a white rim.
Range: Western Australia to central New South Wales, Indo-Pacific, Canary Islands, Caribbean.
Synonyms: *Hydatina stromfelti* Odhner, 1932, *Bulla vesicaria* Solander, 1786.

Family Bullinidae

The shells are thin, with an inflated last whorl and a short spire. They are sculptured with spiral grooves. Rudman (1972c) has created a separate family for the genus *Bullina* based on anatomical differences, the presence of an operculum and the shape of the radula. The New Zealand species were reviewed by Rudman (1971b).

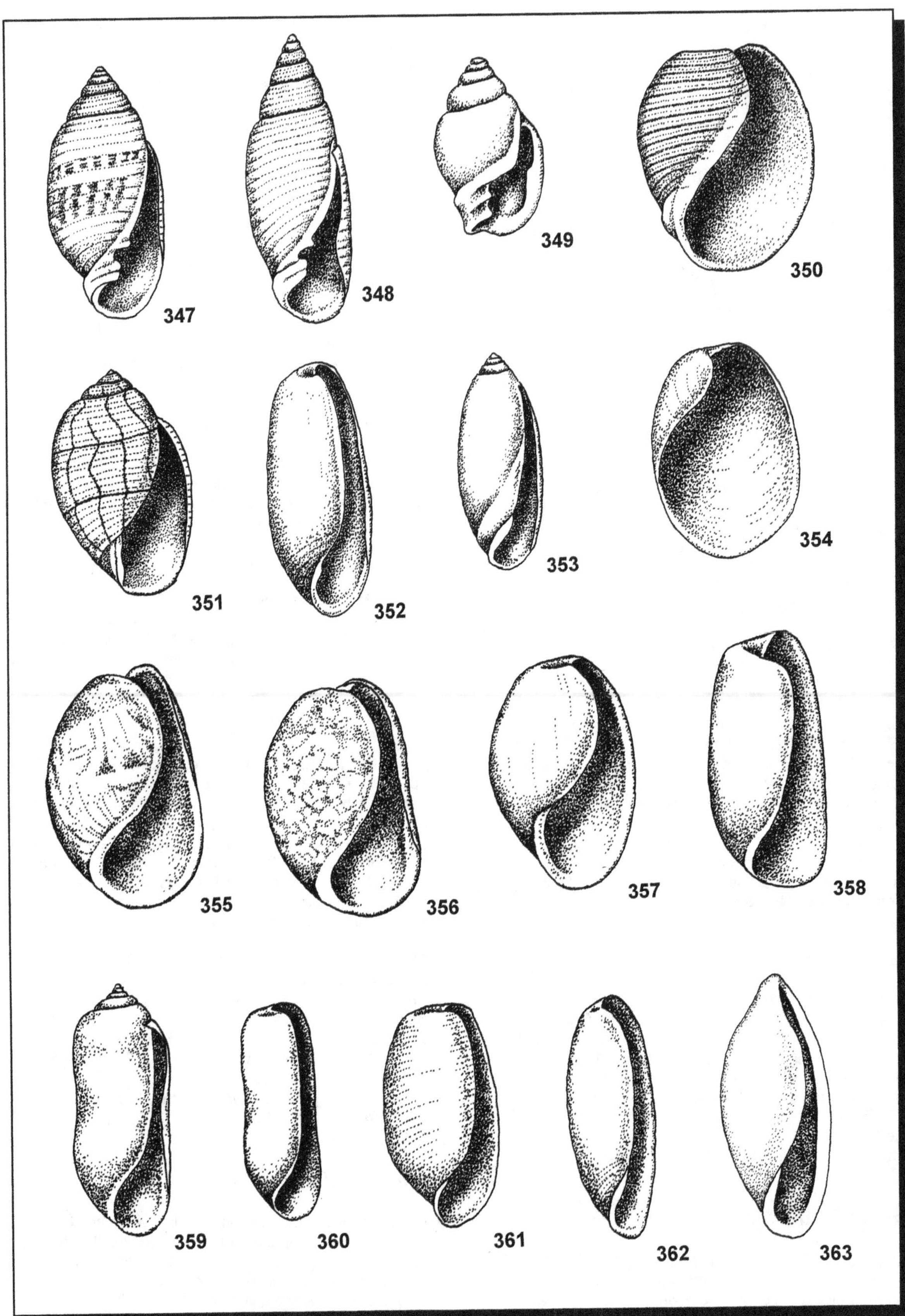
347
348
349
350
351
352
353
354
355
356
357
358
359
360
361
362
363

351. *Bullina lineata* (Gray, 1825)

The shell is inflated and thin. The last whorl is large and rounded. The spire whorls are rounded; the sutures are impressed. The sculpture consists of many fine spiral grooves. The columella is simple, reflected over the umbilical area. The colour is white, with a characteristic pattern of two fine spiral pink bands, crossed by wavy axial lines.
Size: 15mm, but often much smaller.
Habitat: On sand near intertidal or subtidal reefs. The animal is translucent white with a frilly mantle with an iridescent blue rim.
Range: Queensland to central New South Wales, Indo-Pacific.

Family Scaphandridae

These shells are mostly white, cylindrical, with little sculpture. The spire may or may not be raised. The columella may have a fold at the base. The animal is carnivorous, living in sand.

352. *Cylichna arachis* (Quoy & Gaimard, 1833)

The shell is thick. The sides of the shell are straight. The apex is sunken; a small round hole marks its position. The shell surface is almost smooth. The columella has an insignificant fold at its base. The colour is white. Lines of brown periostracum encircle the last whorl.
Size: 24mm.
Range: Northern New South Wales to Western Australia, including Tasmania.

353. *Acteocina fusiformis* (A. Adams, 1854)

The shell is thick, shaped like a grain of rice. The aperture is narrow. The spire is elevated; the sutures are incised. The shell surface is highly polished. The columella has a fold near its base, with callus covering the columella and part of the adjacent area. The colour is milky white.
Size: 7mm.
Range: Central New South Wales to South Australia, including Tasmania.
Synonyms: *Tornatina apicina* Gould, 1859 and *T. brenchleyi* Angas, 1877.

Family Philinidae

These shells are fragile and white, with only one or two whorls. The last whorl is large and inflated. The shell is entirely internal. Rudman (1972*a,d*) has studied the genus *Philine*, which has about 100 members worldwide. The radular characteristics and internal anatomy of the animals vary but Rudman (1972*d*) argues against subdivision of the genus. The animals live in sand and have been found at great depths. They eat small bivalves, which they crush with their gizzard plates.
One species can be found on Sydney's beaches.

354. *Philine angasi* (Crosse & Fischer, 1865)

The shell is very thin and fragile. The last whorl is inflated, enveloping the spire and occupying nearly the entire shell. The sculpture consists of rough growth lines. The colour is translucent white.
Size: 15mm.
Range: Central New South Wales to South Australia, including Tasmania.

Family Bullidae

The shells are globose, with an inflated last whorl, which envelops the entire spire. The position of the apex is marked by a circular hole. The animals live in sand or rubble and feed on green algae. Rudman (1971*a*) and Willan (1977) have studied the Indo-Pacific species and it seems that many of the described species are conspecific (W. Rudman, personal communication). The radula of *Bulla quoyi* has a large rectangular central tooth with upwards pointing sides and many denticles.
Two species can be found in the Sydney area.

355. *Bulla quoyi* Gray, 1843

This species is characterised by its bulbous shape, large size and brown colouring; the interior is milky white.
Size: 42mm.
Range: Central New South Wales to southern Western Australia, including Tasmania, New Zealand.
Synonyms: *B. botanica* Hedley, 1918.

356. *Bulla angasi* (Pilsbry, 1893)

A much narrower, more elongate and thicker shell than *B. quoyi*. The colour is mostly red with black or dark brown markings. The inside and the columella are white.
Size: 25mm.
Range: Queensland to central New South Wales, Southwest Pacific.

Family Haminoeidae

Formerly called Atyidae, this family is well represented in tropical and temperate Australia. The shells are thinner and more rounded than those of the Scaphandridae. The spire is completely enveloped by the last whorl. The characteristics of the aperture are simple. The animals live from the intertidal zone to the edge of the continental shelf. The animals are mostly adapted to a burrowing life and have an uninteresting colour. Burn (1978) discusses the taxonomy of this family. Rudman (1971*c*) has studied the animal of the genus *Haminoea*. It has a large headshield and a short foot extending halfway down the shell. When in motion, the animal produces a mucous tube through which it glides without becoming clogged with sand. The radular ribbon of the genus is wide. The animals are herbivores.
The large tropical genus *Atys* does not live in Sydney; Sydney species are mostly small and thin. Two species are discussed here; it is possible that more can be found.

357. *Liloa brevis* (Quoy & Gaimard, 1833)

The shell is cylindrical and thin. The apex is not visible; it is covered entirely by previous whorls. The shell surface is rough, with irregular growth lines, and is not polished. The aperture is rather broad. The colour is translucent white.
Size: 20mm.
Range: Northern New South Wales to South Australia, including Tasmania.

358. *Haminoea tenera* A. Adams, 1850

The shell is thin, inflated and globose. The apex not visible, it is covered entirely by previous whorls. The aperture is narrow at the top, becoming broad at the base of the shell. The columella is s-shaped. The colour is translucent light brown, tending to be darker towards the outer lip. The columella is white.
Size: 9mm.
Range: Central New South Wales to South Australia, including Tasmania.

Family Retusidae

The shells are mostly very small, cylindrical and elongate. They may have a raised or sunken spire. The characteristics of the aperture are simple. The taxonomy of this family is confused. Little is known about the Australian species of this family. Burn and Bell (1974) describe a new species from Victoria. It feeds on Foraminifera.
Five species that were found on Sydney's beaches are described here; it is possible that more species can be found.

359. *Retusa hofmani* Angas, 1872

The shell is cylindrical. The spire is raised and blunt. The last whorl is shouldered and slightly contracted in the middle. The shell surface is smooth but not polished. The aperture is narrow. The shell is dirty white.
Size: 6mm.
Range: Central New South Wales to Victoria, including Tasmania.

Order Sacoglossa

Family Cylindrobullidae

These shells are external, thin, very fragile and made mostly of chitinous (horny) material.

364. *Cylindrobulla fischeri* A. Adams & Angas, 1864

The shell is cylindrical, thin and fragile. The spire is flat; the last whorl occupies the entire shell height. The spire is

360. *Cylichnina iredaleana* (Hedley, 1915)

The shell is thin and cylindrical. The last whorl is narrow, a little contracted in the middle; the apex is marked by a narrow hole. The aperture is narrow. The shell surface is smooth, but rough and not polished. The colour is white.
Size: 3mm.
Range: Central New South Wales to Victoria, including Tasmania.

361. *Cylichnina pygmaea* A. Adams, 1854

The shell is broad and thin. The last whorl completely covers the spire; the apex is marked by a narrow hole. The last whorl is inflated and not contracted in the middle. The shell surface is matt, marked with microscopic spiral striae. The columella has a small fold at its base. The colour is translucent white.
Size: 5mm.
Range: Central New South Wales to Victoria, including Tasmania.
Synonyms: *C. atkinsoni* Tenison-Woods, 1876.

362. *Volvulella rostrata* (A. Adams, 1850)

The shell is large for the family, cylindrical and thick. The spire is completely enveloped by the last whorl; a narrow round hole marks the position of the apex. The sides of the last whorl are rounded and never become entirely straight. The columella is covered with thin callus and is smooth. The shell surface is porcellaneous; the colour is white.
Size: 9mm.
Range: Central New South Wales to Victoria, including Tasmania.
Remarks: This shell can easily be confused with *Cylichna arachis*, from which it can be separated by its rounded, and never straight sides.

363. *Volvulella tragula* (Hedley, 1903)

The shell is very small and elongate. The last whorl envelops the entire spire. There is no apical hole. The aperture is elongate, narrow above, widening below. The outer lip is thin. The colour is white.
Size: 3mm.
Range: New South Wales.

flat. The aperture is narrow above and widens below. There is a narrow slit in the outer lip just below the suture. The shell surface is smooth except some axial growth lines and a sharp keel at the shoulder (the highest point of the shell). The colour is translucent light brown.
Size: 14mm.
Range: Central New South Wales to Victoria.

Order Aplysiomorpha

Superfamily Aplysioidea

Family Aplysiidae

Also called sea hares, these animals feed on algae in shallow water. They possess two ear-like tentacles and a lump on their back inside which the shell is located. Their free mantle flaps enable some species to swim free for short distances. The internal shell is thin and flat.

365. *Aplysia parvula* Mörch, 1863

The shell is mostly chitinous, thin, fragile and cup-shaped. The apex is curved inwards and to the left. The sculpture consists of fine concentric growth lines. The shell is covered by a thin periostracum, which extends beyond the margins. The colour is translucent brown.
Size: 12mm.
Habitat: Seagrass beds. The animal is often yellowish brown with a dark rim (Wells and Bryce, 1988).
Range: All Australian states.

366. *Aplysia sydneyensis* Sowerby, 1869

The shell is mostly chitinous, thin, fragile and flat; the apex is curved slightly inwards and to the left. The sculpture consists of fine concentric growth lines. The colour is light brown.
Size: 20mm.
Range: All Australian states.

367. *Dolabella auricularia* (Lightfoot, 1780)

The shell is calcareous, thick and flat. The apex is curved to the left and covered with a thick pad of callus. The sculpture consists of fine concentric growth lines. The colour is white.
Size: 41mm.
Range: Western Australia to central New South Wales, Indo-Pacific.

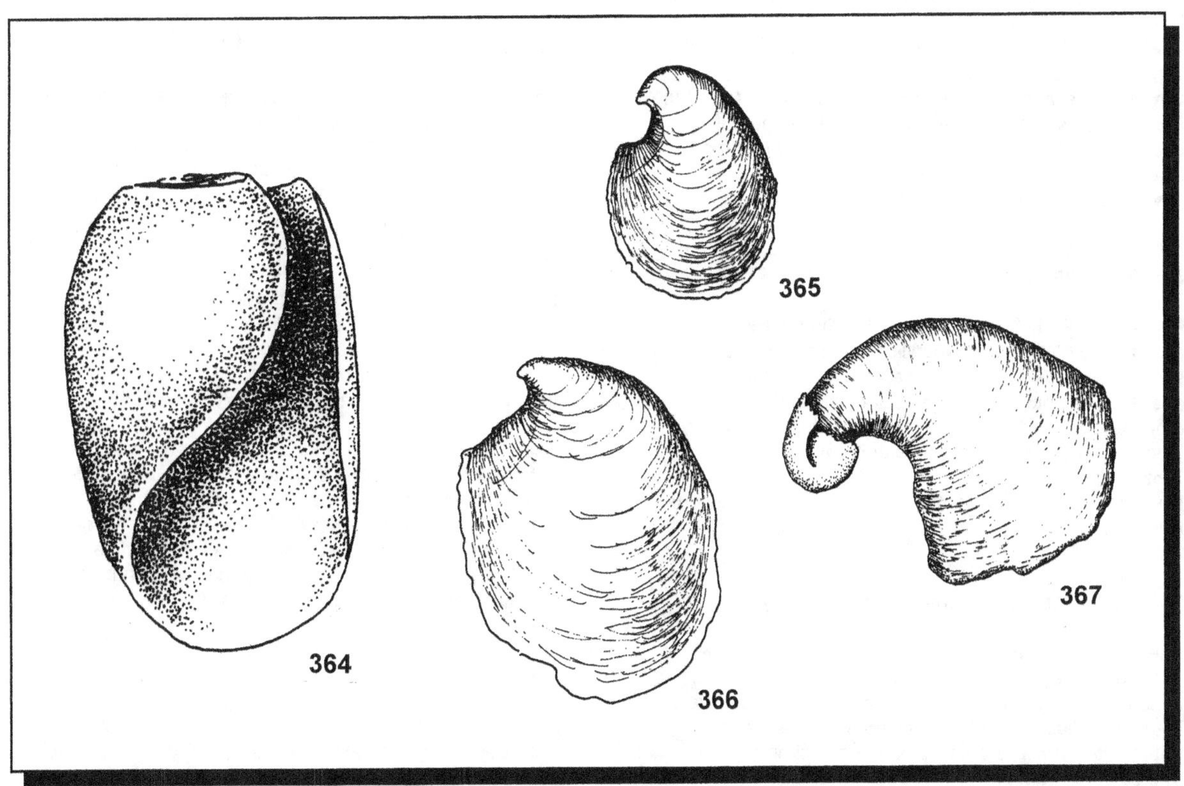

Order Notaspidea

Superfamily Umbraculoidea

Family Umbraculidae

These shells are large and limpet-shaped, with irregular margins. The apex is barely raised. The animals are much larger than the shell. They feed on sponges and are found from the intertidal zone to quite deep water.

Subclass Pulmonata

Order Archaeopulmonata

Superfamily Ellobioidea

Family Ellobiidae

The species belonging to the Ellobiidae have thick, mostly brown shells, with no or little sculpture. Characteristic for the family are the apertural features, which may include a thickened lip, columellar teeth as well as teeth on the inside of the outer lip.
The animals live in mangrove areas in the supra-littoral zone and feed on detritus.
Several species can be found in the Sydney metropolitan area, five of which are described and figured here. *Laemodonta typica* H & A. Adams, 1853 and *L. punctigera* H. & A. Adams, 1853 are two additional species, which have been reported from Sydney (Shea, 1991).

369. *Marinula xanthostoma* H. & A. Adams, 1854

The shell is thick. The whorls are flat; the sutures are slightly incised. The last whorl is rounded. The shell surface is almost smooth. The aperture is teardrop-shaped. The columella has a thick callus and three prominent teeth, the top one of which is the largest. The outer lip is simple. The colour is uniform pink.
Size: 9mm.
Range: Northern New South Wales to southern Western Australia.·

370. *Ophicardelus ornatus* (Férussac, 1821)

The shell is thick and elongately rounded. The whorls are flat; the sutures are hardly visible. The shell surface is almost smooth but not polished. The columella is covered by a thin callus, which is slightly reflected below and bears two teeth. The outer lip is thin and simple.
The colour is dark brown to black, with two or more spiral yellow bands on the last whorl. The columella teeth are slightly lighter in colour.
Size: 12mm.

368. *Umbraculum umbraculum* (Lightfoot, 1786)

The shell is flat, limpet-shaped, with an only slightly elevated apex. It is almost smooth, with just some faint radiating ribs. The colour is white; the inside is yellowish with a brown marking inside the apex.
Size: 95mm, but mostly smaller.
Habitat: On rocky reefs. The animal is yellow and warty.
Range: New South Wales.
Synonyms: *U. sinicum* Gmelin, 1791.

Habitat: In mud between mangroves.
Range: Southern Queensland to South Australia.
Synonyms: *Auricula australis* Quoy & Gaimard, 1834.

371. *Ophicardelus sulcatus* (H. & A. Adams, 1855)

Thee shell is thick and rounded. The whorls are flat; the sutures are hardly visible. The sculpture consists of fine spiral grooves, which are strongest at the top of the whorls. The whorls are very lightly shouldered. The columella has two teeth. The outer lip is thin and simple. The colour is very dark brown with two or more yellow spiral bands.
Size: 12mm.
Habitat: In mud between mangroves.
Range: Northern Territory to Victoria.

372. *Ophicardelus quoyi* (H. & A. Adams, 1855)

The shell is thick and rounded. The spire is short; the sutures are incised. The sculpture consists of at least one incised spiral groove at the top of each whorl. The columella is reflected, with three teeth, the middle one of which is the largest. The outer lip has a median callus bearing a tooth-like projection. The colour is dark brown, with two very weak yellow spiral bands.
Size: 9mm.
Habitat: In mud between mangroves.
Range: Queensland to Victoria.

373. *Leuconopsis inermis* Hedley, 1901

The shell is very small and short-spired. The whorls are flat; the sutures are hardly incised. The sculpture consists of fine axial growth lines and in some shells spiral grooves. The columella is reflected, with a small tooth. The outer lip is simple and thin. The colour is white.

Size: 2.5mm.
Range: New South Wales.

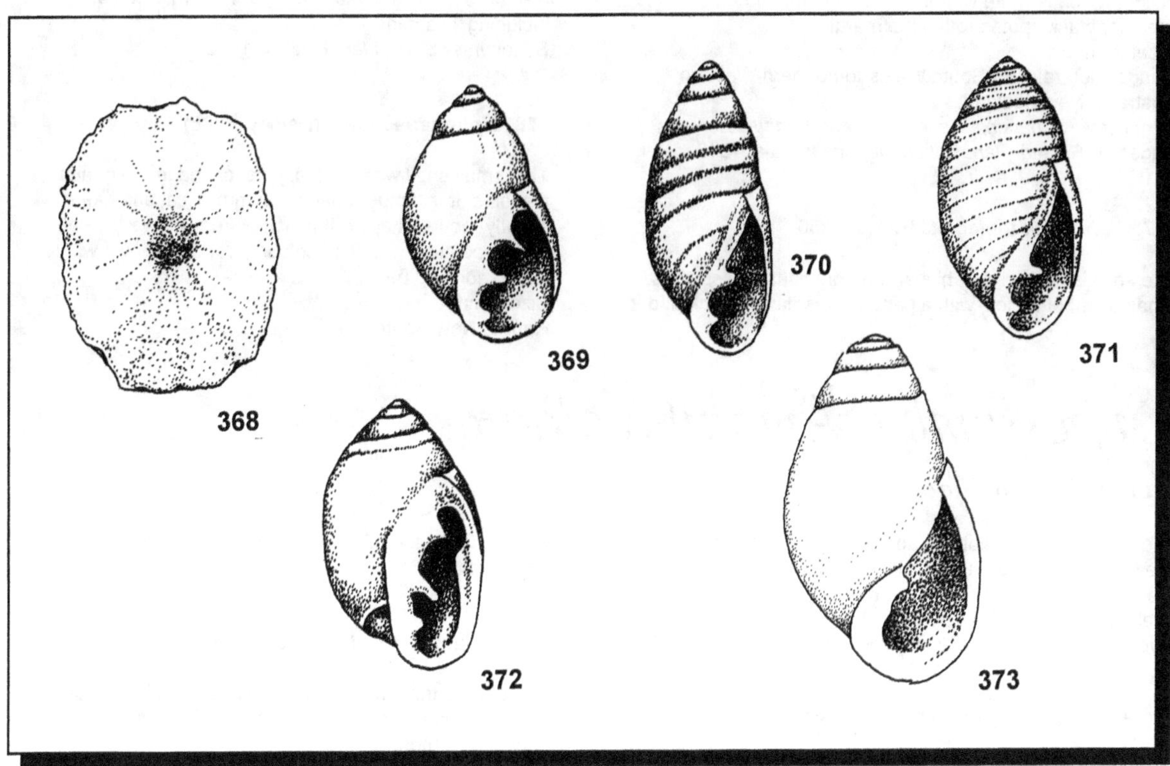

Order Basommatophora

Superfamily Siphonarioidea

Family Trimusculidae

A small family of limpet-like shells, closely related to the Siphonariidae. The animals live on rocks in the intertidal zone. They feed on phytoplankton, which is filtered out of the water with a mucus screen.

374. *Gadinalea nivea* Hutton, 1883

The shell is flat, almost circular, the outer margin is often irregular. It is sculptured with sharp radiating ribs of unequal size. The colour is entirely white.
Size: 15mm.
Habitat: Attached to the underside of stones in the intertidal zone. The animals do not move, but live in colonies, closely packed together in several layers; the shell shape is determined by the available space for growth. Walsby *et al.* (1973) have described the ecology of this species.
Range: Northern New South Wales to southern Western Australia, including Tasmania, New Zealand.
Synonyms: *Gadinia conica* Angas, 1867.

Family Siphonariidae

Limpet-like shells, with strong radiating ribs. They have a siphonal groove on the underside of the shell, making the shell asymmetric. The animals live in the intertidal zone and feed on algae. They possess a broad radula with a central tooth and many laterals. Jenkins (1981, 1983*a*, *b*) has studied the southern Australian Siphonariidae.

375. *Siphonaria denticulata* Quoy & Gaimard, 1833

This species has a dark coloured shell with irregular strong radiating ribs. The interior is chocolate brown with white radiating bands and a mostly white scalloped margin.
Size: 24mm.
Habitat: On rocks intertidally, common.
Range: Queensland to central New South Wales.

376. ***Siphonaria zelandica*** Quoy & Gaimard, 1833

The shell is very flat with irregular radiating rounded ribs. It is characterised by its light colour, especially on the inside, which is white with a light brown spatula and irregular black spots around the margin.
Size: 22mm.
Range: Central New South Wales to northern Western Australia, New Zealand.
Synonyms: *S. baconi* Reeve, 1856 and *S. bifurcata* Angas, 1867 and *Planesiphon elegans* Iredale, 1940.

377. ***Siphonaria funiculata*** Reeve, 1856

The shell is smaller and higher than previous two species. It has a smooth shell, with a pattern of radiating black and white lines. The inside is chocolate brown, with the pattern from the outside shining through at the margins.
Size: 24mm.
Habitat: On stones intertidally.
Range: Southern Queensland to western Victoria, including Tasmania.
Synonyms: *S. virgulata* Hedley, 1915.

378. ***Siphonaria nutata*** (Hedley, 1908)

This small shell was originally described in the genus *Capulus*. It is limpet-shaped, symmetrical and has a slightly recurved apex. It is sculptured with very weak broad radiating ribs. The colour is reddish brown with white radiating bands.
Size: 5mm
Range: New South Wales.

Superfamily Amphiboloidea

Family Amphibolidae

The shells are thin, globose and umbilicate. The animals live in mangroves or mudflats in the intertidal zone; they are detrital feeders. They have an operculum, which enables them to survive periods of low tide.
Two species live in the Sydney region.

379. ***Salinator solida*** (von Martens, 1878)

The shell has rounded whorls, is thick, and has a pattern of brown wavy lines arranged in bands on a white background.
Size: 10mm.
Habitat: In mud between mangroves.

Range: Queensland to Western Australia, including Tasmania.

380. ***Salinator fragilis*** (Lamarck, 1822)

The shell is thin, fragile, more bulbous and lower spired than *S. solida*. It is translucent brown with darker encircling bands.
Size: 11mm.
Habitat: Intertidal sand flats.
Range: Queensland to Western Australia, including Tasmania.

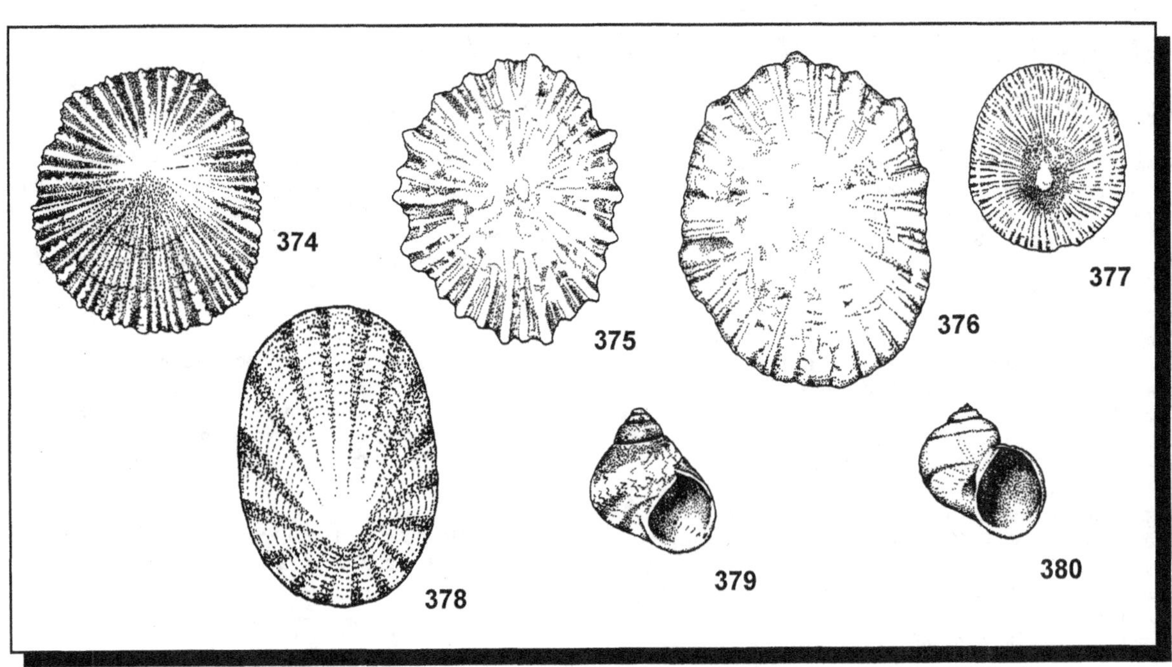

Class Bivalvia

Subclass Protobranchia

Order Solemyoida

Superfamily Nuculanoidea

Family Nuculanidae

The shells are elongate, rounded anteriorly and beaked posteriorly. The sculpture often consists of concentric ribs. The hinge is taxodont, and divided into two plates. The ligament and resilium are variable.
One single valve of the species described below was found in the Sydney area. Iredale and McMichael (1962) list twelve additional species from New South Wales, most from deep water.

Subclass Pteriomorpha

Order Arcoida

Superfamily Arcoidea

Family Arcidae

The shells are thick and heavily predominantly radially sculptured. The valves are usually inequilateral, the posterior end being the longest. The hinge is taxodont, with many small teeth. The hinge plate is long, mostly straight and narrow, and not interrupted below the umbos. The taxonomy of the Arcidae is confused. Iredale (1929*b*) has described many new species from northern Queensland, but no one has worked on the taxonomy of the Australian species since.
The animals live in sand or attached to the undersides of stones. They have a large grooved foot and many species have a byssus.

382. *Anadara trapezia* (Deshayes, 1840)

The shell is heavy and thick, sculptured with about twenty-four strong radiating ribs. It is covered in a thick, dark brown flaky periostracum. The colour is white.
Size: 60mm.
Habitat: In subtidal sand in sandy bays, the animal is often collected for food.
Range: Northern Queensland to Victoria, southern Western Australia, Tasmania. Subfossil only in South Australia. Cotton (1961) describes a failed attempt to reintroduce the species in South Australia.
Remarks: The shell of this species varies greatly with age; juveniles are almost equilateral; adult shells are inequilateral and posteriorly elongate.

381. *Nuculana crassa* (Hinds, 1843)

The shell is thick. The sculpture consists of fine concentric ribs and a furrow from the umbos to the posterior-ventral margin. The inside is polished. The hinge is divided into two plates, separated by a triangular depression to which the ligament is attached. Both hinge plates have rather long, comblike teeth. The colour is white.
Size: 17mm.
Range: Northern New South Wales to Victoria, including Tasmania.

383. *Barbatia pistachia* (Lamarck, 1819)

The shell is elongate and thin for the family. The sculpture consists of fine irregular radiating ribs, crossed by rough concentric growth lines. The ventral margin is slightly excavated, the valves gaping slightly to allow for the passage of the byssus. The hinge has many irregular teeth. The colour is white with dark brown areas on the anterior and posterior ends of the shell. Fresh specimens are covered in a dark brown, hairy periostracum.
Size: 41mm.
Habitat: On the underside of stones on rocky reefs.
Range: Central New South Wales to Victoria.

384. *Barbatia squamosa* (Lamarck, 1819)

The shell is elongate and flat. The sculpture consists of radiating ribs crossed by concentric ribs, forming nodules at the intersections. There are two slightly stronger ribs at a weak ridge from the umbos to the posterior-ventral margin. The hinge plate is slightly curved; the teeth become progressively larger at further distance from the umbos. The inner margin is crenulate. The colour is entirely white, the outside is covered in a light brown hairy periostracum.
Size: 30mm.
Range: Northern Queensland to northern Western Australia, including Tasmania, New Zealand.

385. *Barbatia (Acar) botanica* (Hedley, 1916)

The shell is small for the family. It is inequilateral; the posterior side is slightly longer. The shell has a squarely elongate shape. The sculpture consists of fine radiating ribs crossed by finer concentric lines, forming pits. There is a rounded keel from the umbos to the posterior-ventral margin. The colour is entirely white; the outside is covered by a light brown periostracum.
Size: 12mm.
Range: New South Wales.
Remarks: *Barbatia squamosa* is more elongate in shape and has a crenulated inner margin.

Superfamily Limpsoidea

Family Glycymeridae

The shells are heavy and thick, almost circular. The hinge is taxodont and very similar to that of the Arcidae, except that the hinge plate is curved. Lamprell and Whitehead (1992) give an overview of the Australian Glycymeridae. The animals have no byssus and live in sand, mostly in shallow water, but some have been recorded from depths of 100m or more.
One species was found on the sandy shores of Botany Bay. Lamprell and Whitehead (1992) give five additional species from New South Wales.

386. *Glycymeris grayana* (Dunker, 1857)

The shell is large, heavy and thick. The sculpture consists of very fine concentric striae. The colour is white with a pattern of red-brown zigzag lines.
Size: 60mm.
Range: Central New South Wales to Victoria, including Tasmania.
Remarks: This species has been known under the name *G. flammeus* of authors.

Family Philobryidae

These shells are very small to minute. They have two hinge plates with interlocking denticles, separated by an excavated chondrophore (area between the hinge plates in which the ligament is situated). The hinge plates are variable in length and shape and are often unequal in size or very small. Several species have hinge teeth as well as denticles. The Victorian species of Philobryid-like bivalves are discussed by Noonan (1988). Laseron (1953) has described some Philobryidae from New South Wales. Tevesz (1977) has worked on the taxonomy of the family, but has only revised the genera. The taxonomy of the Australian species is confused and in need of a revision. The animals live attached by their byssus to the lower part of red or brown algae. When detached from the substrate, they can crawl by extending the foot and pulling the shell along the bottom (Tevesz, 1977).

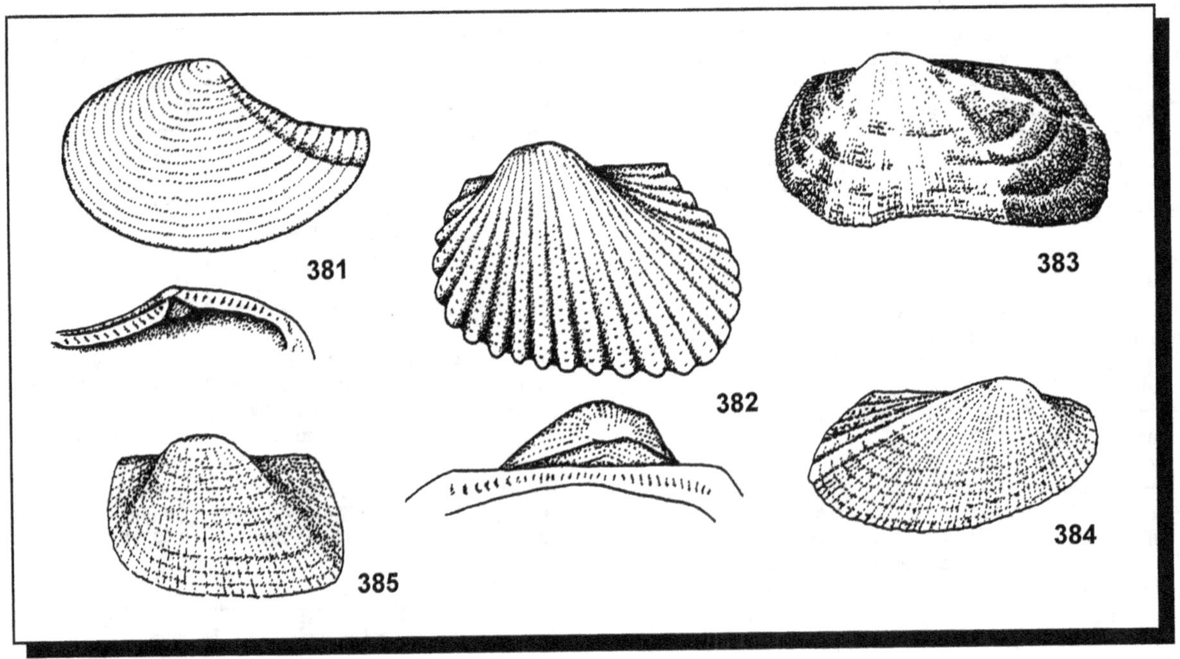

387. ***Philobrya rubra*** (Hedley, 1904)

The shell is inflated and inequilateral. The umbos are hooked; the ventral margin is rounded. The shell surface is almost smooth. The hinge area is curved, with a curved chondrophore, which is oblique, long and separates two hinge plates of unequal size, the subumbonal being the smaller. There are no teeth. The ventral margin is smooth except for five nodules posteriorly. The colour is red, sometimes with lighter bands.
Size: 3mm.
Range: Central New South Wales to Victoria.

388. ***Lissarca picta*** (Hedley, 1899)

The shell is inequilateral. The outside is smooth and featureless. The hinge plates are straight and very thin, the anterior much shorter than the posterior. The hinge has two large teeth anteriorly and three large teeth posteriorly in each valve. The margin has groups of three denticles in the posterior-dorsal, posterior-ventral and anterior-ventral margin. The colour is pink, purple or brown, often in bands.
Size: 2.5mm.
Range: Central New South Wales to Victoria.

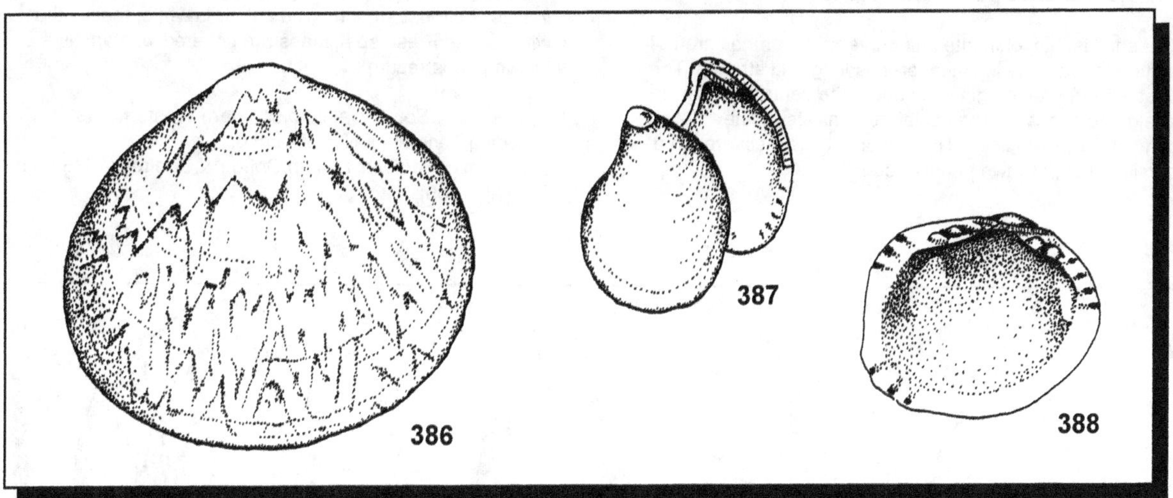

Order Mytiloida

Superfamily Mytiloidea

Family Mytilidae

Elongate, equivalve, strongly inequilateral shells with terminal or almost terminal umbos. The ligament is long and internal; the hinge teeth are absent. The shell colour is mostly dark; the interior is nacreous. The New South Wales Mytilidae were most recently discussed by Laseron (1956c), but his work is now outdated. Wells and Bryce (1988) give an overview of the Western Australian species; several of these species can also be found in New South Wales.

389. ***Mytilus galloprovincialis*** Lamarck, 1819

The shell is fairly large, flat, beaked, with a rounded posterior-ventral margin. The umbos are terminal. The sculpture consists of rough concentric growth lines. The colour is black with blue or brown areas. The interior is blue and white.
Size: 62mm.
Range: Central New South Wales to southern Western Australia, including Tasmania, New Zealand, Japan, China, South Africa, western and southern Europe, southwest coast of the USA.
Remarks: Seed (1992) has recently worked on the mussels belonging to the *galloprovincialis-edulis* group, which includes this Australian population, formerly known as *M. planulatus* Lamarck, 1819.

390. ***Trichomya hirsuta*** (Lamarck, 1819)

The shell is rounded posteriorly and beaked anteriorly. The umbos are terminal. The anterior-ventral margin is slightly concave; the valves gape slightly in this area. The sculpture consists of very fine radiating striae, which are crossed by rough growth lines. The shell is bluish in colour, covered in a thick brown periostracum, bearing a thick mat of barbed hairs, which are easily lost in worn specimens.
Size: 39mm.
Habitat: In clumps subtidally. In Kurnell groups of animals were found living at the base of seaweed.
Range: Northern Queensland to South Australia, including Tasmania.

391. *Modiolus peronianus* Laseron, 1956

The shell is inflated and thin. The umbos are not quite
terminal. The ligament area is straight. The ventral margin
is slightly excavated. The sculpture consists of fine
concentric growth lines. The colour is red or purple, often
with darker bands. Fresh specimens are covered in a dark
brown, hairy periostracum.
Size: 38mm.
Range: Southern Queensland to southern New South
Wales.

392. *Xenostrobus pulex* (Lamarck, 1819)

The shell is thin, elongate and curved. The umbos are not
quite terminal. The ligament area is long and straight. The
posterior-ventral margin is rounded; the ventral margin is
straight to concave. The sculpture consists of fine
concentric growth lines. The colour is bluish, covered in a
persistent dark brown periostracum.

Size: 28mm.
Habitat: In sandy bays.
Range: Central New South Wales to southern Western
Australia, including Tasmania.
Remarks: Wilson (1967) has described the three
Australian species belonging to this genus.

393. *Lanistina impacta* (Hermann, 1782)

The shell is inflated and rounded. The umbos are near the
anterior end of the shell. The shell surface is divided into
three areas, the posterior and anterior areas are
sculptured with fine radiating ribs. The centre of the
valves is almost smooth. The colour is white, maculated
with purple. Fresh specimens are covered with an olive
brown periostracum.
Size: 24mm.
Range: New South Wales to southern Western Australia,
including Tasmania, New Zealand.
Synonyms: *Modiolus nanum* Cotton & Godfrey, 1938 (non
Dunker, 1856).

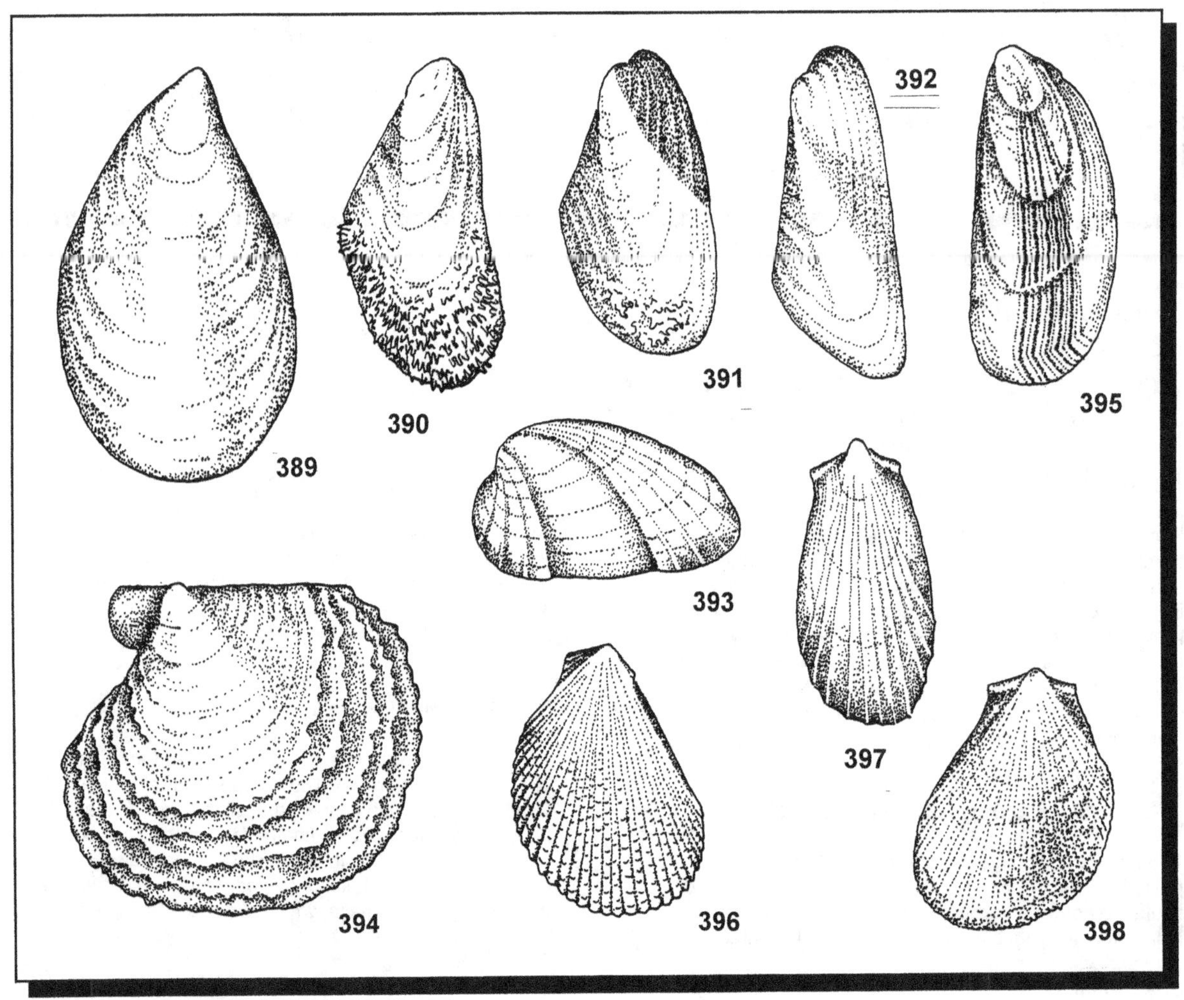

Order Pterioida

Suborder Pteriina

Superfamily Pterioidea

Family Pteriidae

The shells are fragile, thin, flat and inequilateral. The sculpture consists of concentric frills. The interior is nacreous.

394. *Pinctada albina sugillata* (Reeve, 1857)

The shell is as described for the family. The ligament area is straight, with two wing-like expansions on either side of the umbos. The hinge has no teeth. The colour is pale brown, sometimes with purple radiating rays.
Size: 50mm.
Range: Northern Territory to Central New South Wales.

Family Malleidae

The shells are irregularly shaped, fragile and flaky, with a nacreous interior. Fischer-Piette (1977) has revised the genus *Vulsella* based on a range of material.

395. *Vulsella vulsella* (L., 1758)

The shell is thin and elongate. The sculpture consists of very fine irregular radiating lines crossed by irregular growth lines. The ligament is short and internal. Hinge teeth are absent. The colour is light to dark brown, often with radiating purple rays.
Size: 55mm, but grows larger.
Range: Queensland to Western Australia.
Synonym: *V. spongiarum* Lamarck, 1819.

Order Limoida

Superfamily Limoidea

Family Limidae

The shells are thin, sculptured with radiating ribs. Both valves bear two auricles on both sides of the umbos. Hinge teeth are absent; the ligament is internal and triangular. This is one of the few families of bivalves that can swim. The mantle bears many fine tentacles. Animals are red.
Lamprell and Whitehead (1992) give an overview of the Australian Limidae.

396. *Lima nimbifer* Iredale, 1924

The shell is inequilateral. The sculpture consists of about 35 radiating ribs, separated by narrow interstices. The ribs have small scales. The colour is white.
Size: 36mm.
Range: New South Wales.
Remarks: Lamprell & Whitehead (1992) synonymise this species with *L. lima* L., 1758, but differences exist in the strength and the number of ribs. Also, the interstices in *L. lima* are much wider and the scales on the ribs are longer.

397. *Limatula strangei* (Sowerby, 1872)

The shell is almost equilateral, elongate and inflated. The umbos are curved inwards above the ligament. The sculpture consists of about 18 sharp, narrow, radiating ribs in the centre of the valves; the anterior and posterior areas are almost smooth. The colour is white.
Size: 32mm.
Range: Southern Queensland to southern Western Australia.

398. *Limaria (Limaria) orientalis* (A. Adams & Reeve, 1850)

The shell is inequilateral, thin and inflated. The sculpture consists of many very fine radiating ribs, which are irregular in strength. The colour is off-white.
Size: 22mm.
Range: Queensland to South Australia.

Order Ostreoida

Suborder Ostreina

Superfamily Ostreoidea

Family Ostreidae

The shells are inequivalve and irregularly shaped. The right valve is attached to a substrate. Thompson (1954) has studied the genera of Ostreidae and the Australian species. Harry (1985) has reviewed the genera of the family.

399. *Saccostrea glomerata* Gould, 1850

The common Sydney Rock oyster, characterised by its irregular shape with deeply scalloped margins. The colour is white and deep purple on the margins.

Size: 61mm.
Habitat: Extremely common on intertidal rocks in Botany Bay and other sheltered bays. Also widely cultivated in estuaries.
Range: Central New South Wales to eastern Victoria.
Synonyms: *Crassostrea commercialis* Iredale & Roughley, 1933.
Remarks: Another species *Ostrea angasi* Sowerby, 1871 used to be common in Sydney, but is now apparently extinct. It is much larger and lacks the purple colouration. It lives further to the south.

Suborder Pectinina

Superfamily Pectinoidea

Family Pectinidae

The shells are equivalve or inequivalve, mostly equilateral or nearly so, and are sculptured with radiating ribs. The hinge teeth are absent. The presence of two auricles on both sides of the umbos is characteristic for this family, but is shared with the Limidae and some species in related families. The Australian Pectinidae are discussed by Lamprell and Whitehead (1992). Rombouts (1991) has reviewed the Pectinidae of the world.
Pectinidae inhabit a variety of habitats and are found both in shallow and deep waters. They are mostly free-living, but some species live attached to a substrate by a byssus or cemented to the right valve. The mantle possesses a rim of eyes. Some species can 'swim', an escape action whereby the valves are quickly opened and closed, propelling the animal backwards.
Pectinidae are uncommon on Sydney's beaches. Five species are described here. For additional species from New South Wales see Lamprell and Whitehead (1992).

400. *Scaeochlamys livida* (Lamarck, 1819)

The shell is inequivalve, often irregularly shaped. The right valve or the left valve may be largest. The sculpture of the left valve consists of about 10 primary radiating ribs bearing scales with one or more secondary ribs in between. The right valve has about 33 small ribs, which are much more equal in size than those on the left valve. The auricles are unequal, and bear scaled ribs. The colour is brown or purple with white maculations, especially near the umbos. Some specimens are orange, yellow or white.

Size: 56mm.
Habitat: Under or between stones intertidally or subtidally. Leads a sedentary life.
Range: Northern Western Australia to southern New South Wales.
Synonyms: *S. peroniana* Iredale, 1939.

401. *Mimachlamys asperrima* (Lamarck, 1819)

The shell is almost equivalve, round and regularly shaped. The sculpture consists of about 27 radiating ribs, each broken up into one larger and two small scaled riblets on either side. The colour is mostly uniform purple. Some specimens are yellow, but never with white spots near the umbos.
Size: 31mm, but grows larger.
Range: Southern Queensland to South Australia, including Tasmania.

402. *Mesopeplum fenestratum* (Hedley, 1901)

The shell is inequivalve and almost equilateral. The sculpture consists of fine broad rounded radiating ribs, which are slightly wider than the interstices between them. The interstices are broken up into smaller riblets, crossed by very fine concentric striae. The colour is white maculated with pink.
Size: 16mm, but grows much larger.
Range: Southern Queensland to Victoria.
Synonyms: *M. caroli* Iredale, 1929.

403. ***Chlamys aktinos*** (Petterd, 1886)

The shell is flat and elongate. The sculpture consists of about 11 primary rounded radiating ribs, between which there is one smaller secondary rib. The auricles are similarly sculptured. The shell surface is overlaid with a fine screen-like pattern, which is especially clear in the interstices. The colour is red or purple, maculated with white.
Size: 33mm.
Range: Southern Queensland to southern Western Australia, including Tasmania.

404. ***Pecten fumatus*** Reeve, 1852

The common southern Australian edible scallop. It has one inflated and one flat, almost concave valve. The sculpture consists of broad, rounded radiating ribs, with interstices of equal width. The colour of the inflated valve is off-white with pink or red areas; the flat valve is pink or red.
Size: 120mm.
Range: Queensland to southern Western Australia, including Tasmania.
Synonyms: *Pecten albus* Tate, 1893, *P. meridionalis* Tate, 1887 and *Notovola preissiana* Iredale, 1949.

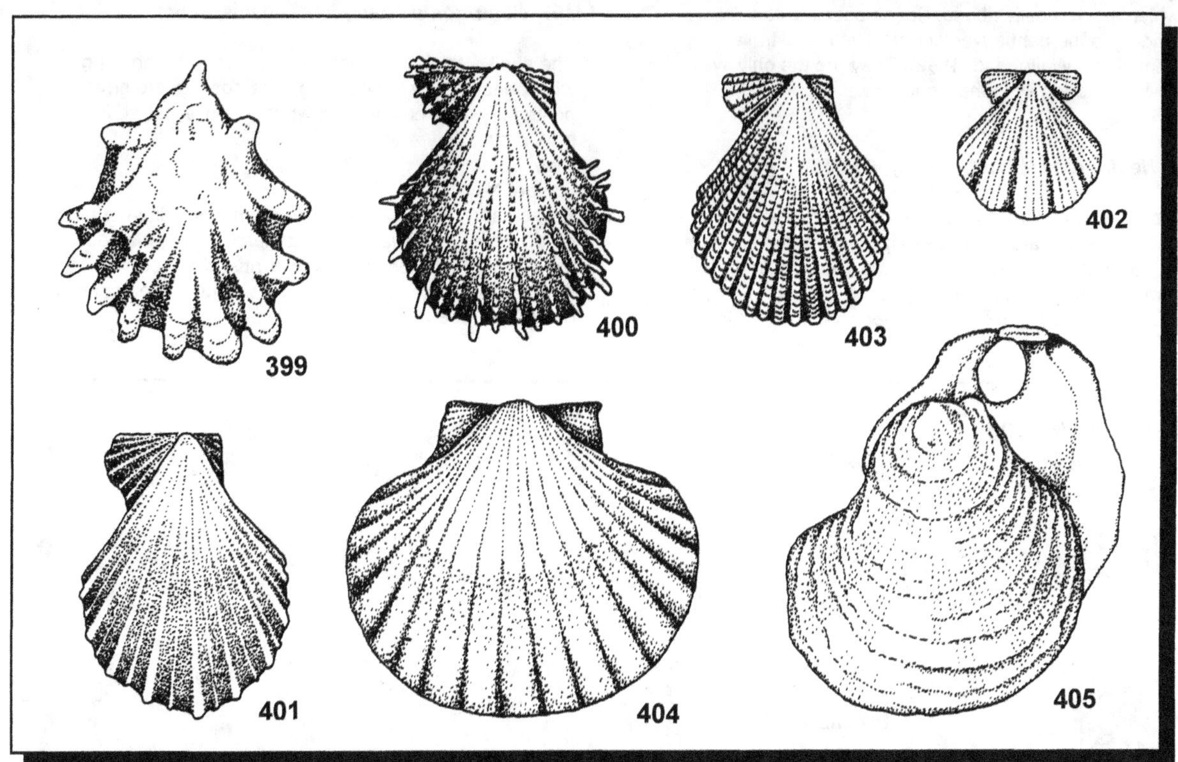

Superfamily Anomioidea

Family Anomiidae

The shells are thin, fragile, inequilateral and irregularly shaped. The right, bottom, valve is flat and possesses a hole just below the umbos to allow for passage of the byssus. Both valves have an internal white area in the centre.
Beu (1977) has studied the Australasian Anomiidae, but his concept of two subfamilies based on the number of muscle scars is now outdated, since the genus *Placunamomia*, the nominal genus for the subfamily Placunamoniinae, is now placed in the family Placunidae (Cunningham-Vaught, 1989).

405. ***Anomia descripta*** Iredale, 1936

The shell is as described for the family. The sculpture consists of rough, irregular concentric growth lines. The left (deep) valve has irregular radiating ribs. The internal white area of the left valve has three muscle scars; the right valve has two muscle scars. The colour of the top valve is orange; the bottom valve is grey.
Size: 54mm.
Range: Southern Queensland to southern New South Wales.
Remarks: Macpherson and Gabriel (1962) describe this species as *Monia ione* (Gray, 1849) (a synonym of *M. zelandica* (Gray, 1843)). However, in that species both valves have radiating sculpture and the left valve has two muscle scars instead of three.

Subclass Paleoheterodonta

Order Trigonioida

Superfamily Trigonioidea

Family Trigoniidae

The members of this family have thick, roundly triangular shells. They have an unusual hinge, which consists of two large teeth in the right and three in the left valve, the sides of which are vertically ribbed. Seven species, all belonging to the genus *Neotrigonia*, live in Australia (Lamprell and Whitehead, 1992). They are the only living species of the family in the world.

406. *Neotrigonia lamarckii* (Gray, 1838)

The shell is heavy, sculptured with about 25 strong radiating ribs, separated by deep furrows, which are wider or narrower than the ribs themselves. The ribs are ornamented with many, closely-packed nodules. The colour is greyish or pink in fresh specimens.

Size: 38mm.
Range: Queensland to central New South Wales.

407. *Neotrigonia strangei* (A. Adams, 1854)

The shell is thick, ornamented with about 22 radiating ribs, which bear very large nodules. The nodules are small posteriorly. The colour is off-white; the periostracum is dark brown.
Size: 22mm.
Range: New South Wales.
Remarks: *N. lamarckii* is larger and has smaller nodules on the ribs. *N. margaritacea* (Lamarck, 1804) also occurs in New South Wales. It has fewer ribs, with nodules smaller and placed further apart than in the two species described here.

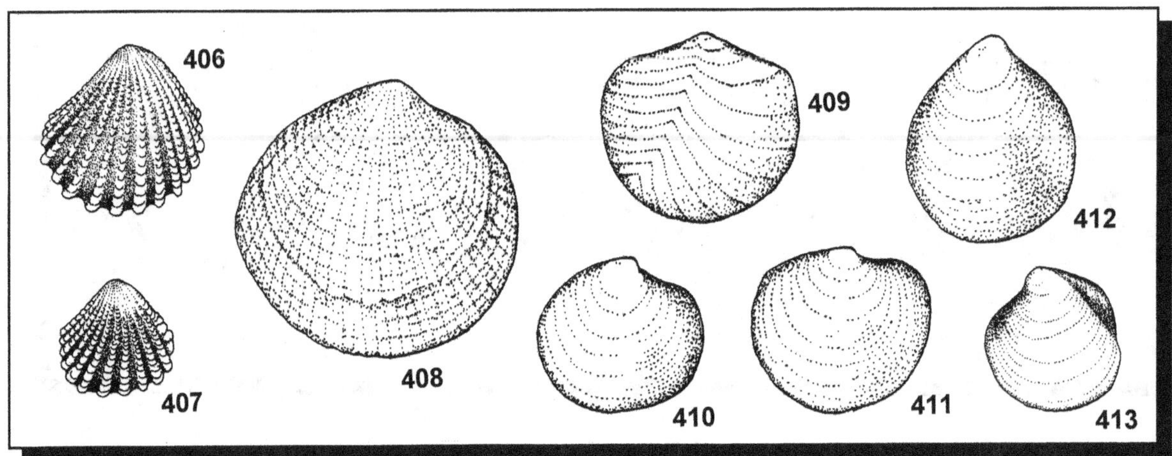

Subclass Heterodonta

Order Veneroida

Superfamily Lucinoidea

Family Lucinidae

The shells are large to small, characterised by their rounded shape and posteriorly placed umbos. The lunule and escutcheon are often visible. The hinge is heterodont, with only cardinal or cardinal and lateral teeth. If lateral teeth are present, they are placed some distance away from the umbos. The ligament is semi-internal; it is set in a groove, but is often still visible from the outside. The pallial sinus is absent. The shells are mostly white. Lamprell and Whitehead (1992) have reviewed the Australian Lucinidae.

408. **Codakia rugifera** (Reeve, 1835)

The shell is large, thick, flat, almost equilateral. The lunule is small. The sculpture consists of concentric ribs, crossed by irregular radiating ribs, which are more prominent at the anterior and posterior ends of the shell. The colour is entirely white.
Size: 48mm.
Range: Central New South Wales to South Australia, including Tasmania.

409. **Divalucina cumingi** (A. Adams & Angas, 1863)

The shell is inflated and rounded. The lunule and escutcheon are absent. The sculpture is a very characteristic v-shaped pattern of flat ribs. The hinge has two cardinal teeth. The muscle scars are well impressed, the anterior much more elongate than the posterior. The colour is white.
Size: 27mm.
Range: Southern Queensland to southern Western Australia.
Remarks: Dekker and Goud (1994) describe the Indo-Pacific species of the *Divaricella* group.

410. **Monilitora ramsayi** (Smith, 1885)

The shell is small and inflated. It is sculptured with fine concentric ribs crossed by very fine radiating striae, giving the shell a pitted appearance. The colour is entirely white.
Size: 15mm.
Range: New South Wales.

411. **Pillucina (Sydlorina) symbolica** Iredale, 1930

The shell is inflated, slightly inequilateral. The sculpture consists of very fine concentric ribs. The colour is off-white.
Size: 8mm.
Range: New South Wales.

Family Diplodontidae

Almost circular shells, which have little or no sculpture. The hinge has cardinal teeth only. The pallial sinus is absent.

412. **Numella adamsi** Angas, 1867

The shell is small but thick, almost equilateral. The umbos are curved towards the anterior end of the shell. The lunule is very small. The hinge has two teeth, one of which is bifid. The sculpture consists of very fine concentric lines; the shell surface is polished. The colour is yellowish to off-white.
Size: 12mm.
Range: Central New South Wales to Victoria.

Family Thyasiridae

The shells are thin, white, inflated, characterised by a wavelike rib from the umbos to the posterior-ventral margin.

413. **Thyasira peroniana** (Iredale, 1930)

The shell is inequilateral; the umbos are closer to the posterior end of the shell. The sculpture consists of fine concentric growth lines and a radiating rib as described for the family. The hinge has two small cardinal teeth and lateral teeth on either side of the umbos. The anterior muscle scar is elongated. The pallial line is distinct; the pallial sinus is absent. The colour is white.
Size: 15mm.
Range: New South Wales.

Superfamily Galeommatoidea

The taxonomy of the Australian species belonging to this superfamily is confused and in need of a revision. Some species can only tentatively be placed in a family (W. Ponder, personal communication).

Family Kelliidae

Shells small, thin, mostly white and with little sculpture. The hinge has one cardinal tooth in the left valve and two in the right valve and one posteriorly placed lateral in both valves. The dorsal margin between the cardinal and lateral teeth is very thin.
Laseron (1956*d*) discusses the New South Wales Kelliidae under the family Leptonidae.

414. **Kellia** sp.

The shell is globose, quadrately oval and inequilateral. The umbos are closest to the anterior end of the shell. The sculpture consists of very fine concentric striae. The shell surface is polished. The colour is translucent white.
Size: 18mm.

Range: Central New South Wales.

Family Galeommatidae

Shells minute to very small, thin and white. Laseron (1956*c*) describes several species.

415. **Marikellia solida** (Angas, 1877)

The shell is small and roundly triangular. The sculpture consists of fine concentric growth lines and a microsculpture of very small round pits. The colour is white.
Size: 4mm.
Range: Central New South Wales.

Family Lasaeidae

Shells small, with variable sculpture within one species. The hinge has one cardinal tooth in the left valve and none in the right valve and two laterals in both valves. The posterior tooth is 'double', with an additional, differently coloured, rim.
The animals live in the intertidal zone. Brooding of young in the mantle cavity is widespread in this family, but the Australian species have planktotrophic development (Ó Foighil, 1989).
Laseron (1956d) discusses the New South Wales Lasaeidae under the family Leptonidae.

416. *Lasaea australis* (Lamarck, 1818)

The shell is roundly triangular, inflated and inequilateral. The sculpture consists of broad irregular concentric ribs; some specimens are almost smooth. The colour is translucent off-white, the hinge areas and the umbos are purple, some specimens are entirely purple.
Size: 6mm.
Habitat: Between *Galeolaria* worm tubes, barnacles, etc. in the low intertidal zone.
Range: Central New South Wales to southern Western Australia, including Tasmania.

Family Montacutidae

The following species are tentatively placed in this family.

417. *Mysella donaciformis* Angas, 1878

The shell is roundly triangular, flat and slightly inequilateral; the posterior end is the longer. The sculpture consists of fine concentric ribs. The ligament is internal, and situated in a deep pit below the umbos. The hinge has one cardinal tooth in the left valve and two tooth-like projections extending from below the umbo in both valves. The colour is white; an olive-grey periostracum covers the entire shell.
Size: 6mm.
Habitat: Sheltered, estuarine habitats.
Range: Central New South Wales to South Australia, including Tasmania.

418. *'Montacuta' dromanaensis* Gatliff & Gabriel, 1912

The shell is rounded, fragile and inequilateral; the posterior end is the larger. The shell surface is almost smooth. The hinge has two well-defined lateral teeth in both valves and two cardinal teeth in the right valve. The colour is translucent white.
Size: 2mm
Havitat: Sheltered, estuarine habitats.
Range: New South Wales to Victoria.

Family 'Leptonidae'

419. *Arthritica helmsi* (Hedley, 1915)

The shell is roundly triangular and inequilateral. The umbos are closest to the anterior end of the shell. The sculpture consists of very fine concentric growth lines and very minute pustules. The colour is off-white with purple maculations.
Size: 3mm.
Range: Central New South Wales to Victoria.

Superfamily Carditoidea

Family Carditidae

The shells are variable in shape, from elongate to nearly circular, and are sculptured with strong radiating ribs. The interior margin is crenulate. The animals live attached to the underside of stones.
Lamprell and Whitehead (1992) illustrate the Australian Carditidae.

420. *Cardita excavata* Deshayes, 1854

The shell is elongate, rough and strongly inequilateral; the umbos are close to the anterior margin. The ventral margin is excavated and gaping to allow for the passage of the byssus. The sculpture consists of rough irregular radiating ribs, the interstices between which are narrow. The ribs bear scales, which are small near the anterior and posterior end of the shell, and large in the middle. The colour is off-white. The interstices between the ribs, the posterior end and the inside are dark purple. Yellow, orange and pink specimens exist.
Size: 29mm.
Habitat: Attached to the underside of rocks intertidally or subtidally.
Range: Southern Queensland to Western Australia.
Remarks: *C. crassicosta* Lamarck, 1819 is larger and is white inside. *C. muricata* Sowerby, 1832 is a tropical species, which has radially striated ribs.

421. *Venericardia amabilis* (Deshayes, 1854)

The shell is thick, rounded and almost equilateral. The sculpture consists of about 28 radiating rounded ribs, which are slightly wider than the interstices between them. The ribs are ornamented with fine nodules. The lunule is large and impressed. The hinge teeth are large and strong. The inner margin is crenulated. The colour is white, irregularly maculated with reddish brown spots. The umbos are tinged with pink. The inside is white.
Size: 17mm.
Range: Southern Queensland to South Australia, including Tasmania.

422. *Venericardia bimaculata* (Deshayes, 1854)

The shell is thick and inequilateral, the posterior end is the longer. The sculpture consists of about 22 weakly nodulose rounded ribs, which are wider than the interstices between them. The lunule and escutcheon are large and clearly visible. The inner margin is crenulated. The colour is white, heavily maculated with brown. The inside is white; the muscle scars are brown. The lunule and escutcheon are dark brown.
Size: 12mm.
Range: Central New South Wales to South Australia, including Tasmania.

Family Condylocardiidae

The shells are minute, often with strong radiating or concentric sculpture. The prodissoconch is large and bordered by at least one concentric rib. Laseron (1953) has reviewed the New South Wales Condylocardiidae.

423. *Condylocardia kunopia* Laseron, 1953

The shell is roundly triangular and somewhat inequilateral; the anterior end is the longer. The prodissoconch is large and clearly visible, with a broad outer rim. The teleoconch is sculptured with about 11 rounded radiating ribs, the interstices between which are narrow. The inner margin is crenulate. The hinge has an obscure cardinal tooth in the right valve. There is one anterior lateral tooth in both valves. The colour is translucent white.
Size: 1.8mm.
Range: New South Wales.

424. *Condylocardia rotunda* Laseron, 1953

The shell is rounded and equilateral. The prodissoconch is large but indistinct. The teleoconch has about 14 rounded, radiating ribs, which are as wide as the interstices between them. The inner margin is crenulate. The hinge has two obscure cardinal teeth. Both valves have a long and well-defined anterior lateral tooth. The colour is translucent white.
Size: 2.1mm.
Range: New South Wales.

425. *Condylocuna ovata* (Hedley, 1906)

The shell is strongly inequilateral. The prodissoconch is large, with a broad, rounded rim. The teleoconch has weak, irregular concentric ribs. The hinge has two obscure cardinal teeth and two lateral teeth in both valves. The colour is translucent white.
Size: 2.0mm.
Range: New South Wales.

426. *Condylocuna projecta* (Hedley, 1902)

The shell is strongly inequilateral, the anterior end is the longer. The prodissoconch is large, and is bordered by two large concentric rings. The teleoconch has strong concentric ribs. The inner anterior margin has several small nodules. The hinge of the right valve has one cardinal and one anterior lateral tooth, there is one massive cardinal tooth in the left valve. The colour is translucent white.
Size: 1.6mm.
Range: New South Wales.

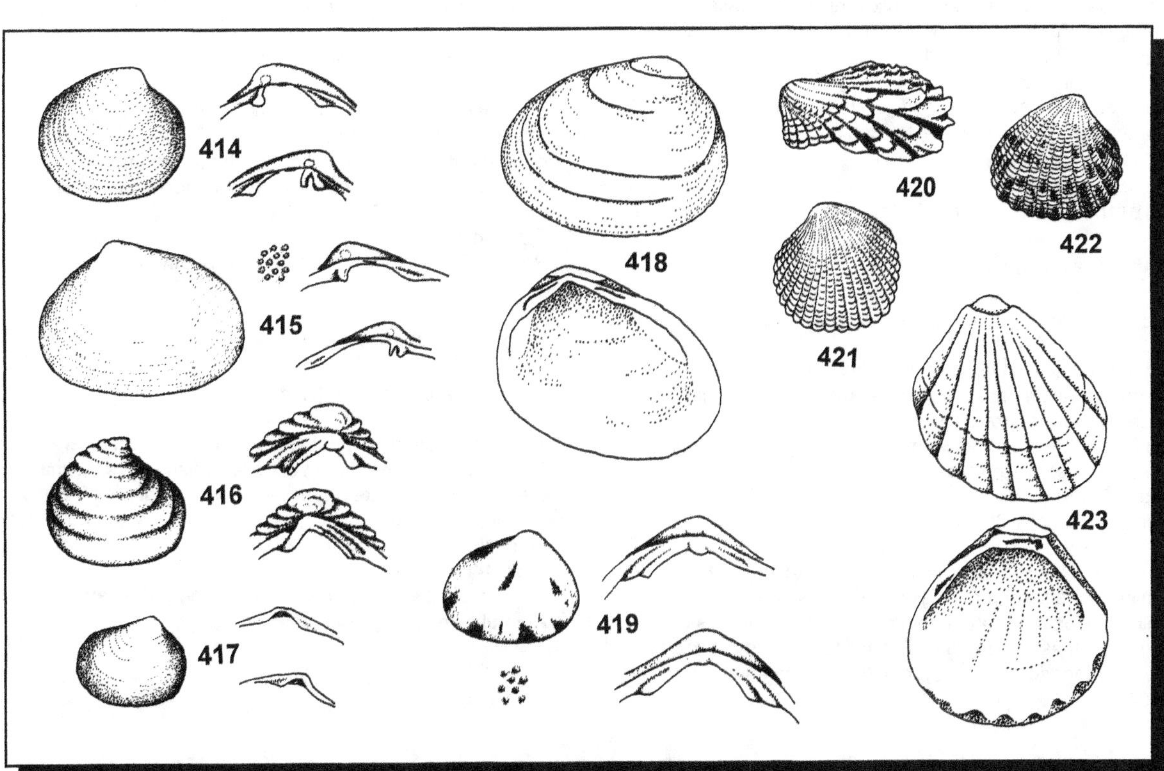

Superfamily Crassatelloidea

Family Crassatellidae

Mostly large and heavy, strongly concentrically sculptured shells; the species discussed here is much smaller than the other members of this family. It is the only species belonging to this family that can be found in Sydney. Lamprell and Whitehead (1992) give an overview of the Australian Crassatellidae. Darragh (1974) has revised the species of the genus *Eucrassatella*.

Superfamily Cardioidea

Family Cardiidae

The shells are rounded, with inflated valves and strong radial sculpture. The hinge has two cardinal and two lateral teeth in each valve. A pallial sinus is absent. The animals live buried in sand and have been recorded from a variety of depths.
Schneider (1992) has recently worked on the taxonomy of the family, including several previously separate families, eg. the Tridacnidae, in the Cardiidae at subfamilial level. He reduced the former subfamily Trachycardiinae to tribe-status within the subfamily Cardiinae.
There have been a few publications on Australian Cardiidae. Wilson and Stevenson (1977) described the Western Australian species of the family. Lamprell and Whitehead (1992) give an overview of the Australian Cardiidae. Poutiers (1992) reviews the Australian species of the subfamily Protocardiinae.
Cardiidae are not common in Sydney. Five species were found and are described and figured here; it is possible that another one or two species could be found.

Subfamily Cardiinae

Tribe Trachycardiini

428. *Acrosterigma kerslakae* Healy & Lamprell, 1992

The shell is almost circular. The sculpture consists of fine rounded radiating ribs, which bear small nodules; the interstices are narrow. The colour is white, irregularly mottled with reddish brown markings. The area anterior to the umbos is dark purple.
Size: 19mm.
Range: Southern Queensland to central New South Wales.
Remarks: This species was named only recently. It is similar to the southern *A. cygnorum* (Deshayes, 1855), which has been reported from the New South Wales coast as far north as Nowra; the present species has not been found further south than Sydney (Healy and Lamprell, 1992).

427. *Talabrica fulvida* (Angas, 1871)

The shell is small, flat, rounded and almost equilateral. The sculpture consists of broad concentric ribs. The interior margin is finely crenulated. The colour is pink externally and internally.
Size: 9mm.
Range: New South Wales.

429. *Acrosterigma reeveanum* (Dunker, 1852)

The shell is large, heavy and elongate. The sculpture consists of about 24 angulated ribs, which are ornamented with small ribs or scales; the interstices between the ribs are narrow and deep. The colour is white, maculated with orange, reddish or pink. The inside is white.
Size: 61mm.
Range: Northern Western Australia to central New South Wales.

Subfamily Fraginae

430. *Afrocardium skeeti* (Hedley, 1906)

The shell is small, thin and somewhat quadrate. It is inequilateral, the posterior end is the longer. The sculpture consists of flat radiating ribs, which are ornamented with sharp scales. The colour is white; the posterior end is maculated with red.
Size: 8mm.
Range: Queensland to central New South Wales.

Subfamily Protocardiinae

431. *Pratulum thetidis* (Hedley, 1902)

The shell is small, thin, globose and almost equilateral. The sculpture consists of very fine radiating ribs, giving the shell a velvet-like appearance. The colour is off-white to pink, often with radiating rays. The umbos, the posterior and anterior ends are often pink.
Size: 14mm.
Range: Southern Queensland to southern Western Australia, including Tasmania.

Subfamily Laevicardiinae

432. *Fulvia tenuicostata* (Lamarck, 1819)

The shell is thin and nearly circular. The sculpture consists of many fine, angulate ribs. The area below the umbos is smooth. The hinge has one cardinal and two lateral teeth in each valve. The colour is off-white to yellowish, maculated with pink. The umbos are frequently purple. Fresh specimens are covered in a thin, flaky periostracum.
Size: 37mm.
Range: Central New South Wales to southern Western Australia, including Tasmania.

Family *Hemidonacidae*

The shells are elongate, and strongly inequilateral; the anterior end is the longer. The valves are beaked posteriorly; the anterior end is rounded. The hinge is similar to that of the Cardiidae. The interior margin is roughly crenulate.
The animal has no siphons and no eyes on the edge of the mantle.

Ponder *et al.* (1981) have revised the species of *Hemidonax* and recognise five living and one fossil species.

433. *Hemidonax pictus* (Tryon, 1870)

The shell is thick, the general shape is as described for the family. The sculpture consists of irregular radiating grooves or ribs, which become stronger posteriorly. The lunule is long and elongate. The colour is white, irregularly marked with brown.
Size: 36mm.
Range: Queensland to central New South Wales.

434. *Hemidonax dactylus* Hedley, 1923

The shell shape is as described for the family; the shell is thin. The sculpture consists of broad radiating bands. The colour is off-white, maculated with brown and purple.
Size: 17mm.
Range: Queensland to central New South Wales.

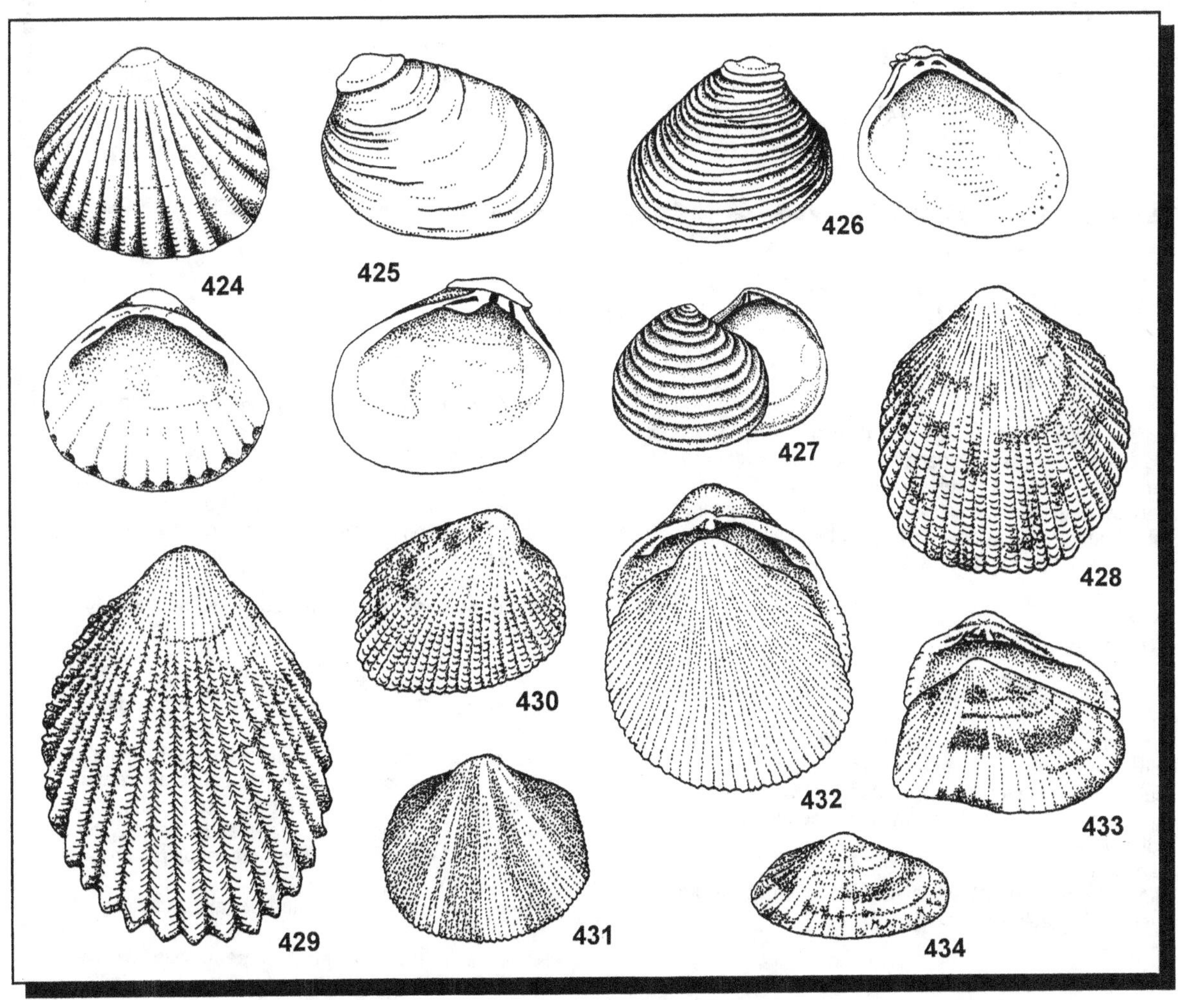

424 425 426 427 428 429 430 431 432 433 434

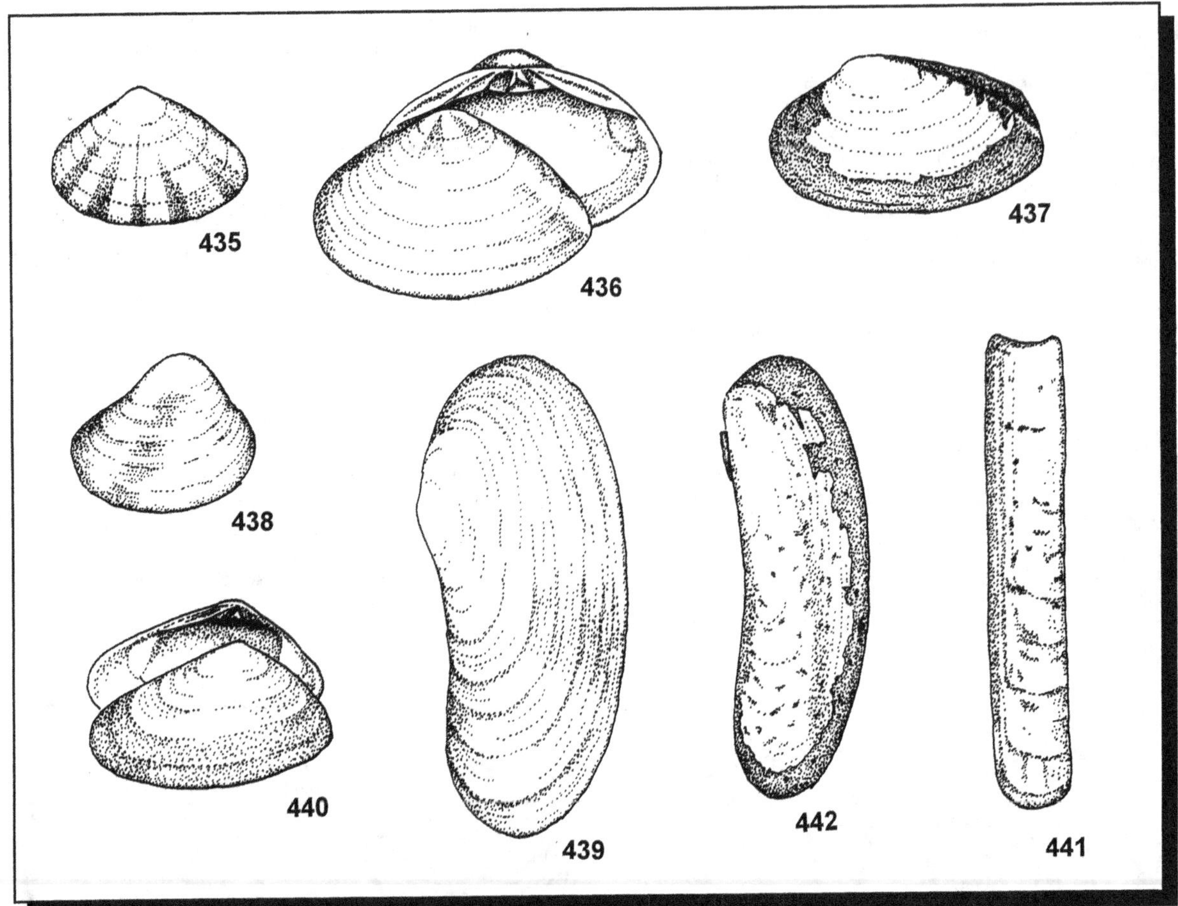

Superfamily Mactroidea

Family Mactridae

The shells are small to large, mostly thin, but not fragile. The ligament is internal, triangular and situated directly under the umbos. Lamprell and Whitehead (1992) give an overview of the Australian Mactridae. Five species are discussed here; it is possible that another two or three species could be found on Sydney's beaches.

Subfamily Mactrinae

435. *Mactra (Nannomactra) jacksonensis* Smith, 1885

The shell is small, broadly triangular, fragile and slightly inequilateral; the posterior end is the longer. The sculpture consists of fine concentric ribs. The colour is off-white, maculated with dark brown or pink, mostly in radiating rays.
Size: 13mm.
Range: Central New South Wales to southern Western Australia, including Tasmania.

436. *Mactra (Nannomactra) pusilla* A. Adams, 1855

The shell is broadly triangular, equivalve and almost equilateral. The sculpture consists of fine concentric striae. A rounded keel runs from the umbos to the posterior-ventral margin. The colour is off-white to grey, with a dirty grey periostracum. The inside is dark purple.
Size: 30mm.
Range: Southern Queensland to Victoria, including Tasmania.

437. *Mactra (Electromactra) antecedens* Iredale, 1930

The shell is elongate, inequilateral, the posterior end is the longer. The sculpture consists of fine concentric striae, with a sharp keel from the umbos to the posterior-ventral margin, the margins gape at both ends. The colour is white, covered in an olive green periostracum.
Size: 33mm.
Range: Queensland to South Australia, including Tasmania.
Remarks: This species has also been called *M. ovalina* Lamarck, 1819, but the type of that species is different

from the species described here (Lamprell and Whitehead, 1992).

438. *Spisula (Notospisula) trigonella* (Lamarck, 1819)

The shell is small, triangular, beaked posteriorly and inflated. The sculpture consists of rough concentric growth lines. The hinge of both valves has one small cardinal and two large lateral teeth. The colour is dirty white, covered in a greyish brown periostracum.
Size: 20mm, but mostly smaller.
Range: Northern Territory to southern Western Australia, including Tasmania.
Synonyms: *N. parva* Petit, 1853, *Mactra corbuloides* Reeve, 1854, *Spisula cretacea* Angas, 1867, *S. producta* Angas, 1867 and *Mactra fluvatilis* Angas, 1871.

Subfamily Lutrariinae

439. *Lutraria rhynchaena* Jonas, 1844

The shell is large and elongate; the valves are gaping. The shell is strongly inequilateral, the posterior end is the longer. The sculpture consists of rough growth lines. The hinge of both valves has a large triangular impression for the ligament and cardinal teeth only. The colour is dirty white, fresh specimens are covered in a dark brown periostracum.
Size: 94mm.

Range: Central New South Wales to southern Western Australia, including Tasmania.

Family Mesodesmatidae

The shells are thick, smooth, elongate and covered in a brown periostracum. The animals live in sand intertidally. Lamprell and Whitehead (1992) give an overview of the Australian Mesodesmatidae.

440. *Paphies (Amesodesma) elongata* Reeve, 1854

The shell is thick and inequilateral, the anterior end is much longer. The ligament is internal; the pallial sinus is small. The sculpture consists of fine concentric growth lines. The shell surface is polished. The colour is white, covered in a resilient thin yellowish periostracum.
Size: 27mm.
Range: Northern Queensland to southern Western Australia, including Tasmania.
Synonyms: *Mesodesma angusta* Reeve, 1854, *Amesodesma perfuga* Iredale, 1930.
Remarks: *Paphies (Atactodea) cuneata* (Lamarck, 1818) is another species that can be found in New South Wales. It is rounder in shape.

Superfamily Solenoidea

Family Solenidae

The shells are elongate, with a straight dorsal and ventral margin, covered in a thin, greenish periostracum. The valves gape widely at both ends.
The animals live buried in sand subtidally. They can leap away from predators, using their powerful foot. They are also capable of swimming (McMahon and O'Byrne McMahon, 1983).
One species can be found in the Sydney area. The Queensland Solenidae are discussed by Lamprell (1986).

441. *Solen vaginoides* Lamarck, 1818

The shell is elongate, equivalve and strongly inequilateral. The umbos are nearly terminal. The anterior and posterior ends are sharply truncate. The hinge of both valves has one cardinal tooth. The sculpture consists of concentric growth lines. The colour is white, mottled with brown.
Size: 70mm.
Range: Central New South Wales to southern Western Australia, including Tasmania.
Remarks: A similar species, *S. sloanii* Hanley, 1843 can be found in northern Australia.

Family Cultellidae

The shells are thin, elongate, curved. The family is represented in Australia by just one species.

442. *Ensiculus cultellus* L., 1758

The shell is thin, elongate, equivalve and strongly inequilateral. The umbos are almost terminal, situated close to the anterior margin of the shell. The anterior and posterior ends are widely gaping. The hinge of both valves has strong cardinal teeth only. The ligament is external. The colour is white, irregularly mottled with red or brown spots. The surface is covered in a thin yellowish periostracum.
Size: 58mm.
Range: Northern Western Australia to central New South Wales.

Superfamily Tellinoidea

Family Tellinidae

The shells are mostly thin, fragile, rounded anteriorly and beaked posteriorly. The hinge has two cardinal and often lateral teeth in each valve. The ligament is external. The animal lives in sand.
There has been no recent revision of the family. Lamprell and Whitehead (1992) give an overview of the Australian Tellinidae.

443. *Tellina (Tellinella) albinella* Lamarck, 1818

The shell is thin, elongate, equivalve and almost equilateral. The posterior end is beaked. The sculpture consists of very fine concentric growth lines, which become lamellae on the posterior end of the shell. There are two ribs from the umbos to the posterior-ventral margin. The colour is white with some areas of pink. All pink specimens exist.
Size: 49mm.
Range: Central New South Wales to southern Western Australia, including Tasmania.
Synonyms: *Tellinota roseola* (Lamarck, 1818).

444. *Tellina (Macomona) deltoidalis* Lamarck, 1818

The shell is thin, somewhat triangular, equivalve and almost equilateral. The sculpture consists of rough growth lines. The shell surface is matt and chalky. The pallial sinus is deep, reaching the anterior muscle scar and forming a triangular shape in the inside of the shell. The posterior end of the shell is beaked and curved in the direction of the right valve. The colour is dirty white; the umbos are often tinged with yellow or orange. The periostracum is dirty brown.
Size: 38mm, but mostly smaller.
Habitat: Estuarine environments, in sand.
Range: Southern Queensland to southern Western Australia, including Tasmania.

445. *Tellina (Pseudacropagia) botanica* Hedley, 1918

The shell is thick and rounded. The right valve tends to be more inflated than left valve. The shell is almost equilateral. The sculpture consists of fine concentric lamellae, crossed by even finer radiating striae, which are more prominent in some areas than in others. The posterior area is slightly beaked, with a shallow furrow from the umbos to the posterior-ventral margin in the left valve and a weak rib in the same position in the right valve. The colour is white, often with yellow umbos.
Size: 39mm.
Range: Southern Queensland to Western Australia, including Tasmania.
Remarks: *T. (P.) victoriae* Gatliff & Gabriel, 1914 is a similar but larger and heavier species, which can also be found in New South Wales. It has a much stronger sculpture, especially radiating sculpture.

Family Semelidae

This family includes species varying in size from large to minute. They resemble the Tellinidae in shape, but are often strongly concentrically sculptured. The hinge has two or three cardinal teeth and usually lateral teeth. The pallial sinus is present, but not as deep as in the Tellinidae. Lamprell and Whitehead (1992) review the larger species of Semelidae. The genus *Ervilia* was recently transferred to this family from the Mesodesmatidae (Morton and Scott, 1990).

446. *Ervilia rubra* (Laseron, 1953)

The shell is small, elliptical and slightly inequilateral; the anterior end is the larger. The prodissoconch is small but obvious and bulbous. The umbos are curved towards the anterior end of the shell. The sculpture consists of very fine radiating ribs, crossed by concentric ribs of equal strength, forming a reticulate pattern. The hinge of both valves has two lateral teeth. In the right valve there is a large cardinal and in the left valve a small cardinal. The colour is pink, fading to white in beach specimens.
Size: 4.6mm.
Range: New South Wales.

Family Psammobiidae

The shells are elongate, thin, fragile and slightly gaping at both ends. Most species have little sculpture, but concentric, radiating or transverse sculpture is present in some species. The hinge has two cardinal teeth in each valve; there are no lateral teeth. The ligament is external. The animals live in sand in a variety of habitats from muddy bays to coral cays. They live mostly intertidally or in shallow water.
Willan (1993) has revised the Australian and New Zealand species based on shell characters. He recognises 37 species belonging to four genera *Asaphis*, *Heteroglypta*, *Gari* and *Soletellina*. The genus *Gari* has nine subgenera; no subgenera are recognised for any of the other genera. Three species are described here, only one of which is common in the Sydney area.

447. *Gari (Psammobia) livida* (Lamarck, 1818)

The shell is thin, elongate, inequilateral; the anterior end is the longer; the posterior end is slightly truncate. The sculpture consists of fine concentric ribs, which are most obvious at the posterior end of the shell. The colour is white, with irregular concentric and often radiating bands of pink or orange.
Size: 23mm.
Range: Southern Queensland to southern Western Australia, including Tasmania.
Synonyms: *Psammotaea zonalis* Lamarck, 1818, *Psammobia puella*, *P. compta*, *P. striata* all Deshayes, 1855, *P. tellinaeformis* Reeve, 1856 (non Deshayes), *P. hamiltonensis* Tate, 1885.

448. *Soletellina alba* (Lamarck, 1818)

The shell is thin, elongate and equivalve; the anterior end is longer than the posterior end. The sculpture consists of irregular concentric growth lines. The ventral margin is almost parallel to the dorsal margin. The colour is purple, with two lighter coloured radiating bands from the umbos to the posterior-ventral margin. . Fresh specimens are covered in a thin brown periostracum.
Size: 52mm.
Range: Queensland to South Australia.
Synonyms: many, including *Soletellina donacioides* Reeve, 1857, *S. incerta* Reeve, 1857, *Florisarka onuphria* Iredale, 1936 and *Solenotellina haynesi* Preston, 1914.
Remarks: *Psammotellina biradiata* (Wood, 1815) is a similar but larger species, which also occurs in New South Wales. It can be separated from the species described here by being lighter coloured and having a more rounded ventral margin.

449. *Heteroglypta contraria* (Deshayes, 1863)

The shell is small, thin, bean-shaped and inequilateral; the posterior end is longer than the anterior end. The sculpture consists of oblique striae on the anterior third, strong radiating ribs on the middle section and strong transverse folds on the posterior third of the shell. The colour is white, yellow or purple.
Size: 18mm.
Range: Northern Queensland to central New South Wales, New Caledonia, Japan to Taiwan, Mauritius, Réunion Island, Djibouti, Aden, Red Sea, probably widespread in the Indo-Pacific (Willan, 1993).
Synonyms: *Heteroglypta hedleyi, H. avecta, H. pansa, H. saltatrix* all Iredale, 1929, *H. nipponica* Kuroda, 1934.

Family Donacidae

The shells are thick, triangular and inequilateral; the anterior end is the longer. The posterior end is beaked and the anterior end is rounded. Shells are weakly sculptured. The hinge has two cardinal teeth and two lateral teeth in each valve. The ligament is external. The interior margin is finely crenulated. The animals live in sand.
There has been no recent revision of the family. Lamprell and Whitehead (1992) give an overview of the Australian Donacidae.

450. *Donax (Plebidonax) deltoides* Lamarck, 1818

The shell is large and thick; the posterior end is sharply beaked. The sculpture consists of fine radiating grooves crossed by irregular growth lines. The colour is white to purple or pink. The interior is marked with purple areas; the interior margin is mostly white.
Size: 51mm.
Habitat: In sand intertidally, the animal is used as bait.
Range: All Australian states.

451. *Donax (Deltachion) brazieri* Smith, 1892

The shell is small and thick. The posterior end is sharply angulated, with a sharp keel running from the umbos to the posterior-ventral margin. The sculpture consists of fine radiating grooves, crossed by concentric growth lines. The colour is white with areas of purple or pink. The interior is frequently marked with large areas of purple.
Size: 17mm.
Range: Southern Queensland to Victoria.
Synonyms: *D. virilis* Iredale, 1930.
Remarks: *D electilis* (Iredale, 1930) from Victoria to Western Australia is smaller and more elongate.

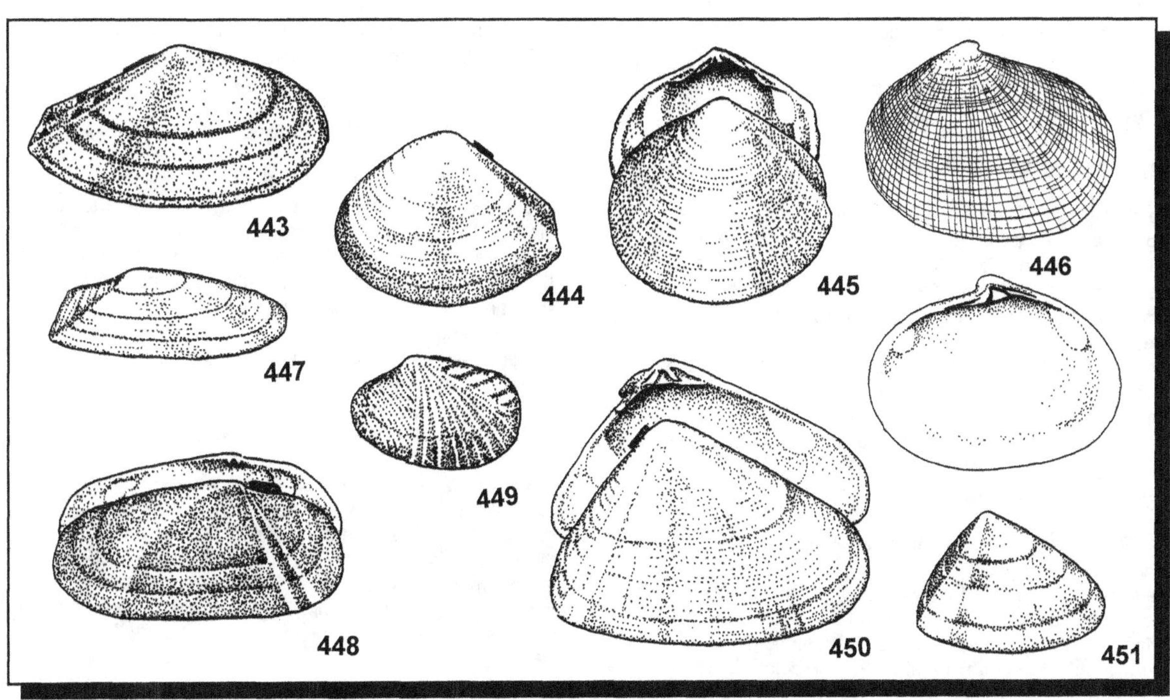

Superfamily Veneroidea

Family Veneridae

This is one of the largest families of the bivalves, members of which live worldwide at a variety of depths, although the majority of species live in shallow water. The shells are equivalve and usually inequilateral. Most members of the family have a well-defined lunule and escutcheon. The sculpture is variable and usually concentric if present. Some species have radiating sculpture as well. The strong sculpture in some venerids is said to deter predators, such as Naticidae. The typical venerid hinge has three cardinal teeth in each valve and may have an anterior lateral tooth.

Although Veneridae are not common on Sydney's beaches, the number of species that can be found is rather large. Nineteen species are described here, representing the most common species. Lamprell and Whitehead (1992) give an overview of the Australian species of Veneridae.

Subfamily Venerinae

452. *Antigona (Antigona) persimilis* (Iredale, 1930)

The shell is heavy, elongate-rounded in shape and inequilateral; the posterior end is the longer. The sculpture consists of crenulated lamellae, which are placed on top of undulating ribs. The lunule is elongate. The colour is white, irregularly mottled with brown; the lunule is brown. The inside is white.
Size: 39mm, but grows larger.
Range: Southern Queensland to central New South Wales.
Remarks: A species from deeper water is *A. (A.) materna* (Iredale, 1929), which has double sets of lamellae. *A. chemnitzi* (Hanley, 1844) is a tropical species.

Subfamily Circinae

453. *Circe (Circe) scripta* (Linnaeus, 1758)

The shell is round and inequilateral; the posterior end is longer than the anterior end. The sculpture consists of rounded concentric ribs. The area below the umbos is flat. The ventral margin is rounded. The colour is white with reddish brown radiating bands of maculations.
Size: 33mm.
Range: Northern Western Australia to central New South Wales.
Synonyms: *C. sugillata* Reeve, 1863
Remarks: This is the only species of this genus that lives in Sydney. Several species of *Circe* occur in tropical Australia, especially in Western Australia.

454. *Gouldiopa australis* (Angas, 1865)

The shell is very small, thin, with inflated valves. It is inequilateral, the posterior end being the largest. The shell surface is smooth, crossed only by concentric growth lines. The hinge has no lateral teeth. The colour is white with three radiating pink bands.
Size: 8mm.
Range: Southern Queensland to northern Western Australia.

Subfamily Sunettinae

455. *Bassina (Callanaitis) disjecta* (Perry, 1811)

The shell is equivalve, almost equilateral and lightweight, with a fragile and delicate sculpture of about seven long, recurved lamellae. The interstices are smooth. The colour is white; the lamellae are often pink.
Size: 53mm.
Range: Central New South Wales to southern Western Australia, including Tasmania.

456. *Bassina (Bassina) jacksoni* (Smith, 1885)

The shell is thin and inequilateral; the posterior end is the longer. The sculpture consists of four to five fine concentric lamellae, which are erect, but low in the central area, becoming larger at both ends, often resulting in a spine at the point furthest away from the umbo. The areas between the lamellae are finely concentrically striated. The colour is light brown with broad darker brown radiating bands. The umbos tend to be purple. The inside is marked with a tinge of purple.
Size: 35mm.
Range: Queensland to central New South Wales.
Remarks: *B. (B.) pachyphylla* (Jonas, 1839) is another species in this subgenus, which can also be found in the Sydney region, which has a smooth and heavy shell, with 3-5 lamellae anteriorly. It is also much larger.

457. *Placamen placidum* (Philippi, 1844)

The shell is thick, equivalve and inequilateral; the anterior end is the longer. The umbos point towards the anterior margin. The sculpture consists of about 14 strong and thick concentric recurved lamellae. The lunule is elongate. The colour is white, sometimes tinged with pink and sometimes with brown radiating bands.
Size: 24mm.
Range: Queensland to southern Western Australia, including Tasmania.

458. *Tawera lagopus* (Lamarck, 1818)

A well-known species, which occurs around southern Australia. It has a heavy, concentrically ribbed shell. The ribs are finely crenulated and the interstices between them are crossed by fine radiating striae. The inside of the ventral margin is crenulated. The colour is white with brown maculations, often arranged in radiating bands. The inside is often pink.
Size: 26mm.

452
453
455
454
456
457
458
459
460
461
462
463
465
466
464
467
469
468
470
471

Range: Central New South Wales to southern Western Australia, including Tasmania.
Remarks: *T. gallinula* (Lamarck, 1818) is a similar species, which can be found in southern New South Wales. It has stronger concentric ribs, weaker radiating ribs and a purple interior.

459. *Timoclea (Chioneryx) scabra* (Hanley, 1844)

The shell is small, triangular and strongly sculptured. It is inequilateral; the posterior end is slightly longer than the anterior end. The sculpture consists of radiating double ribs, crossed by fine concentric lamellae. The inside of the ventral margin is sharply crenulated. The colour is light brown with some radiating white bands. The umbos are often purple. The inside of the shell is dark chocolate brown or purple.
Size: 8mm.
Range: Queensland to central New South Wales.
Synonyms: *T. ethica* (Iredale, 1930).

460. *Timoclea (Chioneryx) cardioides* (Lamarck, 1818)

The shell is small, rather thin, elongate and triangular. It is inequilateral; the posterior end is slightly longer than the anterior end. The sculpture consists of fine, closely-set radiating ribs, crossed by fine concentric lamellae. The inside of the ventral margin is crenulated. The colour is white with some small brown maculations. The areas around the umbos are dark brown; the inside of the shell is white.
Size: 14mm.
Range: Central New South Wales to southern Western Australia, including Tasmania.

Subfamily Pitarinae

461. *Callista (Notocallista) disrupta* (Sowerby, 1853)

The shell is thick, heavy and inequilateral; the posterior end is slightly longer than the anterior end. The sculpture consists of irregular growth lines, giving the shell a rough appearance, often forming broad concentric folds. The shell surface is porcellaneous, which is especially obvious in fresh specimens. The colour is off-white, maculated with many zigzag lines of purplish brown, often arranged in radiating bands.
Size: 50mm.
Range: Southern Queensland to Victoria.
Remarks: *N. kingii* (Gray, 1827) is a similar species, which is more smooth and has a thinner shell. *N. diemenensis* (Hanley, 1844) is also similar, but less rough and more uniformly coloured.

Subfamily Tapetinae

462. *Gomphina fulgida* Hedley, 1918

A shell characterised by its thick, smooth, shiny valves, with only fine concentric growth lines. The valves are almost equilateral. The colour of typical specimens is white with a pattern of brown zigzag lines. Fresh specimens are covered in a thick, yellowish periostracum.
Size: 26mm.
Range: Southern Queensland to southern New South Wales.
Remarks: *G. undulosa* (Lamarck, 1818) is a similar species, which can be found from Victoria to Western Australia. It is more triangular.

463. *Katelysia rhytiphora* (Lamy, 1937)

This is the only species of the genus *Katelysia* to occur in Sydney. The shell shape is elongate, with the umbos situated close to the anterior end of the shell. The sculpture consists of crowded rounded ribs, which often fuse into each other at the anterior end of the shell. The colour is dirty white, sometimes tinged with yellow or with grey maculations.
Size: 44mm.
Range: Central New South Wales to southern Western Australia, including Tasmania.

464. *Eumarcia fumigata* (Sowerby, 1853)

The shell is elongate and strongly inequilateral; the umbos are situated at 1/3rd of the shell width from the anterior margin, which is rounded; the posterior end of the shell is beaked. The shell surface is smooth, with only concentric growth lines, and porcellaneous, covered by a yellowish periostracum. The lunule and escutcheon are elongate and indistinct. The colour is brownish, often with radiating bands or dark or white patterns. The inside of the shell is marked with an orange tinge. The lunule and escutcheon are often darker coloured.
Size: 33mm.
Habitat: In sand in bays, sometimes in large numbers, especially in summer.
Range: Southern Queensland to Victoria.

465. *Irus (Irus) crenatus* (Lamarck, 1818)

The shell is elongate, irregularly shaped and rough. It is inequilateral; the umbos are situated about 1/3rd of the shell width from the anterior margin. The sculpture consists of many radiating ribs, crossed by irregular, sometimes lamellose, concentric ribs, which tend to be stronger at both the anterior and posterior ends of the shell. The lunule is small and deep, often only visible in large specimens. The colour is off-white or yellowish, maculated with streaks of purple. The interior is heavily tinged with purple.
Size: 29mm.
Range: Central New South Wales to southern Western Australia, including Tasmania.

466. *Irus (Irus) crebrelamellatus* (Tate, 1887)

Very similar to the previous species but more elongate.
Size: 24mm.
Range: Queensland to southern Western Australia, including Tasmania.

467. *Irus (Irus) cumingii* (Deshayes, 1854)

The shell is irregularly shaped. The right valve overlaps
the left valve. It is inequilateral; the posterior end of the
shell is slightly larger than the anterior end. The sculpture
consists of radiating ribs crossed by strong frilly
concentric lamellae, which are larger at the anterior and
posterior ends of the shell. The colour is milky purplish-
white. The interior is deep purple.
Size: 22mm.
Habitat: in mussel clumps intertidally.
Range: Southern Queensland to southern Western
Australia, including Tasmania.

468. *Tapes dorsatus* (Lamarck, 1818)

The shell is large and inequilateral, with the umbos
situated at 1/3rd of the shell width from the anterior
margin. The sculpture consists of irregular concentric ribs,
which often fuse into each other at the anterior and
posterior ends of the shell. The colour is dirty brown, often
with darker radiating bands. The inside is white with an
orange tinge.
Size: 85mm.
Range: Northern Western Australia to central New South
Wales, Indo-Pacific.
Synonyms: *T. turgida* (Lamarck, 1818) and *T. watlingi*
Iredale, 1958.

469. *Venerupis anomala* (Lamarck, 1818)

The shell is small to medium-sized, thin and bean-shaped.
The valves are inequilateral; the umbos are situated 1/4th
of the shell width from the anterior margin. The sculpture
consists of fine concentric growth lines, crossed by even
finer radiating striae, giving the shell a velvet-like
appearance. The colour is white; the umbos are often
marked with a tinge of pink. The posterior part of the shell
is often maculated with brown or grey.
Size: 28mm, but mostly smaller.
Range: Southern Queensland to southern Western
Australia, including Tasmania.

Order Myoida

Suborder Myiina

Superfamily Myoidea

Family Corbulidae

Shells heavy and thick, strongly inequivalve, with the right
valve overlapping the left valve. The family is in need of a
revision.

Synonyms: *Pullastra fabagella* (Deshayes, 1854).
Remarks: This is one of the most common species of
Veneridae on Sydney's beaches.

Subfamily Dosiniinae

470. *Dosinia sculpta* (Hanley, 1845)

This is a rather variable species with a wide Indo-Pacific
distribution. The shell is usually rather large, round, heavy
and equilateral. The sculpture consists of many crowded,
often irregular, concentric ribs. At both the anterior and
posterior ends of the shell these ribs fuse and become
lamellose and are crossed by radiating striae. The lunule
and escutcheon are clearly visible. The colour is white,
often with yellow umbos.
Size: 46mm.
Range: Western Australia to central New South Wales.
Remarks: *D. caerulea* Reeve, 1850 is a similar southern
Australian species, which has also been found in Sydney.
It has a more elongate shape and lacks the concentric
lamellae and radiating sculpture on the anterior and
posterior end of the shell.

471. *Dosinia crocea* Deshayes, 1853

The shell is small and inequilateral; the posterior end is
slightly larger than the anterior end. The lunule is very
small, but distinct. The sculpture consists of very fine
concentric ribs. The shell surface is polished and
porcellaneous. The colour is white. The lunule and the
dorsal margin are brown.
Size: 15mm.
Range: Central New South Wales to South Australia,
including Tasmania.

472. *Corbula stolata* (Iredale, 1930)

The shell is heavy and inequivalve; the right valve
overlaps the left valve. The posterior end of the valves is
beaked, with a ridge from the umbos to the posterior-
ventral margin. The sculpture consists of irregular
concentric ribs. The colour is white, covered in a brown
periostracum.
Size: 18mm.
Range: Central New South Wales to Victoria.

Superfamily Hiatelloidea

Family Hiatellidae

This family consists of rock-boring species, which accounts for their often irregular shape. Beu (1971*b*) has discussed the taxonomy of the genus *Hiatella*. It appears that there are only two species, one of which, *H. arctica* (Linnaeus, 1767), can be found worldwide and the other, *H. australis*, in Australia.

Superfamily Pholadoidea

Family Pholadidae

The shells are elongate, thin, with the valves gaping at both ends. The hinge is without teeth or ligament. Only one species was found in the Sydney region.

474. *Pholas australasiae* Sowerby, 1849

The shell is thin and elongate, with the valves gaping widely at both ends. It is inequilateral; the posterior end of the shell is much longer than the anterior end. The hinge and ligament are absent. Part of the dorsal margin is

Subclass Anomalodesmata

Order Pholadomyoida

Superfamily Pandoroidea

Family Laternulidae

The shells are thin, translucent, fragile and made up of a nacreous material. The animals live in sand intertidally.

475. *Laternula creccina* (Reeve, 1860)

The shell is thin and elongate; the valves are widely gaping. The shell is inequilateral; the anterior end is shorter than the posterior end and slightly beaked and curved. The sculpture consists of concentric growth lines. The hinge has one spatula-like tooth in each valve. The colour is milky translucent white.
Size: 40mm.
Range: Queensland to South Australia, including Tasmania.

473. *Hiatella australis* (Lamarck, 1818)

The shell is irregularly shaped, but mostly squarely elongate. The valves are widely gaping. The ligament is external. The sculpture consists of rough concentric growth lines, interrupted by a ridge from the umbos to the posterior-ventral margin. The colour is entirely chalky white, fresh specimens are covered with a brown periostracum.
Size: 38mm, but New South Wales specimens mostly around 10mm.
Range: All Australian states.

reflected over the umbos. In live specimens, an additional plate is situated on top of the umbos. Each valve has a large, curved, tooth-like projection internally. The sculpture consists of concentric lamellae, which bear peaks at regular intervals. The colour is white.
Size: 42mm.
Range: All Australian states.
Remarks: *Pholas obturamentum* Hedley, 1893 is another southern Australian species described from Sydney. It is shorter and has a more strongly beaked anterior end.

Family Myochamidae

The shells are strongly inequivalve, with one deep and one flat valve. The sculpture is mostly concentric, but may be radiating and is always irregular. The shell material is nacreous. Lamy (1935) revised the species of this family. Tevesz (1975) studied the ecology of the Australian species *Myadora pandoriformis*. It lives buried in the sand with the deep valve downwards. It has adaptations to living in muddy conditions, including the structure of the gill and an unusual way to clean the foot of adhering particles.

476. *Myadora pandoriformis* (Stutchbury, 1830)

The shell is inequilateral and slightly elongate. The sculpture consists of concentric ribs, with a ridge from the umbos to the posterior-ventral margin. The colour is

pearly white.
Size: 18mm.
Range: Queensland to Victoria.

477. *Myadora brevis* (Sowerby, 1829)

The shell is thin, inflated and inequilateral. The umbos are strongly curved towards the posterior end. The sculpture consists of wavy irregular concentric ribs, crossed by two rounded ribs from the umbos to the posterior-ventral margin. The colour is pearly white.
Size: 18mm.
Range: Queensland to South Australia, including Tasmania.

478. *Myochama anomoides* Stutchbury, 1830

The shell is thin, inflated and elongate. The umbos are curved towards the posterior end. The anterior end is rounded; the posterior end is slightly beaked. The sculpture consists of irregular broad radiating ribs, crossed by irregular concentric ribs. The colour is brownish.
Size: 26mm.
Range: Central New South Wales to South Australia, including Tasmania.

Family Cleidothaeridae

The shells are heavy, strongly inequivalve, fixed to a substrate by their deep valve. The family, with the genus *Cleidothaerus* as its only genus, is restricted to Australia and New Zealand (Iredale, 1939). The species described here is the Australian representative; the New Zealand species has been studied by Morton (1974).

479. *Cleidothaerus albidus* (Lamarck, 1819)

The shell is large, strongly inequivalve, with the bottom valve deep and triangular and the top valve almost flat. The sculpture consists of irregular growth lines, part of the bottom valve is attached to a substrate. The colour is pink, fresh specimens are covered with a brown periostracum.
Size: 45mm.
Habitat: On exposed rocks intertidally and subtidally.
Range: Central New South Wales to South Australia, including Tasmania.

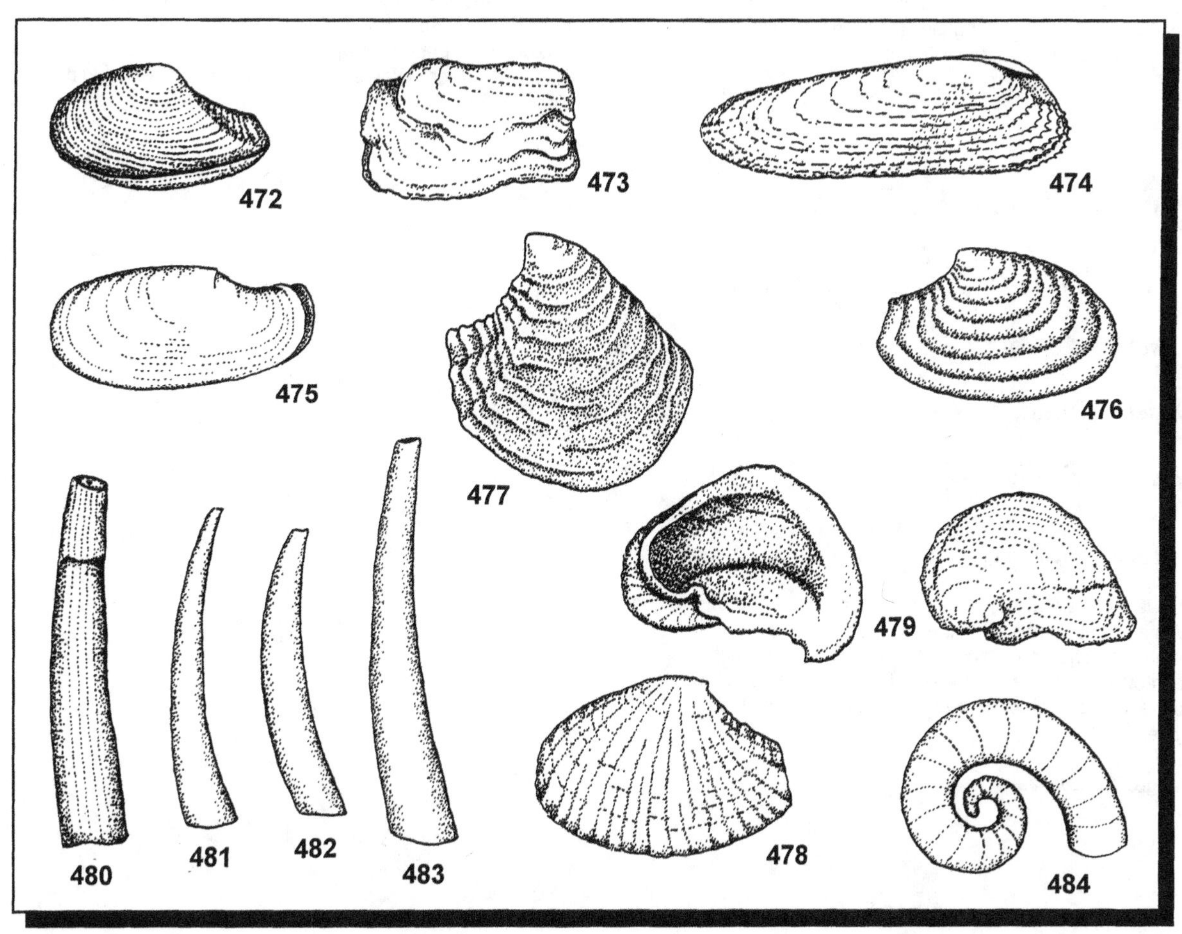

Class Scaphopoda

Order Dentaliida

Family Dentaliidae

This group of shells is extremely poorly documented, but Lamprell and Healy will soon publish a revision of the Australian species. Four species were found in the Sydney region; all are described and illustrated here (with thanks to Kevin Lamprell for identification).

480. *Dentalium (Dentalium) franciscense* Verco, 1911

The shell is large for the family, thick and only slightly curved. The sculpture consists of 14-16 longitudinal ribs. The colour is white.
Size: 18mm, but grows up to 28mm.
Range: Western Australia to New South Wales.

481. *Compressidens platyceras* (Sharp & Pilsbry, 1897)

The shell is small, strongly curved and strongly tapering. The shell surface is sculptured with irregular oblique growth rings, with fine longitudinal striae towards the apex. The colour is white or dirty brown.

Size: 7mm.
Range: southern Queensland to Victoria.

482. *Cadulus simillimus* Watson, 1879

The shell is small, thin and translucent. It is only slightly curved, slightly inflated in the middle and somewhat contracted at both extremities. The shell surface is smooth and polished. The colour is translucent white with an opaque ring near the apex.
Size: 6mm.
Range: Northern Western Australia to Victoria.

483. *Laevidentalium lubricatum* (Sowerby, 1860)

The shell is medium-sized, tapering and only very slightly curved. The shell surface is sculptured with irregular raised transverse annulations, low and rounded, with many transverse growth rings.
Size: 14mm, but grows up to 65mm.
Range: Northern Western Australia to Victoria, including Tasmania.

Class Cephalopoda

Subclass Coleoida

Order Sepiida

Family Spirulidae

484. *Spirula spirula* L., 1758

This is the internal shell of a type of squid, which probably lives at great depths, as very few animals have been found. The shell is coiled, but the whorls do not touch each other. The shell is divided into chambers, which are connected to each other by small holes. The colour is white.
Size: 22mm.
Range: Worldwide.

References

Abbott, R.T., (1960). The genus *Strombus* in the Indo-Pacific. Indo-Pacific Mollusca 1, 33-146.

Adams, A., and Angas, G.F., (1863). Descriptions of new species of shells from the Australian seas, in the collection of George French Angas. Proceedings of the Zoological Society of London 1863, 418-435.

Allan, J.K., (1958). Some species of Lamellariidae from the eastern Australian coast. Journal of the Malacological Society of Australia 2, 48-57.

Ansell, A.D., and Morton, B., (1987). Alternative predation tactics of a tropical naticid gastropod. Journal of Experimental Marine Biology and Ecology 111,109-119.

Baker, H.B., (1923). Notes on the radula of the Neritidae. Proceedings of the Academy of Natural Sciences of Philadelphia 75, 117-178.

Beechey, D., (1989). Two interesting shells from Kurnell. Sydney Sheller, September 1989, 3.

Beechey, D., (1991). An interesting shell No. 2. Sydney Sheller, September 1991, 3-4.

Behrens, D.W., (1980). The Lamellariidae of the North eastern Pacific. The Veliger 22, 323-339.

Beu, A.G., (1970a). The mollusca of the genus *Monoplex* (family Cymatiidae). Transactions of the Royal Society of New Zealand 11, 225-237.

Beu, A.G., (1970b). The mollusca of the genus *Charonia*. Transactions of the Royal Society of New Zealand 11, 206-223.

Beu, A.G., (1971a). Synonymies in the molluscan family Cymatiidae. Journal of the Malacological Society of Australia 2, 101-111.

Beu, A.G., (1971b). New light on the variation and taxonomy of the bivalve *Hiatella*. New Zealand Journal of Geology and Geography 14, 64-66.

Beu, A.G., (1977). Notes on the Australian Anomiidae (Mollusca: Bivalvia). Transactions of the Royal Society of New Zealand 9, 225-243.

Beu, A.G., (1981). Australian gastropods of the family Bursidae Part 1. The families of Tonnacae, the genera of Bursidae and revision of species previously assigned to *Tutufa* Jousseame, 1881. Records of the Australian Museum 33, 248-324.

Beu, A.G., (1985). A classification and catalogue of living world Ranellidae (= Cymatiidae) and Bursidae. Conchologists of America Bulletin 13, 55-66.

Beu, A.G., (1988). Taxonomy of gastropods of the families Ranellidae (= Cymatiidae) and Bursidae. pt. 5. Early history of the families, with four new genera and recognition of the family Personidae. Saito Ho-on Kai Special Publication, 69-96.

Beu, A.G., and Cernohorsky, W.O., (1986). Taxonomy of gastropods of the families Ranellidae (= Cymatiidae) and Bursidae. pt. 1. Adoption of Ranellidae, and review of *Linatella* Gray, 1857. New Zealand Journal of Zoology 13, 241-266.

Beu, A.G., and Knudsen, J., (1987). Taxonomy of the gastropods of the family Ranellidae (=Cymatiidae) and Bursidae part 3. A review of the trifid-ribbed species of *Cymatium (Turritriton)*. Journal of the Royal Society of New Zealand 17, 73-91.

Bieler, R., (1992). *Tenagodus* or *Siliquaria* ? Unraveling taxonomic confusion in marine 'worm-snails' (Cerithioidea: Siliquariidae). Nautilus 106, 15-20.

Bieler, R., (1993). Architectonicidae of the Indo-Pacific. Abhandlungen des Naturwissenschaftlichen Vereins in Hamburg (NF) 30, 376 pp.

Bouchet, P., (1989). A marginellid gastropod parasitizes on sleeping fishes. Bulletin of Marine Science 45, 76-84.

Bratcher, T., and Cernohorsky, W.O., (1987). Living Terebras of the world: a monograph of the recent Terebridae of the world. American Malacologists Inc.,240 pp.

Brown, L.D., (1993). Biochemical genetics and species relationships within the genus *Haliotis* (Gastropoda: Haliotidae). Journal of Molluscan Studies 59, 429-443.

Burn, R., (1978). A review of Australian species of *Austrocylichna, Nipponatys, Cylichnatys* and *Diniatys*,Journal of the Malacological Society of Australia 4, 93-112.

Burn, R., and Bell, K.N., (1974). Description of *Retusa chrysoma* Burn sp. nov. (Opistobhranchia) and its food resources from Corner Inlet, Victoria. Memoirs of the National Museum of Victoria 35, 115-119.

Cate, C.N., (1977). A review of the Eratoidae (Mollusca: Gastropoda). The Veliger 19(3), 341-366.

Cate, C.N., (1979). A review of the Triviidae (Mollusca: Gastropoda). San Diego Society of Natural History Memoirs 10, 1-126.

Cernohorsky, W.O., (1972). Indo-Pacific Nassariidae. Records of the Auckland Institute and Museum 9, 125-194.

Cernohorsky, W.O., (1976). The Mitridae of the world. pt. 1. the subfamily Mitrinae. Indo-Pacific Mollusca 3, 273-528.

Cernohorsky, W.O., (1991). The Mitridae of the world. pt. 2. The subfamily Mitrinae concluded and subfamilies Imbricariinae and Cylindrimitrinae. Monographs of Marine Mollusca 4, 1-164.

Coan, E., (1965). A proposed reclassification of the family Marginellidae. Veliger 7, 184-193.

Coleman, N., (1975). What shell is that? Landsdowne Press, Sydney, 298 pp.

Cotton, B.C., (1951). Australian and Recent tertiary mollusca, family Cerithiopsidae. Records of the South Australian Museum 9, 383-395.

Cotton, B.C., (1961). South Australian Mollusca, Pelecypoda. W.L. Hawkes, Government Printer, Adelaide,363 pp.

Cotton, B.C., and Godfrey, F.K., (1934). South Australian shells (including descriptions of new genera and species). part XI Trochidae. South Australian Naturalist 15, 77-92.

Cunningham-Vaught, K., (1989). A classification of the living mollusca. American Malacologists Inc., Melbourne, Florida,189 pp.

Darragh, T.A., (1974). A preliminary revision of the living species of *Eucrassatella* (Pelecypoda: Crassatellidae). Journal of the Malacological Society of Australia 6, 3-9.

Darragh, T.A., (1991). A revision of the Australian genus *Tylospira* Harris, 1897 (Gastropoda: Struthiolariidae). Alcheringa 15, 151-175.

Dekker, H., and Goud. J., (1994). Review of the Indo-West-Pacific species of *Divaricella* sensu auct. with descriptions of two new species and a summary of the species from other regions. Vita Marina 42, 115-136.

Ewers, W.H., and Rose, C.R., (1966). Polymorphisms in *Velacumantus australis* (Gastropoda: Potamididae) and its relationship to parasitism. Australian Journal of Zoology 14, 49-64.

Fischer-Piette, E., (1977). Révision des Aviculidae II. *Vulsella*. Journal de Conchyliogie 114, 29-39.

Garrard, T.A., (1972). A revision of Australian recent and tertiary Turritellidae. Journal of the Malacological Society of Australia 2, 267- 337.

Garrard, T.A., (1975). A revision of Australian Cancellariidae (Gastropoda: Mollusca). Records of the Australian Museum 30, 1-62.

Garrard, T.A., (1977). A revision of the Australian Architectonicidae (Gastropoda: Mollusca). Records of the Australian Museum 31, 506-585.

Harry, H.W., (1985). Synopsis of the supraspecific classification of the living oysters (Bivalvia: Gryphidae and Ostreidae). The Veliger 28, 121-158.

Healy, J.M., (1993). Transfer of the gastropod family Plesiotrochidae to the Campaniloidea based on sperm ultrastructural evidence. Journal of Molluscan Studies 59, 135-146.

Healy, J.M., and Lamprell, K., (1992). New species of Veneridae, Cardiidae, Crassatellidae, Tellinidae and Mactridae from Australia (Veneroida, Bivalvia, Mollusca). Journal of the Malacological Society of Australia 13, 75-97.

Hedley, C., (1915). Studies on Australian Mollusca, pt. XII. Proceedings of the Linnean Society of New South Wales 39, 695-755.

Hedley, C., (1916). Studies on Australian Mollusca, pt. XIII. Proceedings of the Linnean Society of New South Wales 41, 680-719.

Hedley, C., (1919). A review of the Australian Tun shells. Records of the Australian Museum 12, 329-336.

Hedley, C., (1922). A revision of the Australian Turridae. Records of the Australian Museum 13, 213-359.

Herbert, D.G., (1986). A revision of the South African Scissurellidae (Mollusca: Gastropoda: Prosobranchia). Annals of the Natal Museum 27, 601-632.

Herbert, D.G., (1991). Foraminivory in a *Puncturella* (Gastropoda: Fissurellidae). Journal of Molluscan Studies 57, 127-129.

Hickman, C.S., and McLean, J.H., (1990). Systematic Revision and Suprageneric Classification of Trochacean Gastropods.Science series, Natural History Museum of Los Angeles County No. 35,167 pp.

Hoagland, K.E., (1986). Patterns of encapsulation and brooding in the Calyptraeidae (Prosobranchia: Mesogastropoda). American Malacological Bulletin 4, 173-183.

Høisæter, T., (1989). Biological notes on some Pyramidellidae (Gastropoda: Ophistobranchia) from Norway. Sarsia 74, 283-297.

Houbrick, R.S., (1980). Review of the deep-sea genus *Argyropeza* (Gastropoda: Prosobranchia: Cerithiidae). Smithsonian Contributions to Zoology 321, 1-30.

Houbrick, R.S., (1985). The genus *Clypeomorus* Jousseaume (Cerithiidae: Prosobranchia). Smithsonian Contributions to Zoology 403, 1-131.

Houbrick, R.S., (1987a). Anatomy of *Alaba* and *Litiopa* (Prosobranchia: Litiopidae): Systematic implications. Nautilus 101(1), 9-18

Houbrick, R.S., (1987b). Anatomy, reproductive biology and phylogeny of the Planaxidae (Cerithiacea: Prosobranchia). Smithsonian Contributions to Zoology 445, 1-57.

Houbrick, R.S., (1987c). Description of a new, giant *Ataxocerithium* species from Australia with remarks on the systematic placement of the genus (Prosobranchia: Cerithiopsidae). The Nautilus 101(4), 155-161.

Houbrick, R.S., (1990a). Aspects of the anatomy of *Plesiotrochus* (Plesiotrochidae fam. n.) and its systematic position in Cerithioidea (Prosobranchia, Caenogastropoda). Proceedings of the third International Marine Biology Workshop: The marine flora and fauna of Albany, Western Australia,WA Museum, Perth Vol. 1, 237-249.

Houbrick, R.S., (1990b). Review of the genus *Colina* H. and A. Adams, 1854 (Cerithiidae: Prosobranchia). Nautilus 104, 35-52.

Houbrick, R.S., (1990c). Anatomy, reproductive biology and systematic position of *Fossarus ambiguus* (Linne) (Fossarinae: Planaxidae; Prosobranchia). Açoreana,Supplement 1990,59-73.

Houbrick, R.S., (1991). Systematic review and functional morphology of the mangrove snails *Terebralia* and *Telescopium* (Potamididae; Prosobranchia). Malacologia 31(1-2), 289-338.

Houbrick, R.S., (1992). Monograph of the genus *Cerithium* Bruguière in the Indo-Pacific. Smithsonian Contributions to Zoology 510, 1-211.

Houbrick, R.S., (1993). Phylogenetic relationships and genetic review of the Bittiinae (Prosobrancia: Cerithoidea). Malacologia 35, 261-313.

Hughes, R.N., (1985). The vermetid gastropods of Hong Kong,the malacofauna of Hong Kong and southern China II. vol 1. Morton, B., and Dudgeon, D., ed., Hong Kong University Press, 127-138.

Hughes, R.N., and Hughes, H.P.I., (1981). Morphological and behavioural aspects of feeding in the Cassidae (Tonnacea, Mesogastropoda). Malacologia 20, 385-402.

Iredale, T., (1924). Results from Roy Bell's molluscan collections. Proceedings of the Linnean Society of New South Wales 49, 179-278.

Iredale, T., (1929a). Queensland molluscan notes No. 1.Memoirs of the Queensland Museum 9, 261-297.

Iredale, T., (1929*b*). Mollusca pt. 1. Great Barrier Reef Scientific Expedition Reports 5, 209-414.

Iredale, T., (1936). Australian molluscan notes No. 2. Records of the Australian Museum 19, 267-340.

Iredale, T., (1939). Note on the genus *Cleidothaerus*. Journal de Conchyliogie 83, 243-244.

Iredale, T., and McMichael, D.F., (1962). A Reference List of the Marine Mollusca of New South Wales. Australian Museum Memoir No. 11, 109 pp.

Jansen, P.I., (1993). The family Trochidae (Mollusca: Gastropoda) in the Sydney metropolitan area and adjacent coast. Australian Zoologist 29, 49-61.

Jansen, P.I., (1994). Some observations on the Australian species of *Gena* (Trochidae). Australian Shell News 85/6, 4-5.

Jenkins, B.W., (1981). *Siphonaria funiculata* Reeve (Siphonariidae, Pulmonata) a rediscription making *S. virgulata* Hedley a geographical variant of *S. funiculata*. Journal of the Malacological Society of Australia 5, 1-15.

Jenkins, B.W., (1983*a*). Rediscriptions and relationships of *Siphonaria zelandica* Quoy & Gaimard to *S. australia* Quoy & Gaimard with a description of *S. propria* sp. nov. (Mollusca: Pulmonata: Siphonariidae). Journal of the Malacological Society of Australia 6, 1-35.

Jenkins, B.W., (1983*b*). A new Siphonariidae (Mollusca: Pulmonata) from southwestern Australia. Journal of the Malacological Society of Australia 6, 113-123.

Kabat, A.R., (1990). Predatory ecology of naticid gastropods with a review of shell boring predation. Malacologia 32, 155-193.

Kabat, A.R., (1991). The classification of the Naticidae (Mollusca: Gastropoda): Review and analysis of the supraspecific taxa. Bulletin of the Museum of Comparative Zoology 152(7), 417-449.

Kantor, Y.I., (1991). On the morphology and relationships of some oliviform gastropods. Ruthenica 1, 17-52.

Knudsen, J., (1991). Observations on *Hipponix australis* (Lamarck, 1819) (Mollusca, Gastropoda, Prosobranchia) from the Albany area, Western Australia. In: The marine flora and fauna of Albany, Western Australia vol. 2,Wells, F.E., Walker, D.I., Kirkman, H., and Lethbridge, R., (eds), Marine Science Association, WAM, 641-660.

Komatsu, S., (1986). Taxonomic revison of the Neritid gastropods. Special Publication of the Mukaishima Marine Biological Station 1986, 1-69.

Kool, S., (1993). Phylogenetic analysis of the Rapaninae. Malacologia 35, 155-259.

Kronenberg, G.C. and Berkhout, J. (1984). Strombidae. Vita Marina 1984, 263-362.

Lamprell, K., (1986). Finger oysters of Queensland. Australian Shell News 54, 9.

Lamprell, K., and Whitehead, T., (1992). Bivalves of Australia, Vol. 1. Crawford House Press, Bathurst,182 pp.

Lamy, E., (1935). Révision des Myochamidae vivants du Muséum d'Histoire Naturelle de Paris. Journal de Conchyliogie 90, 236-257.

Laseron, C.F., (1948). New South Wales Marginellidae. Records of the Australian Museum 22, 35-48.

Laseron, C.F., (1950). Review of the Rissoidae of New South Wales. Records of the Australian Museum 22, 257-287.

Laseron, C.F., (1951*a*). Revision of the New South Wales Cerithiopsidae. Australian Zoologist 11, 351-367.

Laseron, C.F., (1951*b*). The New South Wales Pyramidellidae and the genus *Mathilda*. Records of the Australian Museum 22, 298-334.

Laseron, C.F., (1953). Minute bivalves from New South Wales. Records of the Australian Museum 23, 33-53.

Laseron, C.F., (1954*a*). Revision of the Liotiidae of New South Wales. Australian Zoologist 12, 1-25.

Laseron, C.F., (1954*b*). Revision of the New South Wales Turridae (Mollusca). Australian Zoology Handbook, Royal Zoological Society of New South Wales,56 pp.

Laseron, C.F., (1955*a*). Revision of the New South Wales Eulimoid shells. Australian Zoologist 12, 83-107.

Laseron, C.F., (1955*b*). The New South Wales Cancellariidae. Records of the Australian Museum 23, 267-272.

Laseron, C.F., (1956*a*). The families Rissoinae and Rissoidae from the Solanderian Zoogeographical provinces. Australian Journal of Marine and Freshwater Research 7, 384-484.

Laseron, C.F., (1956*b*). The family Cerithiopsidae (Mollusca) from the Solanderian and Dampierian zoogeographical provinces. Australian Journal of Marine and Freshwater Research 7, 151-182.

Laseron, C.F., (1956*c*). New South Wales mussels. Australian Zoologist 12, 263-283.

Laseron, C.F., (1956*d*). A revision of the New South Wales Leptonidae. Records of the Australian Museum 24, 7-24.

Laseron, C.F., (1957). A new classification of the Australian Marginellidae (Mollusca), with a review of the species from the Solanderian and Dampierian zoogeographical provinces. Australian Journal of Marine and Freshwater Research 8, 274-311.

Laseron, C.F., (1959). The family Pyramidellidae from North Australia. Australian Journal of Marine and Freshwater Research 10, 177-267.

Laxton, J.H., (1971). Feeding in some Australasian Cymatiidae (Gastropoda: Prosobranchia). Journal of the Linnean Society of London (Zoology) 50, 1-9.

Lindberg, D.R., (1986). Name changes in the 'Acmaeidae'. The Veliger 29, 142-148.

Loch, I., (1989). And thereby hangs a tail. Australian Shell News 67, 1-2.

Loch, I., (1992). *Ataxocerithium*. Australian Shell News 78, 1-3.

Loch, I., (1994). *Smaragdia*. Australian Shell News 85/86, 1-2.

Luque, A.A., Templado, J., and Burnay, L.P., (1988). On the systematic position of the genera *Litiopa* Rang, 1829 and *Alaba* H. & A. Adams, 1853. Malacological Review Supplement 4, 180-193.

Macpherson, J.H., (1955). Preliminary revision of the families Patellidae and Acmaeidae in Australia. Proceedings of the Royal Society of Victoria 67, 229-259.

Macpherson, J.H., and Gabriel, C.J., (1962). Marine molluscs of Victoria. Melbourne University Press, National Museum of Victoria, 475 pp.

Marshall, B.A., (1983). A revision of the recent Triphoridae of southern Australia. Records of the Australian MuseumSupplement 2, 1-119.

Marshall, B.A., (1988). Skeneidae, Vitrinellidae and Orbitestellidae (Mollusca: Gastropoda) associated with biogenic substrata from bathyal depths off New Zealand and New South Wales. Journal of Natural History 22, 949-1004.

Marwick, J., (1957). Generic revision of the Turritellidae. Proceedings of the Malacological Society of London 32, 144-166.

May, W.L., (1923). Illustrated index of Tasmanian shells. Government printer, Tasmania, 100 pp.

McClatchie, S., (1979). Grazing of *Zeacumanthus subcarinatus* (Gastropoda) on Ulva lactuca. Mauri Ora 7, 39-45.

McLean, J.H., (1984). Systematics of Fissurella in the Peruvian and Magellanic faunal provinces (Gastropoda: Prosobrancia). Contributions in Science, Natural History Museum of Los Angeles County 354, 1-70.

McLean, J.H., (1989). New slit-limpets (Scissurellacea and Fissurellacea) from hydrothermal vents part 1. Systematic descriptions and comparisons based on shell and radular characters. Contributions in Science, Natural History Museum of Los Angeles407, 1-29.

McMahon, R.F., and O'Byrne McMahon, C., (1983). Leaping and swimming as predator escape responses in the jacknife clam, *Ensis minor* (Bivalvia: Pharellidae). Nautilus 97, 55-58.

Moore, D.R., (1962). The systematic position of the family Caecidae (Mollusca: Gastropoda). Bulletin of Marine Science of the Gulf and Carribean 12, 695-701.

Moore, D.R., (1968). Observations on the Caecidae. American Malacological Union, Annual Report 1968, 39.

Morton, B., (1974). Some aspects of the biology and functional morphology of *Cleidothaerus maorianus* Finlay (Bivalvia: Anomalodesmata: Pandoracea). Proceedings of the Malacological Society of London 41, 201-222.

Morton, B., (1991). Aspects of predation by *Tonna zonatum* (Prosobranchia: Tonnoidea) feeding on holothurians in Hong Kong. Journal of Molluscan Studies 57, 11-19.

Morton, B., and Scott, P.H., (1990). Relocation of *Ervilia* Turton, 1822 (Bivalvia) from the Mesodesmatidae Mesodesmatoidea) to the Semelidae (Tellinoidea). The Veliger 33, 299-304.

Murray, F.V., (1962). Gelatinous masses spawned by some Naticids (sand-snails). Australian Journal of Science 25, 62.

Noonan, P., (1988). Philobryid-like bivalves of Victoria. Australian Shell News 62, 2-4.

Numanami, H., and Okutani, T., (1991). Lamellariid gastropods collected by Japanese antarctic research expeditions from near Syowa Station and Breid Bay, Antarctica. Proceedings of the NIPR Symposium on polar biology 4, 50-68.

O'Foighil, D., (1989). Planktonic larval development is associated with a restricted geographic range in *Lasaea*, a genus of brooding, hermaphroditic bivalves. Marine Biology 103, 349-358.

Pawlik, J.R., O'Sullivan, J.B., and Harasewych, M.G., (1988). The egg capsules, embryos and larvae of *Cancellaria cooperi* (Gastropoda: Cancellariidae). Nautilus 102, 47-53.

Pelseneer, P., (1924). Organisation et position systématique du genre *Ringicula*. Annales de la Société Royale Zoologique de Belgique 55, 53-58.

Ponder, W.F., (1965). The family Eatonellidae in New Zealand. Records of the Auckland Institute and Museum 6, 47-99.

Ponder, W.F., (1972). Notes on some Australian genera and species of the family Muricidae (Neogastropoda). Journal of the Malacological Society of Australia 2, 215-248.

Ponder, W.F., (1975a). The identity of the common keyhole limpet of southeastern Australia (Fissurellidae). Australian Zoologist 18, 215-218.

Ponder, W.F., (1975b). The reinstatement of the name *Astralium tentoriiformis* Jonas for *Bellastraea sirius* of authors. Journal of the Malacological Society of Australia 3, 121-126.

Ponder, W.F., (1980). Cephalic brood pouches in *Planaxis* and *Fossarus* (Fossaridae and Planaxidae, Cerithiacea, Gastropoda). Journal of the Malacological Society of Australia 4, 257-258.

Ponder, W.F., (1983). Review of the genera of the Barleeidae (Mollusca: Gastropoda: Rissoacea). Records of the Australian Museum 35, 231-281.

Ponder, W.F., (1984). A review of the genera of the Iravadiidae (Mollusca: Gastropoda: Rissoacea) with an assessment of the relationships of the family. Malacologia 25, 21-71.

Ponder, W.F., (1985a). The anatomy and relationships of *Emblanda emblematica* (Hedley) (Mollusca: Mesogastropoda: Emblandidae n. fam.). Records of the Australian Museum 37, 343-351.

Ponder, W.F., (1985b). A review of the genera of the Rissoidae (Mollusca: Mesogastropoda: Rissoacea). Records of the Australian Museum Supplement 4, 1-221.

Ponder, W.F., (1987). The anatomy and relationships of the pyramidellacean limpet *Amathina tricarinata*. Asian Marine Biology 4, 1-34.

Ponder, W.F., (1988). The truncatelloidean (= rissoacean) radiation - a preliminary phylogeny. Malacological Review Supplement 4, 129-166.

Ponder, W.F., and Creese, R.G., (1980). A revision of the Australian species of *Notoacmea*, *Collisella* and *Patelloida* (Acmaeidae). Journal of the Malacological Society of Australia 4, 167-208.

Ponder, W.F., and de Keyzer, R., (1992). A revision of the genus *Diala* (Gastropoda: Cerithioidea: Dialidae). Invertebrate Zoology 6, 1019-1075.

Ponder, W.F., and Taylor, J.D., (1992). Predatory shell drilling by two species of *Austroginella* (Gastropoda: Marginellidae). Journal of Zoology (London) 228, 317-328.

Ponder, W.F., and Warén, A., (1988). Appendix. Classification of the caenogastropoda and heterostropha - a list of the family-group names and higher taxa. Malacological Review Supplement 4, 288-326.

Ponder, W.F., and Yoo, E.K., (1976). A revision of the Australian and Tropical Indo-Pacific tertiary and recent species of

Pisinna (=Estea) (Mollusca: Gastropoda:Rissoidae). Records of the Australian Museum 30, 150-247.

Ponder, W.F., and Yoo, E.K., (1977). A revision of the Eatonellidae of Australia (Mollusca, Gastropoda, Littorinacea). Records of the Australian Museum 31, 606-658.

Ponder, W.F., and Yoo, E.K., (1980). A review of the genera of Cingulopsidae with a revision of the Australian and tropical Indo-Pacific species (Mollusca: Gastropoda: Prosobranchia). Records of the Australian Museum 33, 1-88.

Ponder, W.F., Colman, P.H., Yonge, C.M., and Colman, M.H., (1981). The taxonomic position of *Hemidonax* Mörch 1871 with a review of the genus (Bivalvia: Cardiacea). Journal of the Malacological Society of Australia 5, 41-64.

Poppe, G.T., and Goto, Y., (1991). European Seashells Vol. 1. Verlag Christa Hemmen, Wiesbaden,352 pp.

Poutiers, J.M., (1992). The Australian Protocardiinae revisited (Bivalvia: Cardiidae). American Malacological Bulletin 9, 139-144.

Powell, A.W.B., (1973). The Patellid limpets of the world (Patellidae). Indo-Pacific Molluca 3(15), 75-205.

Radwin, G.E., (1977). The family Columbellidae in the Western Atlantic. Veliger 19, 403-417.

Radwin, G.E., (1978). The family Columbellidae in the western Atlantic. pt. IIb. the Pyreninae (continued). Veliger 20, 328-344.

Radwin, G.E., and D' Attillio, A., (1976). Murex shells of the world. Stanford University Press, Stanford,284 pp.

Reid, D.G., (1986). The Littorinid molluscs of mangrove forests in the Indo-Pacific region. The genus Littoraria. British Museum (Natural History), 227 pp.

Reid, D.G., (1988). The genera *Bembicium* and *Rissellopsis* (Gastropoda: Littorinidae) in Australia and New Zealand. Records of the Australian Museum 40, 91-150.

Robertson, R., (1973). The genus *Gabrielona* (Phasianellidae) in the Indo-Pacific and West-Indies. Indo-Pacific Mollusca 3(14), 41-61.

Robertson, R., (1983*a*). Observations on the life history of the wentletrap *Epitonium albidum* in the West Indies. American Malacological Bulletin 1, 1-12.

Robertson, R., (1983*b*). Axial shell rib counts as systematic characters in *Epitonium*. Nautilus 97, 116-118.

Robertson, R., (1985). Archaeogastropod biology and the systematics of the genus *Tricolia* (Trochacea: Tricoliidae) in the Indo-West-Pacific. Monographs of Marine Mollusca 3, 1-103.

Rombouts, A., (1991). Guidebook to Pecten shells. Crawford House Press, Bathurst, Australia,157 pp.

Rosewater, J.R., (1970). The family Littorinidae in the Indo-Pacific Part I. The subfamily Littorininae. Indo-Pacific Mollusca 2(11), 417-506.

Rosewater, J.R., (1972). The family Littorinidae in the Indo-Pacific Part II. The subfamilies Tectariinae and Echininae. Indo-Pacific Mollusca 2(12), 507-528.

Rosewater, J.R., (1980). Subspecies of the gastropod *Littorina scabra*. Nautilus 94, 158-162.

Rudman, W.B., (1971*a*). Structure and functioning of the gut in the Bullomorpha (Opisthobranchia) part 1. Herbivores. Journal of Natural History 5, 647-675.

Rudman, W.B., (1971*b*). The genus *Bullina* in New Zealand. Journal of the Malacological Society of Australia 2, 195-203.

Rudman, W.B., (1971*c*). On the opisthobranch genus *Haminoea* Turton and Kingston. Pacific Science 25, 545-559.

Rudman, W.B., (1972*a*). Structure and functioning of the gut in the Bullomorpha (Ophistobranchia). II. Acteonidae. Journal of Natural History 6, 311-324.

Rudman, W.B., (1972*b*). The anatomyof the genus *Hydatina* and the functioning of the mantle cavity and alimentary canal. Zoological Journal of the Linnean Society 51, 121-139.

Rudman, W.B., (1972*c*). Studies on the primitive opisthobranch genera *Bullina* Férussac and *Micromelo* Pilsbry. Zoological Journal of the Linnean Society of London 51, 105-119.

Rudman, W.B., (1972*d*). The genus *Philine* (Opisthobranchia: Gastropoda). Journal of the Malacological Society of London 40, 171-187.

Schilder, F.A. (1933). Monograph of the subfamily Eratoinae. Proceedings of the Malacological Society of London 20, 244-285.

Schneider, J.A., (1992). Preliminary cladistic analysis of the bivalve family Cardiidae. American Malacological Bulletin 9, 145-155.

Seed, R., (1992). Systematics, evolution and distribution of mussels belonging to the genus *Mytilus*: an overview. American Malacological Bulletin 9, 123-137.

Shea, M., (1991). Elusive Ellobiids. Australian Shell News 76, 1-2.

Taylor, J., Kantor, Y., and Sysoev, A., (1993). Foregut anatomy, feeding mechanisms, relationships and reclassification of the Conoidea (=Toxoglossa) (Gastropoda). Bulletin of the Natural History Museum, London 59, 125-170.

Tevesz, M.J.S., (1975). Note on the structure and habits of *Myadora* (Pelecypoda). The Veliger 18, 162-165.

Tevesz, M.J.S., (1977). Taxonomy and ecology of the Philobryidae and Limopsidae (Mollusca: Pelecypoda). Postilla 171, 1-64.

Thompson, J.M., (1954). The genera of oysters and the Australian species. Australian Journal of Freshwater and Marine Research 5, 132-168.

Walls, J.G., (1978). Cone shells: a synopsis of the living Conidae. T.F.H. publications, New Jersey, 1011 pp.

Walsby, J.R., Morton, J.E., and Croxall, J.P., (1973). The feeding mechanism and ecology of the New Zealand pulmonate limpet, *Gadinalea nivea*. Journal of Zoology London 171, 257-283.

Warén, A., (1984). A generic revision of the family Eulimidae. Journal of Molluscan Studies Supplement 3, 1-96.

Warén, A., and Crossland, M.R., (1991). Revision of *Hypermastus* Pilsbry 1889 and *Turveria* Berry, 1956 (Gastropoda: Prosobranchia: Eulimidae), two genera parasitic on sand dollars. Records of the Australian Museum 43, 85-112.

Weaver, C.S., and Dupont, J.E., (1970). The living volutes. Delaware Museum of Natural History, 375 pp.

Wells, F.E., (1990). Revision of the recent Australian Turridae referred to the genera *Splendrillia* and *Austrodrillia*. Journal of the Malacological Society of Australia 11, 73-117.

Wells, F.E., (1991). A revision of the recent Australian species of the turrid genera *Clavus*, *Plagiostropha* and *Tylotiella* (Mollusca: Gastropoda). Journal of the Malacological Society of Australia 12, 1-33.

Wells, F.E., and Bryce, C.W., (1988). Seashells of Western Australia (revised edition). Western Australian Museum, 207 pp.

Willan, R.C., (1977). The nomenclature of three Pacific *Bulla* species. Journal of the Australian Malacological Society 4, 57-68.

Willan, R.C., (1993). Taxonomic revision of the family Psammobiidae (Bivalvia: Tellinoidea) in the Australian and New Zealand region. Records of the Australian Museum Supplement 18, 1-132.

Wilson, B.R., (1967). A new generic name for three recent and one fossil species of Mytilidae (Mollusca: Bivalvia) in southern Australia, with descriptions of the species. Proceedings of the Malacological Society of London 37, 279-295.

Wilson, B.R., (1993). Australian Marine Shells, prosobranch gastropods, pt. 1. Odyssey Publishing, Perth, 408 pp.

Wilson, B.R., (1994). Australian Marine Shells, prosobranch gastropods, pt. 2. Neogastropods,Odyssey Publishing, Perth, 370 pp.

Wilson, B.R., and Gillett, K., (1985). A field guide to Australian shells - prosobranch gastropods. Reed, Sydney, 287 pp.

Wilson, B.R., and Stevenson S.E., (1977). Cardiidae of Western Australia. Western Australian Museum Special Publication No. 9, 114 pp.

Glossary of terms

accessory boring organ: an organ secreting chemicals used to dissolve shells of
prey species. Known from the Naticidae and Muricidae

autotomy: shedding of body parts, like the dropping of the tail by lizards. Displayed
by some species that are unable to fully retract into their shell

byssus: a bunch of threads protruding from the bivalve shell, usually somewhere
near the umbo, anchoring the shell to a substrate

chondrophore: a ligament pit that protrudes from the hinge plates

dextral: the normal direction of coiling of gastropods; the aperture is on the right with
the apex up

dioecious: an animal is either male or female

direct development: larvae hatch as crawling juveniles (as opposed to planktotrophic
development)

foot: the organ that is used for crawling

hermaphrodite (protandrous): an animal that is both male and female; a protandrous
hermaphrodite is an animal that changes sex during life

heterodont hinge: (of a bivalve shell) the hinge has few teeth of unequal size

holotype/type specimen: the one specimen on which the original description of a
species was based. The vast majority of holotypes are housed in museums

ligament: a horny band of material keeping the two valves of a bivalve shell together;
can be situated externally (ligament at the dorsal margin) or internally
(ligament in ligament pit or resilium situated somewhere near the hinge area)

mantle: the organ that secretes the shell. Parts of it are usually visible when the
animal is in motion

monoecious: an animal has both male and female sex organs

nacre: the interior shiny layer present in most archaeogastropods and some bivalves. It has been used for the production of buttons and ornaments

operculum: a horny or calcareous plug attached to the foot of a gastropod, used to seal off the aperture of the shell

pelagic: surface-living

periostracum: the outer layer of the shell; thin, brown and often flaky or hairy. Not present in all species

periphery: the widest point of the last whorl of the gastropod shell

planktotrophic development: larvae hatch as swimming juveniles, which feed in the plankton; other swimming larvae do not feed (they carry yolk) and are called lecitotrophic.

proboscis: the snout of a gastropod

protoconch/prodissoconch: the larval shell of a gastropod (protoconch) or bivalve (prodissoconch)

radula: organ used for feeding. It consists of a varying number of rows of teeth. Each row may have a central (also called rachidian) tooth, and lateral and marginal teeth. Most gastropods have a radula; no bivalves have one

resilium: (in bivalves) process to which the ligament is attached

sexual dimorphism: shells or other features differ between the sexes

sinistral: shell coiling is clockwise; unusual in gastropods

synonym: a more recent or otherwise invalid name for a species

taxodont hinge: (of a bivalve shell) the hinge has many teeth of almost equal size

teleoconch: the part of the shell that follows the protoconch; the adult shell

veliger: the larval stage

Index

Numbers in bold print indicate species number; numbers in normal print are page numbers

Aclididae		56
Aclophoropsis		52
Acrosterigma		102
Acteocina		85
Acteonidae		83
aculeata, Crepidula	**142**,	41
acutispira, Nodilittorina	**96**,	31
acutissima, Eulima	**206**,	55
adamsi, Numella	**412**,	99
Adelphotectonica		77
Adeorbis		40
Aesopus		64
Afrocardium		103
Agatha		82
aktinos, Chlamys	**403**,	97
Alaba		26
Alaginella		70
alba, Soletellina	**448**,	107
albicilla, Nerita	**10**,	11
albidus, Cleidothaerus	**479**,	113
albina sugillata, Pinctada	**394**,	95
albinella, Tellina	**443**,	106
albizona, Pisinna	**109**,	34
alitterata, Etrema	**295**,	74
Alocospira		66
alticostata, Patelloida	**5**,	9
Alvania		34
amabilis, Venericardia	**421**,	100
Amathina		82
Amathinidae		82
Amblychililepas		13
Amoria		65
Amphibollidae		90
Amphithalamus		33
ampullus, Vaceuchelus	**40**,	18
amputatum, Caecum	**132**,	38
Anabathridae		32
Anabathron		32
Anadara		91
anemone, Conus	**298**,	74
angasi, Austrodrillia	**289**,	72
angasi, Bulla	**356**,	85
angasi, Cysticus	**280**,	70
angasi, Philine	**354**,	85
angasi, Prototyphis	**215**,	57
angasi, Rissoina	**122**,	36
Angewia		57
angulata, Adeorbis	**137**,	40
annulus, Cypraea	**147**,	43
anomala, Macteola	**304**,	76
anomala, Venerupis	**469**,	111
Anomia		97
Anomiidae		97
anomoides, Myochama	**478**,	113
antecedens, Mactra	**437**,	104
Antigona		108
antipodes, Scutus	**27**,	15
Antisabia		40
aplustre, Conus	**300**,	74
Aplysia		87
Aplysiidae		87
applenum, Ataxocerithium	**183**,	50
arachis, Cylichna	**352**,	85
arbutum, Mipus	**225**,	59
Architectonicidae		77
Arcidae		91
Arthritica		100
articulata, Pictobalcis	**210**,	56
Asperdaphne		76
asperrima, Mimachlamys	**401**,	96
aspersus, Euchelus	**38**,	18
Assiminea		37
Assimineidae		37
Astelena		22
Asteracmea		9
Astralium		16
Ataxocerithium		50
atkinsoni, Macrozafra	**252**,	64
atkinsoni, Sinezona	**13**,	11
atramentosa, Nerita	**9**,	10
atropurpurea, Eatoniella	**98**,	31
aurantiaca, Cronia	**220**,	59
auratum, Bembicium	**91**,	30
auricularia, Dolabella	**367**,	87
australasia, Ranella	**179**,	50
australasiae, Pholas	**474**,	112
australiae, Onoba	**115**,	34
australis, Agatha	**339**,	82
australis, Engina	**228**,	60
australis, Gouldiopa	**454**,	108
australis, Hiatella	**473**,	112
australis, Lasaea	**416**,	100
australis, Opalia	**192**,	52
australis, Truncaria	**250**,	64
australis, Velacumantus	**84**,	28
australis, Zemira	**264**,	67
Austrocochlea		19
Austrodrillia		72
Austroginella		68
Austroliotia		15
Austropusilla		77
avicennia, Zafra	**254**,	65
Badepigrus		32
badia, Mitra	**285**,	71
ballinensis, Granuliscala	**193**,	53
Bankivia		23
Barbatia		91
Bassina		108
Batillariidae		27
beddomei, Zella	**244**,	64
Bedeva		57
Belloliva		67
bellulum, Spectamen	**62**,	22
Bembicium		30
beraudiana, Austrodrillia	**291**,	73
bicarinata, Notogibbula	**53**,	21
bicolor, Etrema	**296**,	74
bicolor, Trigonostoma	**288**,	72
bifasciata, Syrnola	**335**,	81
bilineata, Heterocithara	**303**,	76
bimaculata, Venericardia	**422**,	100
binivitta, Mesoginella	**271**,	68
botanica, Austroliotia	**29**,	15
botanica, Barbatia	**385**,	92
botanica, Paradaphne	**312**,	77
botanica, Tellina	**445**,	106
brasiliana, Hinea	**86**,	28
brazieri, Colubraria	**227**,	60
brazieri, Donax	**451**,	107
brazieri, Favartia	**214**,	57
brazieri, Haliotis	**15**,	12
brazieri, Hastula	**288**,	72
brazieri, Parviterebra	**247**,	64
brevis, Liloa	**357**,	86
brevis, Linopyrga	**325**,	81
brevis, Myadora	**477**,	113
brunneus, Clanculus	**42**,	18
Buccinidae		59
buccinoides, Assiminea	**124**,	37
Bulla		85
Bullidae		85
Bullina		85
Bullinidae		83
burchardi, Nassarius	**232**,	61
Cabestana		49
Cacozeliana		27
Cadulus		114
Caecidae		38
Caecum		38
caelatura, Chrysallida	**328**,	81
callifera, Monilea	**64**,	23
Calliostoma		22
Callista		110
Callomphala		37
Calypraeidae		41
calyptraeiformis, Sigapatella		
		143, 41
Cancellaria		71
Cancellariidae		71
candida, Notomella	**25**,	15
Cantharidella		21
caputserpentis, Cypraea	**148**,	43
carbonaria, Mitra	**282**,	70
carchedon, Epitonium	**200**,	53
Cardiidae		102
cardioides, Timoclea	**460**,	110
Cardita		100
Carditidae		100
carneola, Cypraea	**149**,	43
Cassidae		48
castanea, Eatoniopsis	**100**,	32
Cellana		9
ceria, Linopyrga	**326**,	81
Cerithidium		26
Cerithiidae		26
Cerithiopsidae		50
chapmani, Patella	**2**,	9
Charilda		79
Charonia		50
Chemnitzia		82
Chicoreus		57
chinensis, Tonna	**172**,	48
Chlamys		97

christyi, Epitonium **199**, 53
Chrysallida 81
Cinctuiga 79
Cingulina 81
Cingulopsidae 32
Circe 108
Cirsonella 24
Cirsotrema 53
Clanculus 18
clandestina, Cypraea **150**, 43
clangulus, Clanculus **43**, 19
Cleidothaeridae 113
Cleidothaerus 113
Clypeola 41
Clypidina 15
coccoradiata, Haliotis **16**, 12
Codakia 99
Coenaculum 56
Colubraria 60
Columbellidae 62
Cominella 59
Compressidens 114
compta, Marita **305**, 76
comptum, Calliostoma **58**, 22
concamerata, Austrocochlea **48**, 19
concatenatus, Cosmetalepas **21**, 13
concinna, Crossea **69**, 24
concinna, Leucotina **346**, 83
Condylocardia 101
Condylocardiidae 101
Condylocuna 101
conicus, Polinices **163**, 46
Conidae 74
constricta, Austrocochlea **19**, 19
contabulatum, Anabathron **101**, 32
contraria, Heteroglypta **449**, 107
Conus 74
convexa, Syrnola **336**, 81
cookii, Mitra **284**, 70
Coralliophila 59
Corbula 111
Corbulidae 111
cornuta, Curveulima **205**, 55
corrugata, Proterato **159**, 45
Cosmetalepas 13
Couthouyia 41
coxi, Paradrillia **293**, 73
crassa, Nuculana **381**, 91
crassa, Rissoina **123**, 36
Crassatellidae 102
Crassitoniella 31
crebrelamellatus, Irus **466**, 110
creccina, Laternula **475**, 112
crenatus, Irus **465**, 110
Crepidula 41
crocea, Dosinia **471**, 111
Cronia 59
Crossea 24
Cultellidae 105
cultellus, Ensiculus **442**, 105
cumingi, Divalucina **409**, 99
cumingi, Irus **467**, 110
Cupidoliva 67
Curveulima 55
Cycloscala 53
Cylichna 85

Cylichnina 86
Cylindrobulla 86
Cylindrobullidae 86
Cyllene 61
Cymatium 49
Cymbiola 65
Cypraea 43
Cypraeidae 43
Cysticus 70
dactylus, Hemidonax **434**, 103
damicornis, Chicoreus **212**, 57
delectabilis, Pseudotorinia **319**, 79
delta, Anabathron **103**, 32
deltoidalis, Tellina **444**, 106
deltoides, Donax **450**, 107
Dentaliidae 114
Dentalium 114
denticulata, Siphonaria **375**, 89
Dentimitrella 62
denudatus, Chicoreus **213**, 57
dermestoidea, Pseudamycla **243**, 62
descripta, Anomia **405**, 97
Diala 26
Dialidae 26
diaphana, Cinctuiga **324**, 79
Dicathais 59
didyma, Neverita **167**, 46
Diodora 13
Diplodontidae 99
disjecta, Bassina **455**, 108
disrupta, Callista **461**, 110
dissimilis, Epigrus **127**, 37
Divalucina 99
Dolabella 87
doliaris, Ringicula **349**, 83
Donacidae 107
donaciformis, Mysella **417**, 100
Donax 107
dorsatus, Tapes **468**, 111
Dosinia 111
dromanaensis, Montacuta **418**, 100
Eatonellidae 31
Eatoniella 31
Eatoniopsis 32
ebeninus, Pyrazus **83**, 27
eburnea filiacea, Cominella **226**, 59
edwini, Microgenia **310**, 76
elata, Hedleytriphora **186**, 52
elegans, Merelina **119**, 36
elegantula, Eucharilda **321**, 79
Ellatrivia 44
Ellobiidae 88
elongata, Paphies **440**, 105
Emblanda 34
Emblandidae 34
emblematica, Emblanda **112**, 34
eminens, Alvania **113**, 34
Engina 60
Ensiculus 105
Epidorona 73
Epigridae 37
Epigrus 37
Epitoniidae 52
Epitonium 53
erosa, Cypraea **151**, 43
Ervilia 106

Ethminolia 22
Etrema 74
Eucharilda 79
Euchelus 18
Euguraleus 76
Eulima 55
Eulimella 79
Eulimidae 55
Eumarcia 110
Eunatica 47
Eurytrochus 21
exaratum, Cymatium **180**, 50
excavata, Cardita **420**, 100
excavata, Nepotilla **311**, 77
exigua, Janthina **204**, 54
eximius, Phasianotrochus **55**, 21
exquisita, Belloliva **262**, 67
exquisitus, Turbo **34**, 16
fabia, Epitonium **198**, 53
fasciata, Bankivia **66**, 23
fasciata, Hedleytriphora **187**, 52
fasciata, Rissoina **121**, 36
Favartia 57
fenestratum, Mesopeplum **402**, 96
fimbriata, Cypraea **152**, 43
fischeri, Cylindrobulla **364**, 86
Fissurellidae 13
flammea, Crassitoniella **97**, 31
floridus, Clanculus **44**, 19
foliacea, Antisabia **136**, 40
Fossarina 21
Fossarus 28
foveolata, Vanikoro **139**, 41
Fractolatirus 62
fragilis, Salinator **380**, 90
franciscense, Dentalium **480**, 114
frauenfeldi, Pisinna **110**, 34
fulgida, Gomphina **462**, 110
Fulvia 103
fulvida, Talabrica **427**, 102
fumata, Pupa **347**, 83
fumatus, Pecten **404**, 97
fumigata, Eumarcia **464**, 110
funiculata, Siphonaria **377**, 90
fusiformis, Acteocina **353**, 85
Gadinalea 89
Galeommatidae 99
galloprovincialis, Mytilus **389**, 93
Gari 106
gaudiosus, Nassarius **230**, 61
Gazameda 28
Gena 21
Gibberula 70
glabra, Mitra **283**, 70
glans particeps, Nassarius **229**, 61
glomerata, Saccostrea **399**, 96
gloriola, Talopena **65**, 23
Glycymeridae 92
Glycymeris 92
Gomphina 110
Gouldiopa 108
gracilis, Couthouyia **138**, 41
gracilis, Merelina **120**, 36
granarium, Cacozeliana **82**, 27
Granata 18
granifera, Tetraphora **188**, 52
Granulina 70

Granuliscala	53
gravicosta, Pyrgiscus	**343**, 82
grayana, Glycymeris	**386**, 92
gregaria, Pseudopisinna	**99**, 32
gunii, Gazameda	**88**, 28
Guraleus	76
Haliotidae	12
Haliotis	12
Haloginella	65
Haminoea	86
Haminoeidae	85
hargravesi, Haliotis	**17**, 13
hasta, Eulimella	**322**, 79
Hastula	72
hayesiana, Asperdaphne	**309**, 76
hedleyi, Clypeola	**144**, 41
hedleyi, Epideira	**292**, 73
Hedleytriphora	52
Heliacus	78
helmsi, Arthritica	**419**, 100
Hemidonacidae	103
Hemidonax	103
henni, Paregila	**333**, 81
Herpetopoma	18
Herviera	81
Heterocithara	76
Heteroglypta	107
Hiatella	112
Hiatellidae	112
hilum, Austropusilla	**313**, 77
Hinea	28
Hipponicidae	40
hirstuta, Trichomya	**390**, 93
hofmani, Chemnitzia	**342**, 82
hofmani, Retusa	**359**, 86
Hydatina	83
Hydatinidae	83
ignava, Herviera	**330**, 81
illibrata, Asteracmea	**8**, 9
imbricata, Granata	**41**, 18
immersa, Zeacrypta	**145**, 42
impacta, Lanistina	**393**, 94
imperialis, Turbo	**35**, 16
impertusa, Gena	**57**, 21
implexus, Heliacus	**318**, 78
incei, Polinices	**164**, 46
inconspicua, Mesoginella	**268**, 68
indistinctus, Odontotrochus	**56**, 21
inermis, Leuconopsis	**373**, 88
infelix, Mesoginella	**267**, 68
Iravadiidae	37
iravadioides, Microdryas	**108**, 33
iredaleana, Cylichnina	**360**, 86
iredalei, Eulima	**207**, 56
Irus	110
jacksonensis, Euguraleus	**301**, 76
jacksonensis, Mactra	**435**, 104
jacksoni, Amphithalamus	**106**, 33
jacksoni, Bassina	**456**, 108
jacobiscala, Cycloscala	**201**, 53
janthina, Janthina	**203**, 54
Janthina	54
Janthinidae	54
javanicensis, Amblychilepas	**19**, 13
johnstoni, Austroginella	**274**, 68
jonasii, Nassarius	**233**, 61
jukesianum, Epitonium	**195**, 53
Katelysia	110
Keliidae	99
Kellia	99
kerslakae, Acrosterigma	**428**, 102
kesteveni, Astralium	**31**, 16
kesteveni, Latitriphora	**189**, 52
kesteveni, Puncturella	**26**, 15
kunopia, Condylocardia	**423**, 101
labiatum, Phalium	**173**, 48
labiosa, Cymatium	**177**, 49
labrolineata, Cypraea	**153**, 43
lachryma, Proterato	**158**, 45
Laevidentalium	114
lagopus, Tawera	**458**, 108
lamarckii, Neotrigonia	**406**, 98
Lamellaria	45
Lamellariidae	45
lampas rubecunda, Charonia	**178**, 50
Lanistina	94
Lasaea	100
Lasaeidae	100
lata, Parvioris	**209**, 56
Latavia	81
Laternula	112
Laternulidae	112
Latitriphora	52
Leiopyrga	23
lene, Anabathron	**102**, 32
Lepsiella	59
Leptonidae	100
letourneauxiana, Turella	**308**, 76
Leuconopsis	88
Leucotina	83
leucozona, Olivella	**260**, 67
Liloa	86
Lima	95
Limaria	95
Limatula	95
Limidae	95
lincolnensis, Dentimitrella	**241**, 62
lineata, Bullina	**351**, 85
lineata, Diodora	**23**, 13
lineolaris, Leiopyrga	**67**, 23
linneana, Eunatica	**169**, 47
Linopyrga	81
Liotella	24
Lissarca	93
Litiopidae	26
Littoraria	31
Littorinidae	30
livida, Gari	**447**, 106
livida, Scaeochlamys	**400**, 96
lodderae, Lodderia	**129**, 37
Lodderena	24
Lodderia	37
Lotiidae	9
lubricatum, Laevidentalium	**483**, 114
lucida, Callomphala	**128**, 37
Lucidestea	36
Lucinidae	98
luhuanus, Strombus	**134**, 38
lurida, Macrozafra	**251**, 64
lutea, Philippia	**315**, 78
luteola, Littoraria	**93**, 31
Lutraria	105
Macrozafra	64
Macteola	76
Mactra	104
Mactridae	104
maculosus, Aclophoropsis	**190**, 52
magnifica, Cymbiola	**257**, 65
Malleidae	95
Mammilla	46
manifesta, Syrnola	**337**, 81
Maoritomella	74
marginalba, Morula	**222**, 59
marginata, Alocospira	**258**, 66
Marginellidae	67
Marikellia	99
Marinula	88
Marita	76
maugeri, Clanculus	**45**, 19
megapicalis, Diala	**76**, 26
melastomus, Polinices	**166**, 46
merces, Ellatrivia	**156**, 44
Merelina	36
Merria	41
Mesodesmatidae	105
Mesoginella	67
Mesopeplum	96
Metanachis	64
metcalfei, Paradrillia	**294**, 73
micans, Pseudoliotia	**130**, 38
Microcarina	24
Microdryas	33
Microgenia	76
Mimachlamys	96
mimula, Patelloida	**6**, 9
minima, Lodderena	**71**, 24
Minolops	22
minora, Epitonium	**196**, 53
minuta, Coenaculum	**211**, 56
Mipus	59
Miralda	81
Mitra	70
Mitraguraleus	76
mitralis, Mitraguraleus	**306**, 76
Mitridae	70
modesta, Paramontana	**307**, 76
Modiolus	94
monile, Alaba	**79**, 26
Monilea	23
Monolitora	99
Monophorus	52
Montacuta	100
Montacutidae	100
morchi, Cirsotrema	**197**, 53
Morula	59
mufria, Patelloida	**7**, 9
Muricidae	56
muscaria, Austroginella	**273**, 68
mustelina, Haloginella	**276**, 68
mutabilis, Strombus	**135**, 39
Myadora	112
Myochama	113
Myochamidae	112
Mysella	100
Mytilidae	93
Mytilus	93
Nanula	19
nanum, Bembicium	**92**, 31
Nassarius	61

Natica 46
Naticidae 46
Neotrigonia 98
Nepotilla 77
Nerita 10
Neritidae 10
Neverita 46
nigellus, Nassarius **231**, 61
nigrita, Amblychilepas **20**, 13
nigrofusca, Monophorus **185**, 52
nigrofusca, Seila **184**, 51
nimbifer, Lima **396**, 95
Ninella 16
nitens, Lucidestea **117**, 36
nivea, Gadinalea **374**, 89
nivea, Pupa **348**, 83
nodiliferus, Morula **223**, 59
Nodilittorina 31
normalis, Fractolatirus **236**, 61
Notoacmea 9
Notogibbula 21
Notomella 15
Notosetia 24
novarensis, Alvania **114**, 34
Nozeba 37
Nuculana 91
Nuculanidae 91
Numella 99
nutata, Siphonaria **378**, 90
nympha, Cupidoliva **263**, 67
nympha, Granulina **279**, 70
oblonga, Alocospira **259**, 66
ochracea, Alaginella **281**, 70
Odontotrochus 21
olivella, Mesoginella **270**, 68
Olivella 67
Olivellidae 66
Olividae 66
Onoba 34
Opalia 52
Ophicardelus 88
opiniosa, Alaba **78**, 26
opulens, Pyrene **238**, 62
orbignyana, Merria **141**, 41
orbita, Dicathais **219**, 59
orientalis, Limaria **398**, 95
ornata, Scissurella **14**, 11
ornatus, Ophicardelus **370**, 88
oryza, Trivirostra **157**, 44
Oscilla 81
Ostreidae 96
Ovaginella 68
ovata, Condylocuna **425**, 101
ovulum, Ovaginella **272**, 68
oxytropis, Psilaxis **316**, 78
pagodiformis, Plesiotrochus **75**, 25
paivae, Bedeva **217**, 57
pallidulus, Aesopus **246**, 64
pandoriformis, Myadora **476**, 112
Paphies 105
papilliferus, Conus **299**, 74
Paradaphne 77
Paradrillia 73
Paramontana 76
Paregila 81
parkinsonia, Sassia **175**, 48
parmophoidea, Tugali **28**, 15

parthenopeum parthenopeum,
Cymatium **181**, 50
Parvioris 56
Parviterebra 64
parvula, Aplysia **365**, 87
pascoei, Linopyrga **327**, 81
Patella 9
Patellidae 8
Patelloida 9
patula, Fossarina **54**, 21
pauperus, Nassarius **234**, 61
Pecten 97
Pectinidae 96
peroniana, Dentimitrella **242**, 62
peroniana, Thyasira **413**, 99
peronianus, Modiolus **391**, 94
peronii, Patella **3**, 9
perplexum, Epitonium **194**, 53
persimilis, Antigona **452**, 108
petterdi, Notoacmea **4**, 9
Phalium 48
Phasianella 17
Phasianotrochus 21
Philine 85
Philinidae 85
Philippia 78
Philobrya 93
Philobryidae 92
Pholadidae 112
Pholas 112
Phyllocoma 57
physis, Hydatina **350**, 83
picta, Lissarca **388**, 93
Pictobalcis 56
picturata, Cantaridella **51**, 21
pictus, Guraleus **302**, 76
pictus, Hemidonax **433**, 103
Pillucina 99
Pinctada 95
Pisinna 34
pistacia, Barbatia **383**, 91
Placamen 108
placidum, Placamen **457**, 108
Planaxidae 28
platyceras, Compressidens
481, 114
plebejus, Clanculus **46**, 19
Plesiotrochidae 25
Plesiotrochus 25
pleurisulcatus, Aesopus **245**, 64
Polinices 46
ponderi, Heliacus **317**, 78
porcellana, Notosetia **73**, 24
Pratulum 103
probabilis, Ethminolia **63**, 22
projecta, Condylocuna **426**, 101
Proterato 45
Prototyphis 57
Psammobiidae 106
Pseudamycla 62
Pseudoliotia 38
Pseudolividae 67
Pseudopisinna 32
Pseudotorinia 79
pseustes, Natica **161**, 46
Psilaxis 78
Pteriidae 95

pulcherrima, Liotella **70**, 24
pulcherrima pulcherrima, Minolia
61, 22
pulchra, Latavia **331**, 81
pulex, Xenostrobus **392**, 94
Puncturella 15
Pupa 83
pupoideus, Badepigrus **104**, 32
pusilla, Mactra **436**, 104
pygmaea, Cylichnina **361**, 86
pyramidalis, Nodilittorina **95**, 31
Pyramidellidae 79
pyramis, Amphithalamus **107**, 33
Pyrazus 27
Pyrene 62
Pyrgiscus 82
pyrum, Phalium **174**, 48
Pyxipoma 29
quoyi, Bulla **355**, 85
quoyi, Ophicardelus **372**, 88
ramsayi, Monolitora **410**, 99
Ranella 50
Ranellidae 48
reeveanum, Acrosterigma **429**, 102
reevei, Adelphotectonica **314**, 77
reticulata, Lepsiella **221**, 59
Retusa 86
Retusidae 86
rhynchaena, Lutraria **439**, 105
rhytiphora, Katelysia **463**, 110
Ringicula 83
Ringiculidae 83
Rissoidae 34
Rissoina 36
rosae, Charilda **320**, 79
rostrata, Volvulella **362**, 86
rotunda, Condylocardia **424**, 101
royana, Cyllene **235**, 61
rubicunda, Onoba **116**, 36
rubra, Ervilia **446**, 106
rubra, Haliotis **18**, 13
rubra, Philobrya **387**, 93
rugifera, Codakia **408**, 99
rugosa, Clypidina **24**, 15
Saccostrea 96
sagittata, Tanea **162**, 46
salebrosa, Pisinna **111**, 34
Salinator 90
Sassia 48
scabra, Timoclea **459**, 110
scabriuscula, Herpetopoma **39**, 18
Scaeochlamys 96
scalarina, Turbonilla **341**, 82
Scaphandridae 85
Scissurella 11
Scissurellidae 11
scitula, Astelena **60**, 22
scripta, Circe **453**, 108
scripta, Pyrene **237**, 62
sculpta, Dosinia **470**, 111
scutulata, Tylospira **133**, 38
Scutus 15
Seila 51
Semelidae 106
semiconvexa, Dentimitrella **239**, 62
serotinum, Ataxocerithium **182**, 50
Serpulorbis 42

siennae, Assiminea **125**, 37
Sigapatella 41
sigaretiformis, Vanikoro **140**, 41
Siliquariidae 29
simiae, Mammilla **168**, 46
simillinus, Cadulus **482**, 114
simplex, Agatha **340**, 82
Sinezona 11
sinuata, Mesoginella **269**, 68
Sinus 47
sipho, Serpulorbis **146**, 42
Siphonaria 89
Siphonariidae 89
skeeti, Afrocardium **432**, 103
Skeneidae 24
Smaragdia 11
sobrina, Eulima **208**, 56
Solen 105
Solenidae 105
Soletellina 107
solida, Marikellia **415**, 100
solida, Mitra **286**, 71
solida, Salinator **379**, 90
solida, Teinostoma **74**, 24
sordidus, Polinices **165**, 46
souverbiana, Smaragdia **11**, 11
speciosa, Phyllocoma **216**, 57
speciosa, Pseudoliotia **131**, 38
speciosum, Calliostoma **59**, 22
Spectamen 22
spengleri, Cabestana **176**, 49
spina, Cingulina **329**, 81
spirula, Spirula **484**, 114
Spirula 114
Spirulidae 114
Spisula 105
squamosa, Barbatia **384**, 91
squamosissima, Coralliophila **224**, 59
stolata, Corbula **472**, 111
strangei, Eurytrochus **52**, 21
strangei, Limatula **397**, 95
strangei, Neotrigonia **407**, 98
Strombidae 38
Strombus 38
Struthiolariidae 38
subbulbosa, Gibberula **278**, 70
subcarinatus, Zeacumantus **85**, 28
Subninella 16
subtilineata, Maoritomella **297**, 74
succinea, Macrozafra **253**, 64
sulcatus, Ophicardelus **371**, 88
sulcifera scobina, Diala **77**, 26
suprasculpta, Miralda **332**, 81
surgerea, Microcarina **72**, 24
sydneyensis, Aplysia **366**, 87
sydneyensis, Fossarus **87**, 28
symbolica, Pillucina **411**, 99
Syrnola 81
Talabrica 102
Talopena 23
Tanea 46
Tapes 111
tasmanica, Austroginella **275**, 68
tasmanica, Gazameda **89**, 28
tasmanica, Nanula **50**, 19
tasmanica, Oscilla **334**, 81

Tawera 108
tayloriana, Dentimitrella **240**, 62
Teinostoma 24
Tellina 106
Tellinidae 106
tenellum, Epitonium **202**, 54
tenera, Haminoea **356**, 86
tentoriiforme, Astralium **30**, 16
tenuicostata, Fulvia **430**, 103
Terebridae 72
Tetraphora 52
thetidis, Pratulum **431**, 103
Thyasira 99
Thyasiridae 99
ticaonica, Diodora **22**, 13
Timoclea 110
tincta, Syrnola **338**, 82
Tonna 48
Tonnidae 48
topaziaca, Nozeba **126**, 37
torquata, Ninella **32**, 16
tragena, Smaragdia **12**, 11
tragula, Volvulella **363**, 86
tramoserica, Cellana **1**, 8
translucida, Alaba **80**, 26
translucida, Mesoginella **266**, 68
trapezia, Anadara **382**, 91
Trichomya 93
Tricolia 16
trigonella, Spisula **438**, 105
Trigoniidae 98
Trigonostoma 72
trilineata, Parviterebra **248**, 64
Trimusculidae 89
Triphora 52
Triphoridae 51
triticea, Belloliva **261**, 67
tritoniformis, Angewia **218**, 57
Triviidae 44
Trivirostra 44
Trochidae 18
Truncaria 64
Tugali 15
turbinata, Mesoginella **265**, 67
Turbinidae 15
Turbo 16
Turbonilla 82
Turella 76
Turridae 72
turrita, Eulimella **323**, 79
Turritellidae 28
Tylospira 38
Umbraculidae 88
umbraculum, Umbraculum **368**, 88
Umbraculum 88
undatoides, Clanculus **47**, 19
undulata, Amoria **255**, 65
undulata, Cancellaria **287**, 71
undulata, Subninella **33**, 16
unifasciata, Nodilittorina **94**, 31
Vaceuchelus 18
vaginoides, Solen **441**, 105
Vanikoridae 40
Vanikoro 41
variabilis, Tricolia **36**, 16
varicifera, Pyrgiscus **344**, 82
variegata, Tonna **171**, 48

Velacumantus 28
Venericardia 100
Veneridae 108
Venerupis 111
ventricosa, Phasianella **37**, 17
Vermetidae 42
victoriae, Mesoginella **277**, 70
violacea, Amathina **345**, 82
vitellus, Cypraea **155**, 43
Vitrinellidae 37
Volutidae 65
Volvulella 86
vulsella, Vulsella **395**, 95
Vulsella 95
weldii, Cirsonella **68**, 24
weldii, Pyxipoma **90**, 29
xanthodon, Cypraea **154**, 43
xanthostoma, Marinula **369**, 88
Xenostrobus 94
Zafra 65
Zeacrypta 42
Zeacumantus 28
zebra, Amoria **256**, 65
zelandica, Siphonaria **376**, 90
Zella 64
Zemira 67
zonale, Sinum **170**, 47